Studies in Modern History

General Editor: J. C. D. Clark, Joyce and Elizabeth Hall Distinguished Professor of British History, University of Kansas

Titles include:

James Mackintosh
VINDICIÆ GALLICÆ
Defence of the French Revolution: A Critical Edition

Robert J. Mayhew
LANDSCAPE, LITERATURE AND ENGLISH RELIGIOUS CULTURE, 1660–1800
Samuel Johnson and Languages of Natural Description

Jeremy Mitchell
THE ORGANIZATION OF OPINION
Open Voting in England, 1832–1868

Marjorie Morgan
NATIONAL IDENTITIES AND TRAVEL IN VICTORIAN BRITAIN

James Muldoon
EMPIRE AND ORDER
The Concept of Empire, 800–1800

Julia Rudolph
WHIG POLITICAL THOUGHT AND THE GLORIOUS REVOLUTION
James Tyrrell and the Theory of Resistance

Lisa Steffen
TREASON AND NATIONAL IDENTITY
Defining a British State, 1608–1820

Lynne Taylor
BETWEEN RESISTANCE AND COLLABORATION
Popular Protest in Northern France, 1940–45

Anthony Waterman
POLITICAL ECONOMY AND CHRISTIAN THEOLOGY SINCE THE
ENLIGHTENMENT
Essays in Intellectual History

Doron Zimmerman
THE JACOBITE MOVEMENT IN SCOTLAND AND IN EXILE, 1746–1759

Studies in Modern History
Series Standing Order ISBN 978–0–333–79328–2 (Hardback)
978–0–333–80346–2 (Paperback)
(*outside North America only*)

You can receive future titles in this series as they are published by placing a standing order. Please contact your bookseller or, in case of difficulty, write to us at the address below with your name and address, the title of the series and the ISBN quoted above.

Customer Services Department, Macmillan Distribution Ltd, Houndmills, Basingstoke, Hampshire RG21 6XS, England

The Jacobites at Urbino

An Exiled Court in Transition

Edward Corp

Professor of British History, University of Toulouse

First published 2009 by
PALGRAVE MACMILLAN

Palgrave Macmillan in the UK is an imprint of Macmillan Publishers Limited, registered in England, company number 785998, of Houndmills, Basingstoke, Hampshire RG21 6XS.

Palgrave Macmillan in the US is a division of St Martin's Press LLC, 175 Fifth Avenue, New York, NY 10010.

Palgrave Macmillan is the global academic imprint of the above companies and has companies and representatives throughout the world.

Palgrave® and Macmillan® are registered trademarks in the United States, the United Kingdom, Europe and other countries.

ISBN-13: 978–0–230–22004–1 hardback
ISBN-10: 0–230–22004–5 hardback

This book is printed on paper suitable for recycling and made from fully managed and sustained forest sources. Logging, pulping and manufacturing processes are expected to conform to the environmental regulations of the country of origin.

A catalogue record for this book is available from the British Library.

Library of Congress Cataloging-in-Publication Data
Corp, Edward T.
    The Jacobites at Urbino : an exiled court in transition / Edward Corp.
        p.   cm. — (Studies in modern history)
    Includes bibliographical references and index.
    ISBN 978–0–230–22004–1
    1. James, Prince of Wales, 1688–1766—Homes and haunts—Italy—Urbino. 2. Jacobites—History—18th century.   3. Great Britain—Court and courtiers—History—18th century.   4. Great Britain—History—Stuarts, 1603–1714.   5. Princes—Great Britain—Biography.   6. British—Italy—History—18th century.   7. Great Britain—Foreign relations—Italy. 8. Italy—Foreign relations—Great Britain.   9. Scots—Italy—History—18th century.   10. Exiles— Great Britain.   11. Stuart, House of.   I. Title.
    DA814.A3C67 2009
    942.07092—dc22
    [B]   2008030142

10   9   8   7   6   5   4   3   2   1
18   17   16   15   14   13   12   11   10   09

Printed and bound in Great Britain by
CPI Antony Rowe, Chippenham and Eastbourne

Contents

List of Illustrations

Acknowledgements

My research in the Vatican and other Italian archives was made possible by a fellowship which I received from the Paul Mellon Centre in 2005. It is a great pleasure to acknowledge and express my gratitude to the Centre for this extremely generous award.

The permanent staff and the other fellows and scholars at the British School at Rome made my four-month stay in Italy as enjoyable and profitable as it could possibly have been. I am particularly grateful to Maria Pia Malvezzi for giving me the necessary introductions to several private and public collections, which enabled me to study numerous portraits and other paintings not normally available or on display. In particular it was thanks to her that I was able to spend several hours one summer morning exploring and photographing the king's apartment in the Palazzo del Re (now called the Palazzo Balestra) at the north end of the Piazza dei SS. Apostoli.

I am also grateful to the staff of the *Università degli Studi* of Urbino for letting me examine the diary of Giovanni Gueroli Pucci, and their other Jacobite archives, in a room with the same view looking west which James III would have known from his apartment. Situated in the building immediately beside the Palazzo Ducale, in what was once the Palazzo Bonaventura, the university is one of the places where the Jacobites regularly attended their *conversazioni*.

Dr Maurizio Ascari very kindly guided me into both the Bologna State Archives and the superb manuscript collection at Bologna University, a short distance from where James III stayed during his two visits to the city in 1717 and 1718.

My research in England was mainly conducted in the British Library, the Bodleian Library and the Royal Archives, where the librarians and archivists were unfailingly helpful. The papers of James III are now preserved at Windsor Castle, and are used here with gracious permission from Her Majesty Queen Elizabeth II.

I must also acknowledge the generous help that I have received in Edinburgh, from the staff of both the Scottish Catholic Archives and the Scottish National Archives. Above all, I must pay tribute to the extraordinary kindness of everyone at the Scottish National Portrait Gallery, which possesses the best collection of Stuart and Jacobite portraits, and an extraordinarily rich photographic library. I have benefited more than

I can say here from the help and support of James Holloway and his colleagues.

Among the many historians whose work has inspired my own, I must mention Professor Jeremy Black, Professor Jonathan Clark, Dr Eveline Cruickshanks, Professor Howard Erskine-Hill, Professor Edward Gregg, Professor Paul Monod, Professor Murray Pittock, Abbot Geoffrey Scott and Professor Daniel Szechi. On more detailed points I am indebted to Professor Xavier Cervantes and Jane Clark for enjoyable and useful discussions of music; to Dr Simona Capelli for sharing her expert knowledge of Antonio David, and for providing invaluable help with one of the illustrations; to Richard Sharp for his comprehensive knowledge of engraved Jacobite portraits; and particularly to Alastair Laing for giving me so much information over so many years, as well as providing me with such active support.

Finally I must pay tribute to the members of my family for all the help they have given me in the preparation of this book. Rosanna Corp introduced me to the *Marche* and shared my enthusiasm for Urbino and the surrounding area. My wife Elizabeth read (and argued about) each chapter, translated all the quotations from French into English, and generously acted as both copy editor and proof reader. In fact, the book could not possibly have emerged in its present form without her contribution.

List of Abbreviations

ASB.	Archivio di Stato di Bologna
ASR. Cam I:	Archivio di Stato di Roma, Camerale I:
CDG	Conti della Depositeria Generale
GT	Giustificazione di Tesoriere
RMC	Registro de' Mandati Camerale
ASV.	Archivio Segreto Vaticano
Albani	Fondo Albani
PAC	Palazzo Apostolico Computisteria
Salviati	Fondo Salviati
SS: Ingh	Segretario di Stato: Inghilterra
BL. Add.	British Library, Additional
Bod. Lib.	Bodleian Library
HMC	Historical Manuscripts Commission
NLS.	National Library of Scotland
RA. SP	Royal Archives, Stuart Papers
SCA. BL	Scottish Catholic Archives, Blairs Letters
SNA. GD	Scottish National Archives, Gifts and Deposits
WDA. Epist. Var.	Westminster Diocesan Archives, Epistolae Variorum

Introduction

The exile of the Stuart kings originated in 1689 when James II was deposed during the Glorious Revolution. From then on, and until the death of his son James III in 1766, there was a Stuart court permanently based abroad, its members hoping and praying that King James would one day be restored.[1] Those who remained loyal to the Stuart kings were known as the Jacobites.

This long period of exile may be divided into two main phases. From 1689 to 1716 the Stuart court was based in or near French territory, mainly at Saint-Germain-en-Laye, but also at Bar-le-Duc in the Duchy of Lorraine (1713–1715) and within the Papal enclave at Avignon (1716–1717). The second phase began in 1719, when the court was established in Rome, where it remained, with one short break at Bologna (1726–1729), until the death of James III at the beginning of 1766. This book is concerned with the important and influential transitional period between these two phases.

In February 1717 political pressure obliged James III to move his court away from Avignon and French territory, beyond the Alps into the Italian peninsula. He arrived in the Papal States and settled at Pesaro on the Adriatic coast in March and remained there until May. He then made his first visit to Rome, where he stayed until July, after which his court was established at Urbino. Although the Stuart court remained at Urbino from July 1717 to October 1718 its future location was uncertain, and no one expected it to remain in the Papal States or move permanently to Rome. But because Urbino was considered to be too cold in winter, an alternative temporary location was found during the autumn of 1718. After much discussion, during which the favoured location was the Pope's palace at Castel Gandolfo, it was decided that the court should settle in Rome until the following spring. Some expected it to return to Urbino, others expected it to go to some other papal palace. Most may have expected it to move back to England. The *terminus ad quem* of this transitional period, therefore, was not when the court actually left Urbino, which was in October 1718, but when it was properly established somewhere else, which turned out to be in Rome, in October 1719.

In order to understand the uncertainty concerning the future location of the court, we need briefly to consider the international situation during these years and the main lines of Jacobite diplomatic and military planning. Until 1715 James III, like his father before him, had been able to rely on the solid support of France. For most of the time that support had been military and financial, and had also provided a residence at Saint-Germain-en-Laye. For some of the time, however, and notably after the Treaty of Utrecht in 1713, French support had been less active and become restricted to financial and moral help. Yet so long as Louis XIV was alive the French government remained keen to have the exiled Stuart king restored.

The death of Louis XIV in 1715 changed this situation. The duc d'Orléans, the Regent for the boy King Louis XV, was dependent on King George I for support in the event of any future French succession dispute. As a result the French government effectively turned against the Jacobites, forcing James III to look elsewhere for military assistance. A transitional period then followed until 1720, by which time James III and his court were established in Rome, when the principal aim of Jacobite policy became the improvement of relations with France.

The international diplomacy of Jacobitism during the period from 1716 to 1720 was determined by the impact of the two major wars fought in Europe at the beginning of the eighteenth century. In southern Europe the War of the Spanish Succession decided both who should be the King of Spain and how the Spanish empire in Europe should be partitioned. In northern Europe the Great Northern War decided which powers should control the Baltic. When James III lost the support of the French government in 1715, and the Jacobite rising failed in both England and Scotland in 1716, his policy was naturally to involve himself in these two sources of conflict with a view to obtaining an ally who would intervene militarily alongside Jacobite forces to help bring about a Stuart restoration.

By the Treaties of Utrecht and Rastadt in 1713–1714 Philip V had been recognised as the King of Spain, and the Spanish Empire in Europe had been partitioned. The Emperor Charles VI had received the Spanish Netherlands, Milan, Naples and Sardinia. The Duke of Savoy had received Sicily. The Spanish were obliged to accept the permanent loss of the Netherlands and Milan, but were determined to regain Naples, Sardinia and Sicily at the first opportunity. Moreover Philip V had been forced to renounce his claims to the throne of France. As such a renunciation ran counter to the doctrine of the divine right of hereditary succession its legality was never accepted by Philip, either for himself or for his sons. If, therefore, the boy King Louis XV were to die before he was able to get married and have children, there was bound to be a major dispute concerning the French succession, in which Philip V, the legitimate heir, would be confronted by the alternative heir, the Regent duc d'Orléans. As the Regent would then need the support of King George I, and both France and Great Britain were determined to maintain the territorial partition settled at Utrecht and Rastadt, James III could in this eventuality put himself forward as the natural ally of Spain. A Stuart restoration brought about with Spanish help would provide Philip V with the backing of Great Britain in the Mediterranean and in any future French succession dispute.

The Great Northern War in the Baltic involved a struggle between Sweden and Russia, in which the latter was supported by Hanover. As George I, in his capacity as Elector of Hanover, had seized both Bremen and Verden from Sweden, James III hoped to obtain the military support of King Charles XII to stage an invasion of northern England. Moreover the relations between King George I and Peter the Great of Russia were becoming strained because of Russia's continued westward expansion. Jacobite policy was therefore to negotiate an alliance with Sweden, and then to try to encourage a rapprochement between Sweden and Russia which might open the way to a Jacobite alliance with Russia as well.

During the period covered by this book, when the Stuart court had left Avignon but was not yet in Rome, Jacobite diplomacy was directed towards obtaining the support of Spain, Sweden and Russia against the Hanoverian government in Great Britain, which was itself supported both by the Regent in France and by the Dutch. The Emperor Charles VI, as the new ruler of Naples and Sardinia, was likely to be on the side of George I and the Regent, but was involved in a war against the Turks in Hungary. Pope Clement XI was on the side of Philip V and James III, but was conscious of the vulnerability of the Papal States to the Emperor's army stationed in Naples and to the British fleet in the Mediterranean.

While the court was at Avignon in 1716 James III concentrated on negotiations for the Swedish alliance. With the cooperation of the Swedish ambassador in London a large sum of money was raised to finance a Swedish landing in northern England, but Jacobite hopes were dashed at the beginning of 1717 when the ambassador's correspondence was intercepted by the Whig government and the plan was discovered. The ambassador himself was expelled, and the proposed invasion was cancelled. During the same month the Whigs negotiated a Triple Alliance with France and the United Provinces.

Jacobite diplomacy then turned towards Russia. In April 1717, while James III was at Pesaro, the Duke of Ormonde left the court to travel on an embassy to St Petersburg in order to negotiate an alliance with Russia. It took him a long time to get there, and his negotiations then made slow progress, but they provided the diplomatic background to James's first visit to Rome that spring and to his arrival in Urbino at the beginning of July.

In August 1717 the news reached Urbino that the Spanish had invaded Sardinia and reconquered the island from the Emperor. Meanwhile negotiations were reopened with Sweden, running parallel to those being conducted by Ormonde in Russia. The rest of the year was thus a period of waiting, but there was positive news from England, where the Hanoverian Whig régime was encountering problems. Major disagreements in April, which had resulted in the resignations from the ministry of Lord Townshend and his brother-in-law Sir Robert Walpole, were followed in December by an open breach between George I and his son George, the Prince of Wales. The latter was ordered to leave St James's Palace, and he established a rival court at Leicester House, thereby providing a focus for division within the enemy camp and encouraging the Jacobite opposition.

The spring and summer of 1718 brought a mixture of good and bad news to the court at Urbino. In June 1718 the Spanish invaded Sicily, captured Palermo and quickly overran the island. They then prepared to invade the Kingdom of Naples. On the other hand the Duke of Ormonde reported in March that his embassy had been a failure. Peter the Great had made the Russian alliance dependent on the successful conclusion of an alliance with both Sweden and Spain, and the renewed negotiations at Stockholm had produced no result. For the time being, therefore, it was clear that no help would be forthcoming from the northern powers, and this was confirmed when the great warrior King Charles XII died in November and was succeeded by his sister Ulrica Eleonora.

July 1718 also brought unwelcome news from Vienna. The Emperor had made peace with the Turks at Passarowitz, and then immediately adhered to the Triple Alliance, to form a new Quadruple Alliance with Great Britain, France and the United Provinces, and thus gain their support in the Mediterranean for the defence of Naples. The Emperor could now definitely be regarded as an enemy. Moreover the benefit for him of the new alliance came very quickly. In August a combined Anglo-Dutch fleet, commanded by Admiral Byng, encountered the Spanish fleet off Cape Passaro (the south-eastern tip of Sicily) and destroyed it in a major naval engagement. The Spanish not only had to cancel their planned invasion of Naples, but lost their communications with both Sicily and Sardinia, where their troops were now left stranded. These developments frightened the Pope who became less enthusiastic in his support for James III, because of the presence of the Anglo-Dutch fleet off the coast of the Papal States, near Rome and his own residence at Castel Gandolfo.

The Battle of Cape Passaro, however, proved to be a blessing for the Jacobite cause, as it finally made the Spanish government resolve to support the restoration of James III. In October 1718 Cardinal Alberoni, the chief minister of Philip V, began preparations to launch a major invasion of England early the following year. War was formally declared between Spain and Great Britain in December, and the Duke of Ormonde, having spent the summer in France, was invited to join the Spanish court and take command of the invasion force. James III had finally obtained what he had wanted since 1716: a definite commitment to restore him to his kingdoms from one of the three countries he had approached.

Meanwhile another extensive correspondence, conducted by his secretariat at Urbino with the leading Jacobites in England, had convinced him that the arrival of a Spanish army commanded by Ormonde would provoke a major Jacobite rising which could quickly topple the divided Hanoverian régime. The period of waiting in Italy, long and wearisome though it might have been on a day to day basis, seemed about to come to an end.

As it turned out, the Spanish fleet sent to invade England was destroyed by a storm off Cape Finisterre, and a small diversionary force sent to Scotland was defeated at Glenshiel. Jacobite hopes were thus unexpectedly dashed, and the Hanoverian régime in Great Britain given an important reprieve. Moreover the whole international situation now turned against James III. The new Queen of Sweden agreed to cede Bremen and Verden to Hanover, thus ending any hope of future support from the northern powers. And Philip V of Spain was forced in 1720 to accept a new Mediterranean agreement, whereby the Emperor kept Naples, the Spanish evacuated both Sardinia and Sicily, and the Emperor and the Duke of Savoy exchanged their islands. This had the effect of strengthening the Imperialists by uniting Sicily with Naples, and elevating the Duke of Savoy to become the King of Sardinia. It was under these circumstances that James III found himself obliged to remain in the Papal States for very much longer than he had originally expected, with his court now permanently established in Rome.

To what extent was the Stuart court established in Rome after 1719 the same as it had been at Saint-Germain before 1713 – or at Whitehall before 1689? How did the experience of residing at Urbino impact on the court and its structure?

The attention given to court studies in recent years has enabled historians to move beyond purely anecdotal or biographical information about a few leading personalities, and to consider the influence on monarchs (or other heads of state) of those who lived in proximity with them, secretaries, household servants or courtiers, including their wives and mistresses. Although rarely all-powerful, these people were often able to influence important decisions, perhaps by argument or other forms of persuasion, but perhaps also by insinuation or ridicule. Studying royal courts as sociological groups has therefore enabled historians to consider not just what each government was trying to achieve, but also how decisions were made and carried out. An examination of the departmental structure and the hierarchy of the court, combined with an understanding of its daily ceremonial, and the distribution and use of the rooms within the royal apartments, has helped us understand who had access to the monarch, and how often, whether it was to influence policy or to secure places and other rewards for themselves and their friends and supporters.

The study of courts has also enabled some historians to break down the artificial barriers erected between apparently separate academic disciplines, such as political, music and art history. By emphasising the function and purpose of the performing and visual arts within their courtly context, it has been possible to rediscover what they meant to contemporaries – to stand back, for example, from connoisseurship concerning brush strokes or the search for prime versions, and identify message, quantity and distribution. The royal and princely courts can therefore be better understood as patrons of the arts and creators or mirrors of fashion.

The Jacobite court, however, was a court *in exile*, cut off from the administration of the kingdom and the royal estates, from the management of Parliament and the legal system. Decisions still had to be made, policies formulated and correspondence conducted, but they concerned a narrower spectrum. The primary political function of the exiled court was to maintain the best possible relations with the host government (the King of France, and then the Pope), and to make plans to bring about a restoration. The spiritual function was to emphasise the divinely appointed status of the king, and (in the case of the Jacobite court) to provide a full measure of religious toleration in a Catholic country. The dynastic function was to contract favourable marriage alliances which would perpetuate the dynasty and bring diplomatic support. The social function was one of public relations, to create a focus of loyalty to the exiled king, and a forum in which his loyal subjects could be entertained. The cultural function, in addition to musical entertainment, was to patronise painters, engravers and medallists in order to distribute the image of the king and his family to people who could not otherwise see them. Subsistence had to be given out, in the form of salaries and pensions, and honours and other rewards had to be distributed – but sparingly, so they would not lose their value. Perhaps above all, confidence had to be inspired, in an environment where a belief could be maintained that there would be an eventual restoration. In this respect James III was helped when in Italy because the Papacy had never extended (and would never extend during his lifetime) even *de facto* recognition to the monarchs of the post-revolution Protestant succession.

To be credible, the court also had to be sufficiently impressive to command respect, yet moderate to avoid seeming over-inflated or even ridiculous. At Saint-Germain and Bar-le-Duc this had involved giving careful attention to the daily ceremonial and to the size and structure of the household departments. For example, some of the most senior posts (Lord Chamberlain, Lord Steward, Master of the Horse) had been left unfilled, and the numbers of people employed reduced from what they had been at Whitehall. The architecture and available accommodation had also dictated changes to the organisation of the departments, particularly the sub-departments of the Household Below Stairs.

In certain respects the Stuart court in Rome was significantly different from what it had been at Saint-Germain. Most obviously it was situated in the middle of a large capital city, and not on the edge of a very small town. It also employed fewer people, so that most of them could live as well as work within the same building as the king and his family. After 1719 the court became increasingly Italian, both in its organisation and its personnel. For example, the most senior posts which had been left vacant at Saint-Germain were reintroduced, but with the Italian equivalent names (*Maestro di Camera, Maggiordomo, Maestro di Stalla*) to disguise the lower status of their holders. These, and other important changes, originated while the court was at Urbino.

The book will begin by explaining how and why the Jacobites moved to Urbino (Chapters 1 and 2), and will then describe the Palazzo Ducale there as it was when occupied by James III and his court (Chapter 3).

The period from July 1717 to October 1718, when the court was at Urbino, was a time of waiting and anxiety, and both the Jacobites and James III himself felt tense and insecure. Urbino was a remote city, cut off from the centres of power and the main communication routes, and offering very little by way of entertainment. As a result there was friction and rivalry, and sometimes even overt hostility, among the people who constituted the court. They can be divided into two main groups. There were the household servants who had been living in exile with the king since long before the Jacobite rising of 1715. And there was a group of new pensioners, most of whom were Scottish, who had remained in Great Britain, participated in the Jacobite rising, and only followed the king into exile after its failure in 1716. The old and the new exiles (who are all identified in Chapter 4) had no previous acquaintance, and had lived very different lives before being thrown together by recent events. Despite their shared loyalty to the king, they seem to have had little else in common, so that there was always a potential divide between the salaried servants and the unemployed pensioners. Each group could, and did, argue that they had demonstrated more loyalty to and made a greater sacrifice for the Jacobite cause than the other.

James III, who had no experience of living in Great Britain, seems to have preferred the company of the new exiles, who had risked their lives and forfeited their estates by rising in his support. He became particularly friendly with two of them, the Duke of Mar and John Hay, and by giving them salaried posts in the royal household he destroyed the harmony which had hitherto prevailed there. Chapter 6 shows how this became increasingly important while the court was at Urbino. The Scottish pensioners themselves, however, were by no means a united group, and the obvious preference shown by the king for his two new favourites resulted in resentment and further discord. As will be shown, differences of religion and personality, as well as differences in nationality, produced friction at the court.

James had been brought up at Saint-Germain surrounded by advisers and senior servants who were older than himself. When he reached Urbino in July 1717 he was 29 years old and keen to replace these people with men of his own age. During 1718 the king's two new favourites were joined by another, James Murray, who had not taken part in the rising of 1715–1716, but who now arrived from London with the confidence of a man who had up-to-date and first-hand experience both of public affairs and of the leading politicians in the British capital. The king, who was clearly feeling the strain of waiting in such a remote Italian hill-top city for his restoration, placed far too much confidence in these men, with unfortunate results. Two of the three new favourites, Hay and Murray, who were heartily disliked by most of the Jacobites, would continue to dominate the court for many years to come.

James was not only relatively young, he was also unmarried. One very striking thing about the court at Urbino is the absence of women. Whereas Mary of Modena and her ladies had set the tone at Saint-Germain, and Queen Maria Clementina and hers would to some extent do the same in Rome, the Stuart court at Urbino was for most of the time an exclusively masculine community. The Jacobites had not only left their wives and daughters behind, but had come to a country where they could not speak the local language. They had also been uprooted from their normal occupations, from local government and the management of their estates. How they organised their lives and entertained themselves will be examined in Chapter 5, while Chapter 7 will show that the Jacobite court in the Palazzo Ducale became for a short time one of the most significant musical centres in the Papal States, a development which has been overlooked by both political and music historians.

James III himself was primarily concerned with planning his restoration and with perpetuating his dynasty through marriage to a well-connected princess. The last chapters of the book show how these two questions, which have already been examined by political historians, had a profound impact on the organisation and location of the court. In 1718 it was decided to move away from Urbino to a new but temporary residence – the papal palace at Castel Gandolfo. It will be shown how and why, contrary to their expectations, James and the Jacobite court moved, and moved permanently, to Rome instead. This change of location, and the way it was managed, had a profound and even traumatic impact on the leading courtiers. Decisions taken at this time were to have enduring consequences for the entire Jacobite movement as well as for the exiled court.

James III had chosen as his bride a young princess, Maria Clementina Sobieska, who was 14 years younger than himself, and then still only a teenage girl. His marriage at Montefiascone in September 1719 took place immediately after his hopes for a restoration had been dashed. It was then that he went with her to live in a palazzo in Rome – called here for the first time by its correct name, the Palazzo del Re – made available to him by the Pope. The way in which the court was to be organised there, and the way the young queen was to be treated, had been arranged by the king and his unpopular favourites while they were at Urbino.

The management of their courts provided all exiled monarchs with a considerable challenge. Decisions had to be taken concerning the allocation of space within the available accommodation, the numbers of people to be employed, the ceremonies to be retained and the favours to be bestowed. Discipline had to be maintained, yet loyalty encouraged and preserved. These were never easy things to decide or achieve, but at least a semi-permanent residence, such as at Saint-Germain or Rome, allowed the monarchs to make their arrangements more readily. Within the field of court studies the experience of James III and the Jacobites at Urbino thus provides us with a particularly interesting example, for theirs was not just an exiled court, but an exiled court in a state of flux, in which previous arrangements had to be reconsidered and modified. How should the king's household and apartment be changed, to take account of political and financial circumstances and of the new accommodation? How should the new queen's household be organised? Or, perhaps more pertinently, should she actually have her own independent household, and should she even be given her own separate apartment? These questions have not been considered by previous historians of Jacobitism, yet they were of the greatest importance at the time, particularly for the upbringing of the Stuart princes.

It is indeed surprising that there has never previously been a study of the Stuart court at Urbino. The fact that one of the most famous buildings in Italy, now visited by over 1.3 million people each year, was occupied in the early eighteenth century by a British court, including a large number of high ranking Scots, is remarkable in itself. The fact that these Scots were almost all Protestants, and that they enjoyed full religious toleration in the Papal States, is also bound to interest us today. More specifically, the arrival of the Jacobite court was of considerable significance because it coincided with the development of the Grand Tour, and thus had an impact on Anglo-Italian relations. The establishment of a permanent British presence in Rome in 1719 had far-reaching implications for all those who chose to visit the papal city in the decades to follow. This book explains how and why that situation came about.

1
From Avignon to Pesaro

The Triple Alliance of Great Britain, France and the United Provinces, signed at The Hague on 4 January 1717, stated that "it is known by experience that the near abode" of the exiled Stuart King "may excite commotions and troubles in Great Britain, and the dominions depending thereon". It was therefore agreed that the King of France should "engage the said person to depart out of the country of Avignon, and take up his residence on the other side of the Alps".[1] Although signed in the name of the six-year-old Louis XV, the treaty represented the policy of Philippe, duc d'Orléans, Regent of France since 1715, and the only member of the French royal family who disliked James III. The Regent's mother, who disapproved of his policy, commented a little later that she was "inexpressibly distressed" by the decision to expel James and force him into a second exile, "because he is the best fellow in the world. He is gentle and courteous and he does not deserve all the misfortunes that are crushing him."[2]

The decision to expel James from the Papal enclave at Avignon, where he had been living since April 1716, was not difficult to implement. The Stuarts were financially dependent on the pension which they received from the French court. Without it Queen Mary of Modena would be unable to maintain her court at Saint-Germain-en-Laye, and the thousands of Jacobites living in France on her charity would starve. The threat of withdrawing the pension was enough to force James into Italy.

The Triple Alliance represented a diplomatic triumph for the Whig government of King George I in London and was extremely unpopular at the French court. Whatever the official policy pursued by the Regent and his successors, James III always retained strong support among those courtiers who had known him at Saint-Germain, Marly, Versailles and Fontainebleau. For the time being, however, the pro-Jacobite group at

11

the French court was overruled,[3] and James had to accept that he was now to be an exile from France as well as from his own Kingdoms of England, Scotland and Ireland. He was well aware, as he explained to the Pope, what a "terrible blow to my interests would be caused by a move to Italy".[4] Hostility to the papacy was even stronger than anti-Catholicism in both England and Scotland.

Once it was known that James would have to leave Avignon and move to Italy, it was necessary to decide where he should re-establish his court, and which of his servants and followers he should take with him. The first decision was relatively straightforward. James was warned as early as October 1716,[5] and when Cardinal Giannantonio Davia, the Legate of the Romagna, heard the news he offered to let him have the Palazzo Ducale at Pesaro for as long as he would like it.[6] James accepted this offer, and began to make his preparations to leave Avignon.

The royal household at Avignon has been described elsewhere.[7] It was greatly reduced from its former size, containing only 33 people. Apart from three of the oldest servants, and one or two others, who returned to Saint-Germain, everyone was instructed to follow James to Pesaro.[8] They were accompanied by 5 new servants who had been recruited at Avignon, so the total remained about the same, at approximately 33. In addition to these James III took with him the members of his political secretariat, the Duke of Mar (Secretary of State, but already counted as a Gentleman of the Bedchamber), Robert Creagh and John Paterson (his under-secretaries) and the indispensable David Nairne (Secretary of the Closet).

It was more difficult to decide what to do with the many other Jacobites, virtually all of them Scottish, who had assembled at Avignon during 1716. There were said to be well over 1500 of them by June, perhaps as many as 2000 by the end of the year, of whom 370 were receiving a regular monthly pension.[9] In the event James divided these people into three categories. A list was drawn up of "his Majesty's Subjects that are to goe to Italy". It included 48 names, but as some of them had become members of the household it can for our purposes be reduced to 42.[10] A second list was drawn up with 62 names, described as "those that are to stay in France; or Flanders".[11] Everyone else was to go to Toulouse. The Duke of Mar summed up the situation at the end of January 1717:

the people of quality here with the King and some of his gentle-men are to follow him to Italy, and the rest are to disperse as they find most convenient till we have occasion for their service. Most of the Highlandmen are going towards Toulouse, and, if they be not in numbers in one place, and behave quietly and discreetly, we hope they will not be disturbed.[12]

The number of people to follow James III to Italy was therefore under 80. They all left Avignon at the beginning of February 1717.[13]

James himself left on the 6th, with a party of about 60 people headed by the Dukes of Ormonde and Mar. His plan was to travel to Chambéry in Savoy, and then across the Alps via the Mont-Cénis pass to Turin. Meanwhile his *équipages* and the remaining 20 people, headed by Lord Edward Drummond and Lord Clermont, both Gentlemen of the Bedchamber, would travel to Marseille and then by sea to Italy, to be waiting for him in the Papal States at Bologna.[14]

The details of James's journey, and his visits to Turin, Piacenza, Parma and Modena, have been given by his biographers and do not need to be repeated here. Everything went according to plan, with one important exception. When they approached Chambéry, the Duke of Mar announced that he had important business to attend to in Paris and deserted the royal party. He took with him one of his under-secretaries (Robert Creagh), leaving the other (John Paterson) to handle his correspondence.[15]

The final staging point of the journey, before James entered the Papal States, was Modena, the birth place not only of his mother, but also of her two closest friends, Lady Almond (Lady of the Bedchamber) and Contessa Veronica Molza (Bedchamber Woman). There he met one of the daughters of Lady Almond and four of the children of Contessa Molza, all of whom he had known well at Saint-Germain.[16] We should remember that James, although a reluctant exile in Italy, was actually himself half-Italian and, of particular importance, able to speak the language.

When James and his party crossed the river Panaro to enter the Papal States on 13 March, they were formally received by Don Carlo Albani, one of the three nephews of Clement XI. The scene was recorded in a large painting by Giuseppe Maria Crespi, in which the king can be seen with the Duke of Ormonde and his leading courtiers.[17] They were then escorted to Bologna, where they found Drummond and Clermont with the *équipages* waiting for them, and the necessary accommodation already prepared in the Casa (sometimes called Palazzo) Belloni, the home of James's banker.[18]

Illustration 1 Giuseppe Maria Crespi, *The Meeting of James III and Don Carlo Albani on the Banks of the River Panaro outside Bologna, 13 March 1717* (1717). The king is shown with five gentlemen, one of whom (on the right of the group) has a black wig. They are intended to represent the Duke of Ormonde (second from left, with his Garter sash shown incorrectly, worn over the wrong, i.e. right, shoulder), some of the Scottish peers, and perhaps Dominic Sheldon or David Nairne

After two days in Bologna, where he saw other old acquaintances from Saint-Germain, James III continued his journey towards Pesaro, leaving behind Drummond and Clermont "and several others" with the *équipages* (as James put it) "so as not to embarrass my route".[19] At Imola, James was greeted at the door of the Archbishop's palace by Cardinal Ulisse Giuseppe Gozzadini, and once again the scene was recorded in a large painting, this time by Antonio Gionima.[20] The party finally reached the Palazzo Ducale in Pesaro on 20 March after what David Nairne described as "a boring journey lasting six weeks".[21] The king was soon joined by Drummond and Clermont, and then by various Scottish peers who had preferred to travel independently.[22]

Pesaro was never intended to be more than a temporary base for the Stuart court, and it did not take James long to realise that it was far from suitable. Dr John Blair, who had been appointed one of his physicians at Avignon, has left a description of the town during that spring which captures the sense of disappointment felt by the Jacobites who had come there from Avignon:

> Pesaro is a town...situat on the Adriatique in a narrow plain bounded with hills around. The plain is prettie fruitfull in corns and vines as also the hills are full of planting but the air is very moist and unhealthy you will very seldome see there a clear day free of fogs which is occasiond by the Adriatique on the one side the high hills and much planting on the other: The water there is not good and most of the Kings Subjects upon their coming were seized with headaches loosness or some other distempers.
>
> In the mercat place you have a fountain the only thing worth notic-ing in the place.... Their Cabarets are the worst I ever see, for they are nesty and they cannot dress meat.... There are no walks but on the sea shore and that did not agree with most of our people besides the sea frequently stinks so confoundedly that theres no abiding on't. On the landside theres a little walk towards a little house belonging to the Duke of Toscany with a garden where most of us took our diversion.[23]

The court remained at Pesaro for two months

The most important person at the court was the Duke of Ormonde, but there were also the Spanish Count of Castelblanco, who had been created Duke of St Andrews,[24] and ten Scottish peers: the 2nd Duke of Perth, the Marquis of Tullibardine (eldest son of the Duke of Atholl), Earl Marischal, the Earls of Linlithgow, Nithsdale, Panmure, Southesk and

Illustration 2 Antonio Gionima, *James III being received by Cardinal Gozzadini at the Archbishop's Palace at Imola, 16 March 1717* (1717). The king is shown with five gentlemen, one of whom (on the right of the group) has a black wig. The Duke of Ormonde is shown with the star of the Order of the Garter, worn correctly on the left side of his coat, but without a blue sash

(eventually) Winton and Viscounts Kilsyth and Kingston. These men, with others such as Charles Fleming (brother of the Earl of Wigton) and Alexander Maitland (brother of the Earl of Lauderdale), and some high ranking military officers, gave the Stuart court considerable prestige, but they also tended to overshadow the few remaining senior members of the Royal Household, Lord Edward Drummond and Lord Clermont, and Dominic Sheldon (the Vice-Chamberlain).

It is not surprising that James III, who had abolished the duty of waiting in the Chamber at Bar-le-Duc, now also abolished waiting in the Bedchamber.[25] He could not continue to give priority to the old servants from Saint-Germain, nor could he give posts to some but not others of the new exiles. He was no doubt also conscious that formal waiting at a court which had been so drastically reduced was inappropriate. He therefore decided that he would be served in his Bedchamber by his valets only, and that he would call on his senior courtiers, old and new, to be present as and when he needed them. The amount of the salaries and pensions for men of equal social rank had already been equalised while the court was at Avignon.[26] Meanwhile the Household Below Stairs, the Table and the Stables were all made the responsibility of Charles Booth, whose position as Groom of the Bedchamber no longer carried any duties, and who was given the Italian title of *Maggiordomo*.[27]

In the unsatisfactory climate of Pesaro and lacking entertainment, despite the performance of three operas in the Teatro del Sole,[28] some of the Jacobites became increasingly dissatisfied and were keen to leave, "finding this place very unwholesome".[29] The Duke of Ormonde left the court during April, at the king's request, to try to negotiate an alliance with Peter the Great of Russia,[30] and Lord Tullibardine left soon after to join the Highlanders in and near Toulouse.[31] As a result the Duke of Perth was said to become "somewhat uneasy, when he found some of his friends had left him in town", so he asked to be allowed to visit Genoa. This prompted Lord Linlithgow and Charles Fleming to ask to be allowed to go to Milan.[32] One Jacobite in Pesaro wrote to the Duke of Mar, then staying at Saint-Mandé near Vincennes, that "our people are daily leaving.... Those of any note are confined to this country [Italy] till they have further directions. Some of the lesser sort are coming towards you [in France]".[33] The lesser sort included Charles Leslie, the Anglican Chaplain, who persuaded James to let him return to Paris because of his health.[34]

The man who seems to have been most dissatisfied was the Earl of Panmure, but this was because he was not consulted on political questions, and felt neglected and slighted. He argued that a royal council should be created to give advice to the King, and was apparently supported by Charles Leslie before his departure. James, however, was keen to persuade the Duke of Mar to return, and in the meantime had no wish to create a redundant royal council. He confided to Mar on 19 May:

> Your poor uncle [Lord Panmure] is in a dismal way, and full of his old splenetic notions, which he has vented a little to me. I have done all I could to quiet him, but I fear it has not done, which I am sorry for, for he is really a worthy man.[35]

But there was another reason why James did not want to listen to Panmure. The latter was a much older man, and James increasingly wanted to surround himself with men of his own age, to replace those who had served him since his childhood and youth at Saint-Germain. His particular favourite, apart from Mar himself, was Mar's brother-in-law John Hay (brother of the Earl of Kinnoul), whom he had appointed to be one of his Equerries at Avignon. He regretted having left him in France, and now wrote that he wanted him to come to Pesaro as quickly as possible. "You know the kindness I have for him", he confided to Mar.[36] It was the beginning of a long and ultimately disastrous friendship.

When one examines the names of the people in the court at Pesaro one cannot but be struck by the absence of women. At Saint-Germain the presence of Mary of Modena and all her ladies – the women in attendance on the prince and princess, and all the wives and daughters of the servants and courtiers – had meant that the court had been a balanced community in which the feminine influence was strong. But the servants at Avignon had left their wives behind at Saint-Germain, and the Scottish Jacobites had mainly fled abroad without their wives and children. So the circumstances of the second exile to Italy, when James III had taken with him as few people as possible, meant that the court had become an essentially masculine community.

The number of women at Pesaro was so small that it can easily be listed. There was a washerwoman called Catherine Macane, and her daughter Anne who had married one of the footmen (Nicolas Prévot) while the court was at Avignon. And there was a scourer in the kitchen, who had been recruited in Avignon, called Magdalen. She was actually a widow, and her married name was Muti. Although she was accompanied by her son, Francesco Muti, she was always known by her maiden name, Magdalen Rebout.[37]

Of course there must have been local women employed to clean, to wash and mend clothes, but they are not mentioned in the archives. It is difficult to know what the effect of such an absence of women must have been on the morale of the court, or what the impact of such a large male community must have been on the life of a small city like Pesaro. Although we do not have the necessary documentary evidence, no account of the court would be complete which did not mention this factor, and we may speculate that the inter-relationship between court and town must have been coloured by it.

Another important aspect of court life, about which more can be said, is the question of religion. The small Catholic city of Pesaro, like Avignon the previous year, had to accept the arrival of a large number of Protestants. Although nearly all the members of the Royal Household were Catholics, the Jacobites who had been allowed to follow the court into Italy were, with few exceptions, Protestants.[38] The Catholics could attend local services in the churches of Pesaro, but the Protestants needed to have their own chaplains and had to be tolerated by the local authorities.

There had been four clergymen to look after the Protestants in Avignon: Charles Leslie, Ezekiel Hamilton, George Barclay and Patrick Cowper. When James III drew up the lists of who should go to Italy and who should remain in France, he reduced the number from four to two. Barclay and Cowper were instructed to remain in France, but Leslie and Hamilton were invited to accompany the court to Italy.[39] Consequently there was ample provision for Protestant services to be held in the court when it first arrived at Pesaro. But it was necessary to obtain formal permission from the Pope for these services to be held, and James was very fortunate that he encountered no obstacles.

The Papal Vice-Legate at Avignon had been Alamanno Salviati, who came from one of the leading aristocratic families of Florence. He had been particularly helpful in allowing the Jacobite Protestants to enjoy religious toleration at Avignon,[40] and shortly after the arrival of the Stuart court at Pesaro the Pope transferred him to join James there.[41] Cardinal Davia remained the Legate for the rest of the Romagna, but Salviati was given responsibility for the area covering both Pesaro and Urbino.[42] While James lived at Pesaro, Salviati lived at Urbino, Davia lived at Rimini, and religious toleration was guaranteed.

James, however, had no Catholic chaplains, and did not even have a Confessor. John Ingleton, who had been his Confessor at Bar-le-Duc, stated that he was "by no means fond of a wandering life" and decided to remain at Saint-Germain. "If I stay here", he wrote, "the King I believe will have none in my place, but make use of those he finds where he is".[43] Ingleton was right, and in Avignon James accepted a local priest named Father Viganego, who was recommended to him by Salviati and Francesco Gontieri, the Archbishop, on the advice of Cardinal Fabrizzio Paulucci in Rome.[44] He employed another local priest, the Abbé Curnier of Saint-Didier, as his chaplain,[45] but he left both men behind when he left Avignon, and now needed to recruit a new Confessor in Pesaro. By good fortune it transpired that there was an Irish Dominican priest named Father John Brown living in a convent at Fano. He was appointed to be the king's new Confessor, and remained at the Stuart court for the next ten years.[46] As no chaplains are mentioned, it seems likely that James again made use of a local priest to officiate services during the short time that he remained at Pesaro.

Although James had been forced to leave France when the Regent threatened to stop paying the monthly Stuart pension, he was himself no longer dependent on French money, either to maintain his own court or to give pensions to those Jacobites he had allowed to follow him to Pesaro. Since November 1716 the Pope had paid him a quarterly pension of 2500 *scudi* (equal to about 9569 *livres*), so from that point onwards he had told William Dicconson, the Treasurer at Saint-Germain, to stop sending him any money and keep his share of the French pension for distribution among the new Scottish exiles living in France.[47] James's new papal pension was not large, but it was sufficient to maintain himself and the 80 people who now made up his household and court.[48]

The costs of preparing and maintaining the Palazzo Ducale at Pesaro were, of course, met by the papal authorities. Just before James's arrival the palazzo was completely cleaned and his own apartment repaired and redecorated. Furniture and other items were transferred to Pesaro from the Palazzo Ducale at Urbino, including enough chairs and tables, candlesticks, beds and pillows for all the Jacobite courtiers. There were crystal drinking glasses, bowls for eating and a supply of wood. Moreover, James found the palazzo had been provisioned with a generous supply of food and drink as a *regalo* (present).[49]

Care was also taken to provide for James's security. An assassin sent by the British government had been discovered at Avignon,[50] and the papal authorities were anxious to prevent a further attempt on the king's life. The four gates through the city walls of Pesaro were therefore hastily repaired, and a detachment of soldiers was sent from Rome to guard them and protect the Palazzo Ducale.[51]

Despite these arrangements, James had no desire to remain at Pesaro, and in May 1717 he determined to go to Rome to meet the Pope. Before leaving he arranged for his portrait to be placed in the Palazzo Ducale as a souvenir of the time he had spent there. As no new portrait had been painted since he left France, and he had no spare portraits to give away, he had to arrange for an old one to be copied. The portrait selected was not very suitable, but was presumably the only one available. It had been painted at Saint-Germain by Alexis-Simon Belle in 1706[52] and was copied for James by a local artist. Richard Rawlinson saw it when he visited the Palazzo Ducale at Pesaro eight years later: "above stairs in one of the rooms", he commented, "is a very wretched picture done by one Lodi under which is the following inscription Jacobo III Anglia Regi".[53] The portrait is still there.[54]

2
The King's First Visit to Rome

Although James had always intended to visit Rome in order to see the Pope,[1] his desire to escape from Pesaro made him decide to go earlier than originally planned.[2] He had two main reasons for going, apart from a general curiosity to see the city itself. He wanted to persuade the Pope to appoint Cardinal Gualterio to be the Cardinal Protector of England, something he had so far refused to do.[3] He also wanted the Pope to allow him to leave Pesaro and move his court to the Palazzo Ducale at Urbino.[4] He informed Mar that "nobody goes with me but [Charles] Booth and John [Hay], and Nairne that will meet me at Rome by another road".[5] The king was, of course, also to be accompanied by servants of lesser status: his *valets de chambre*, his doctor, his coachman, and various footmen and grooms.

James and his party left Pesaro on Saturday, 22 May[6] and intended to reach Rome in three days, on Tuesday, 25 May. But the journey was much longer and more tiring than expected, because they travelled down the Adriatic coast to visit the shrine of the Virgin at Loretto, before turning inland to join the Via Flaminia. By Monday evening they had only reached Terni. James's new valet, Felix Bonbled, had to be sent on with a letter for Cardinal Gualterio, announcing that his master would not be able to reach Rome until one day later than expected, on the evening of Wednesday, 26 May.[7] Meanwhile David Nairne, accompanied by the Duke of St Andrews and Dr Lawrence Wood (the king's physician) left Pesaro on Monday, 24 May and travelled directly down the Via Flaminia, arriving in Rome the same evening.[8] It was the first time Nairne had been in Rome since 1691, and he was delighted to be back. He commented at the end of that week that "I wish there was no objection against this place's being his séjour for good and all, till he could go where he ought to be, for I never could be of opinion it was his interest to choose such an exile as Pesaro or Urbino."[9] Once the party was reunited in Rome, James and his servants, but not the Duke of St Andrews, stayed at the Palazzo Gualterio on the Corso.[10] The building, which was rented from Cardinal Pietro Ottoboni, was on the west side of the street, immediately beside the church of San Lorenzo in Lucina, immediately to the south of the Palazzo Ruspoli.[11]

This first visit to Rome by James III is very fully documented. In addition to various letters sent from Rome by Hay, by Nairne, and by James III himself, we have the "Journal du Séjour de S.M.B. à Rome" written by Nairne,[12] and two "Relazioni della venuta à Roma del Re d'Inghilterra Giacomo III", with a description of the "onore verso di lui" by the Pope, written by a member of the papal secretariat.[13] We also have details of the *regali* given to James by the Pope, and the financial accounts of the entertainments provided by the *Camera Apostolica*.[14]

The list of places visited by James in Rome between 27 May and his departure in early July is impressive. It includes all the major churches and ancient monuments, and several of the more important palazzi. The king was generally accompanied on his visits by Cardinal Gualterio, the Pope's nephew Don Carlo Albani, and by his own cousin Prince Fabrizio Colonna. The latter's mother showed him the famous gallery in the Palazzo Colonna, which was considered "one of the most beautiful things in Rome, quite as fine as the Grand Gallery at Versailles".[15] James also visited some of the villas which had been built outside Rome, notably the Villa Ludovisi, which was the home of the Principessa di Piombino, a relation of Alamanno Salviati, whom he had met in Avignon the previous year.[16] She was to become one of James's closest friends over the next 15 years.[17]

James also made a point of seeing those of his subjects who were already resident in Rome. On 9 June he visited the English College near the Palazzo Farnese, and on the 10th he visited the Scots College opposite the Palazzo Barberini. Then, on the 22nd, he received a visit from "le Recteur et les Ecoliers du College Irlandois".

The king also took advantage of being in Rome to have a new portrait painted. The artist selected for him by Cardinal Gualterio was Antonio David, who had lived in Rome since 1686, and who had made his reputation by painting several cardinals.[18] Gualterio described him as "the best painter we have",[19] and Nairne echoed this in his "Journal", where he wrote that David was "considered the best painter in Rome for portraits and for catching a sitter's likeness".[20] James III sat four times to David between 30 June and 2 July, and left him to finish the portrait after his departure.

Illustration 3   Antonio David, *James III* (1717)

This portrait of James is particularly important in the iconography of the king. It was the first to be painted since 1714, when he had been at Bar-le-Duc. In the intervening years, Queen Anne had died and had been succeeded by George I of Hanover. In addition James had shown his gratitude to the Scottish Jacobites by deciding that his two major chivalric orders should be made compatible, so that the insignia of the Thistle might thenceforth be worn with those of the Garter.[21] The portrait by Antonio David reflected these two changes. James is shown for the first time as the legitimate king, with a closed crown placed on a table beside him, and a view of London in the background. He is also shown with the St Andrew medal of the Thistle suspended from a green ribbon worn around his neck, resting on the blue sash of the Garter. Until this point all his portraits had shown him with the Garter only, and none of them had included the Thistle. Henceforth, he would never be painted without both orders.[22]

The original painting was intended for Mary of Modena at Saint-Germain,[23] but James knew that he would have to repay all the hospitality he was receiving in Rome by distributing copies to his numerous friends and supporters. The portrait was therefore assumed at the time to be of particular significance.

Another important cultural aspect of James's visit to Rome was his exposure to Italian (or rather Roman) music. The Master of the Music at Saint-Germain (Innocenzo Fede) had come from Rome, so James was already very familiar with Italian music, particularly the sonatas and cantatas performed in the royal apartments, and the *petits motets* performed in the *Chapelle Royale*.[24] But Fede had left Rome back in 1686, and James had left Saint-Germain in 1712, so it is unlikely that he was familiar with the latest styles. In recent years, moreover, he had had much less opportunity to listen to church music of the quality that he had known in France and Lorraine.

James was known to be particularly keen on French opera, but had not attended a performance for several years. While he was at Avignon Salviati had organised a concert with 12 instrumentalists and 9 singers,[25] and there had been balls. Salviati's accounts include payments "for twelve violinists, who played at four balls given by the Vice Legate at his palace for the King of England during the carnival",[26] but we do not know what kind of music (French or Italian) was performed. At Pesaro James had heard three Italian operas and does not seem to have been particularly impressed by them.[27]

Nairne's "Journal" tells us something about the performances, but unfortunately not about the music which James heard in Rome. On 3 June the king was entertained by Donna Teresa, the wife of Don Carlo Albani: "refreshments were provided and Domenico Scarlatti, a great musician, played the harpsichord and sang". A few days later, when James visited the gallery in the Palazzo Colonna, Nairne noted that "there were two of the best voices in Rome, and an admirable symphony". James also visited the Church of SS. Apostoli, beside the Palazzo Colonna, specifically to hear "the music at High Mass". At the Villa Pamphili on 27 June there was "some very beautiful music, the best that His Majesty had so far heard and the most to his taste". These comments tell us very little, beyond the fact that James was hearing the best music which his Roman hosts could provide. At the Villa Pamphili, James particularly appreciated "a Cantata composed especially for His Majesty" with words by Cardinal Pamphili himself.

But was the composer instructed to write music in the Italian style, or in "le goût français"? We are not told. At any rate the music at the Palazzo Ruspoli on 30 June was definitely Italian, composed by Francesco Gasparini: "2 or 3 cantatas rehearsed and performed by two young women, one of whom is the best female voice in Rome at the moment".[28] Once the Stuart court had acquired a permanent residence, the style of music to be performed was bound to be discussed, and James's exposure to this Italian music in Rome was therefore likely to have been influential.

In addition to seeing the sights of Rome itself, James also made two excursions to the surrounding area. One was a day trip to Tivoli. The other, which was more important and lasted three days, was to Castel Gandolfo and the surrounding area in the Alban hills.

The visit to Castel Gandolfo was organised by Don Carlo Albani and paid for by the *Camera Apostolica*.[29] James travelled out there on 15 June and arrived at the papal palace, high up overlooking Lake Albano, in the evening. Nairne described the reception which followed:

> As soon as His Majesty arrived, fires were lit at regular points all round the Lake of Castell [*sic*], with two magnificent illuminations among them, and numerous small cannon shots were heard from guns placed on the edge of the lake, which measures 6 miles round, and which is turned into a sort of amphitheatre by the surrounding hills. From the middle of the lake fireworks were set off which were seen to great effect from the windows of the Palace, after which the King sat down to eat.[30]

While the king ate his dinner with Don Carlo Albani, musicians played on a balcony which had been specially constructed under a large canopy in the shape of a royal closed crown. Behind them the wall had been painted for the occasion, and showed James being restored to his Kingdom of England, "disembarking from a ship with a large company of his followers and being greeted on the beach by a crowd".[31]

On the following day, James visited Frascati and the monastery of Grotta Ferrata, before having dinner with Prince Colonna in his villa at

Marino. Nairne noted that Colonna had thoughtfully placed a portrait of Mary of Modena "in the apartment into which His Majesty first entered...and placed under a canopy".[32] On the way back to Castel Gandolfo, James visited Cardinal Ottoboni, the Cardinal Protector of France, in his villa at Albano.

That evening James was given a musical entertainment of some significance. Don Carlo Albani had gone out of his way to make his hospitality as French as possible. Thus "all the meat was prepared in the French manner, and excellent Champagne was served" – a considerable compliment given the problems of transportation from Reims to Rome. Even the music was especially composed in the French style by Domenico Scarlatti. Using an Italian adaptation of part of a libretto set by André Campra for his *tragédie-lyrique* called *Télémache*, Scarlatti had composed a cantata entitled *Il Ritorno di Telemacho*. It was performed against the wall painting showing James disembarking on the English coast. Scarlatti's music "lasted about three-quarters of an hour, and was much appreciated",[33] and was sung by Checchino and Pasqualino, the two most famous castrati in Rome at the time, supported by a chorus of 14 and an orchestra of 47 instrumentalists.[34] The cantata itself has not survived, but it was probably incorporated into the opera *Telemaco*, performed at the Teatro Capranica in Rome the following January, and attributed in its entirety then and ever since to Domenico's father, Alessandro Scarlatti. The cantata is the only work of its kind which Domenico Scarlatti is known to have written, and the opera has recently been described as "peculiar" in the history of Italian baroque opera, "in that its libretto and scenic style is entirely in the French style" and its music "displays the utmost instrumental magnificence".[35]

Even before they went to Castel Gandolfo James III told the Duke of Mar how the three men he had taken with him to Rome were reacting to the experience: "I believe Nairne will live a year longer and Booth as much shorter for this journey; our friend John [Hay] is delighted with all he sees here."[36] Nairne confirmed this a few days later: "we have had fine music and seen fine pictures and statues, all which, as old as I am, I am not philosopher enough to despise, especially the music part, in which you will not condemn me quite as much as Mr Booth does."[37] The disapproval so obviously shown by Booth, only recently appointed *maggiordomo*, offended James III and was to have important implications for the Stuart court in the coming months.

Beyond the sight-seeing, and these various entertainments, James's main purpose in coming to Rome had been to see Pope Clement XI. During the course of his visit, James had five private audiences with the

Pope at the Quirinale, each of which lasted two hours, and saw him on two other occasions.[38] By the end of his second audience, James had achieved one of his objectives: it was agreed that when he left Rome he would go straight to the Palazzo Ducale at Urbino, without the need to return to Pesaro.[39] During his farewell audience on Saturday, 5 July he achieved his other objective, to have Gualterio officially appointed to be the Cardinal Protector of England.[40] Nairne commented that "I think it is a great deal to the King's credit as well as satisfaction to have gaind that great point amongst other things by his journy to Rome".[41]

Illustration 4   Antonio David, *Pope Clement XI* (c.1720)

In addition to the private audiences James also visited Pope Clement at the Quirinale on 14 June with the Portuguese ambassador, and was given a crucifix made of "Montegrande crystal, garnished with gold".[42]

These visits, and various others to and from the cardinals and princes in Rome, involved a ceremonial which was much more elaborate than that to which he had been accustomed in France. Hay observed that "this place is so full of ceremony that it is a perfect torture to have to do with any of the inhabitants". James apparently received people in the English manner, but had to accept the Roman ceremonial when he was himself received: "The King does as he pleases, and lets them do as they please."[43] Once again it was Booth who allowed his disapproval to show. Nairne remarked that, "as for the ceremonial part, I cannot say I like it, for nobody does, but I can bear it more patiently than Mr Booth".[44]

By this time, however, Nairne, Booth and Hay were no longer the only Jacobite courtiers in Rome. Before he left Pesaro, James had left clear instructions that none of his other courtiers should follow him to Rome until eight days after his own departure.[45] By the end of May the period of waiting was over, and a large group of Jacobites set out, arriving in Rome during the first week of June. They included five peers: the Earls of Nithsdale, Panmure and Southesk and Viscounts Kilsyth and Kingston. The presence in Rome of such a distinguished group of Scottish lords prompted the Pope to visit the Scots College. There, in the college chapel on 10 June, Clement XI said mass in the presence of James III and his courtiers.[46]

The arrival of the Scottish peers, however, raised important questions of ceremonial. They argued that they should have the privilege of being presented to the Pope wearing swords and hats. As this was something which no Italian *conte* was permitted to do, the Scottish peers were obliged to justify their request to the papal authorities. There is an interesting Italian document in the archives of the Scots College at Rome, anonymous and undated, which is entitled "Some Reasons why the Earls of Great Britain claim the right to kiss the feet of the Pope wearing a sword and a hat".[47] The author of the document pointed out that although an English or Scottish Earl was called a *conte* in Italy, this was only because "there is no word in the Italian language to translate their actual rank in the peerage".[48] Far from being the equivalent of Italian *conti*, the Earls were peers of the realm with the right to sit in the upper house of Parliament. There were very few of them, and they had considerable landed estates. Their rank was thus equivalent to that of a German Landgrave, considerably higher than that of an Italian *conte*.

The document further argued that Earls should not be equated with other English and Scottish noblemen simply because they were all called "Mylordes". Most of the "Mylordes" who came to Rome were young men who had not yet inherited from their fathers, and might even be younger sons, whereas the system of primogeniture meant that anyone with the rank of Earl was actually the eldest son and already head of the family. The request was evidently successful. In his description of James III's farewell audience with the Pope on 3 July, Nairne recorded that

> the visit lasted two hours. When His Majesty was ready to leave, he invited the Lords and a few other gentlemen from his suite into the room and presented them to His Holiness and they kissed his foot. In consideration for His Majesty, the Lords were allowed to enter wearing their swords and hats. There were 5 Lords: Southesk, Nithsdale, Panmure, Kilsyth and Kingston.[49]

Given that the Stuart court was destined to return to Rome within a short time, and remain there permanently, this audience established a precedent of considerable social importance, which would apply in future to Dukes and Marquesses as well as Earls and Viscounts.

That evening the Pope sent the king several presents to take with him as souvenirs of his visit. They included "a casket containing the holy relics of a martyr, another filled with Agnus Dei medallions, a piece of the true cross set in crystal and enclosed in a reliquary, and a rosary of lapis lazuli, with some Indulgences, and certificates of authenticity for all the items".[50] James also received 21 books, making 28 volumes in total, containing descriptions and engravings of everything of interest in Rome.[51] These books would form a significant part of the royal library at the Stuart court.

James III finally left Rome on the evening of Sunday, 4 July, "accompanied in his coach by Mr Hay, and in another by Mr Booth, with 3 or 4 valets and other servants".[52] In the morning they reached the Palazzo Farnese at Caprarola, where they rested for most the day, before moving on in the cool of the evening to spend the night at Soriano, a country house belonging to Don Carlo Albani. Nairne, meanwhile, was left behind in Rome to conclude business with Cardinal Gualterio. From Soriano the king moved on slowly up the Via Flaminia, through Terni, to Foligno, which he reached on Thursday, 8 July, and where he remained for a day to allow Nairne to catch up. The party then travelled on, and finally arrived at the Palazzo Ducale at Urbino on the evening of Sunday, 11 July. The household servants had already arrived from Pesaro, and the Stuart court was re-established in its new and permanent residence.[53]

3
The Palazzo Ducale

Urbino is a small city situated in hilly countryside about 20 miles to the south-west of Pesaro. To modern eyes the city itself appears charming and the surrounding hills ruggedly beautiful. But that was not the way they appeared to the Jacobites who lived there from July 1717 to October 1718. After a brief honeymoon period they soon grew weary of the place and increasingly critical of its geographical position. As an escape from Pesaro it served its purpose well enough, but James III and his courtiers soon became very conscious of the disadvantages of living in such a remote and inconvenient place.

To begin with Urbino could only be reached by travelling along extremely bad roads. Those from Pesaro on the Adriatic or from Tuscany in the west were the worst, but even the more normal access routes from the Via Flaminia were notoriously bad. People travelling up from Rome had to turn off the Via Flaminia at the small town of Acqualagna, travel up to Fermigniano, and then up the steep and dangerous final hill to Urbino. People coming from the coastal town of Fano reached Fermigniano by turning off further east, after the small town of Fossombrone, and then following the river Metauro. They then also had to travel up the final hill to Urbino. One Jacobite has left us with the following description of these alternative access routes:

At the end of the town next to [i.e. before] Acqualagna ... the way is some better ye wayes broader and the precipices no so frightfull. The hills on each side barren but the pass not so strait. At Acqualagna we quit the post road (which goes by Fossombrone and Fano to Pesaro) and came to Urbino reckoned to be about ten miles from Acqualagna. The way is so very bad and hilly that we were obliged to gett more horses and oxen to draw our chaises: all the way you see nothing but hills upon hills jumbled together without any valey.[1]

From Urbino to Fossombrone its said to be 13 myles a very bad road being amongst hills and full of precipices very hazardous at any time but more...when the whole ground is covered with snow.... about six or seven miles from Urbino [there is] a pretty good road to Fossombrone thro a smal strath where runs the river Metaurus.[2]

In short Urbino was a remote city, cut off from main roads and trade routes, which no one would ever pass through and no one would ever visit without making a special effort.

To make matters worse, Urbino was itself "seated on the tops and declivity of two hills",[3] so that there was virtually no flat land either inside or outside the city. In July 1717, only 12 days after his arrival, John Hay wrote that "we have a few promenades and must of necessity go down and up hill to get at them, so that, except one have something within doors that is agreeable, one must pass his time here but very indifferently".[4] When the Duke of Mar arrived at Urbino several months later he was even more critical:

the place of the country we are in is a damned one. We have... nothing but hills, not so much as the least valley near us, so that our promenade...[is] on roads cut out of the sides of one hill to the top of another, where there is nothing to be seen but hills on three sides and hills too on the fourth quite to the sea.[5]

He added on another occasion (and the comment is significant coming from a Scot): "for the part of the country it [Urbino] stands in there are few places in the Highlands of Scotland that are not champaign level countries in respect of it."[6]

Under these circumstances it was inevitable that the Jacobites would soon become dissatisfied with Urbino, and that one of the main problems for James III would be to keep his courtiers entertained. We may again conveniently quote the Duke of Mar:

we are here as it were out of the world, at least Europe.... I do not wonder the people of this country give themselves to music, architecture, etc., since they are in a manner out of communication with the world, and must have things not depending on it to entertain themselves.[7]

The Stuart court at Urbino increasingly devoted itself to indoor entertainments: sports, billiards, cards and particularly music.

To make matters worse the Jacobites disliked the weather at Urbino for much of the year. Not surprisingly they found it too hot in the summer, but that was not the only problem: "we have had terrible hot weather and been plagued by the Corina, a wind which is scarce to be borne, and 'tis as bad here, I believe, as anywhere."[8] The wind continued even when the heat declined. A letter from late July records that the court was suffering from bad weather, made worse by the wind called the *corina* or *scirocco*.[9] They apparently hoped for a mild winter, but were in for a disappointment, as Urbino became covered in snow. Mar commented in February that "we have now here a very cruel winter.... I could not believe that there were ever such bad winters in any place in this country and will think the better of our own island afterwards."[10] With such difficult communications to the Via Flaminia and the outside world, "the snows and mountains of Urbino...make it a real prison in winter".[11] So they looked forward to the spring, and in March the king wrote optimistically that "the spring is delightful after the snows".[12] A few weeks later he wrote that "though this country is as bad as the Highlands, the climate is excellent and much better than Pesaro".[13] But he was too optimistic. The wind and rain returned in the middle of April,[14] and the mountains were still covered in snow: "we see snow and feel frost".[15] Once again Urbino could be compared with Scotland. Mar wrote on the following day that "next to a certain country, if not before it, I believe Urbino excells" for cold and rain.[16] At the end of the summer he described the place as "abominable".[17]

Under these circumstances one might reasonably wonder why James III had been so keen to transfer his court to Urbino in the first place. He had definitely wanted to get away from Pesaro, and perhaps he had been misinformed about the weather. But the most important reason was surely the presence in Urbino of the superb Palazzo Ducale, for the most part unoccupied at the time. Presumably James had visited it while he was at Pesaro, and seen that it was able to provide all the necessary facilities for the reestablishment of the exiled Stuart court as it had been at Bar-le-Duc, if not Saint-Germain-en-Laye. There is not a hint of criticism of the palazzo to be found in any of the letters already quoted. Indeed virtually every one contrasts the disappointing surroundings and climate with the building, which is "very noble",[18] "excellent"[19] and "fine".[20]

The palazzo had been built on one of the two hills of Urbino by Duke Federico da Montefeltro in the second half of the fifteenth century, to replace a medieval castle which had previously occupied part of the same position, overlooking the Western approach to the city.[21] It was essentially a square three-storey brick building faced with marble, constructed around a central courtyard, with some additional wings projecting from three of the corners. On the west side only, where the land fell steeply away, there were also some extensive basements, almost all that remained of the original medieval castle.

Illustration 5   A View of Urbino (showing the main road leading uphill from the Porta di Valbona, with the Palazzo Ducale on the right), anonymous engraving published in Bernardino Baldi, *Memorie concernenti La Città di Urbino dedicate alla Sacra Real Maestà di Giacomo III, rè della Gran Brettagna etc.*, edited by Francesco Bianchini (Rome, 1724), title page

The principal architectural features of the palazzo, for which it was as famous then as it is today, were the twin round towers built either side of the central loggia of the Duke's apartment. That apartment, and similar ones above and below it, extended towards the west from the north-west corner of the palazzo, and enjoyed spectacular views over the surrounding hills. Beside it, and extending towards the north from the same north-west corner, was another wing which linked the palazzo, via a private inner staircase, with the adjacent fine sixteenth-century cathedral, which had a renaissance cupola. This wing was built around an irregular courtyard containing an enclosed garden.

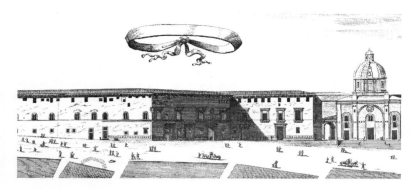

Illustration 6 The Palazzo Ducale and the Cathedral of Urbino, as seen from the Piazza Maggiore, anonymous engraving published in Bernardino Baldi, *Memorie concernenti La Città di Urbino dedicate alla Sacra Real Maestà di Giacomo III, rè della Gran Brettagna etc.*, edited by Francesco Bianchini (Rome, 1724), pp. 48–49

In the south-east corner of the palazzo, diagonally opposite the Duke's apartment, the east wing had been extended to provide additional accommodation, and then extended even further to create a second courtyard. This, however, was unfinished: one corner remained open, while the extension of the palazzo from the south-west corner had only a single storey.

Since the death of the last Duke of Urbino in 1631, the duchy had devolved to the papacy and been governed by a papal legate, who resided at Pesaro. As a result the Palazzo Ducale (now more properly called the Palazzo Apostolico) had lost its function as a princely residence. A papal vice-legate had retained one of the apartments, and various rooms, particularly on the ground floor, had been handed over to the city for public use. Otherwise the building had been stripped of its rich furnishings and left unoccupied. Such, then, was the palazzo into which the Stuart court moved in July 1717.

There had been very little time to make it ready, and the papal accounts show that the necessary painting, cleaning and repairs (particularly of the windows) continued for several weeks after the king's arrival. Although a great deal of furniture had already been sent from Rome, further items (including chairs, tables and beds) did not arrive until the autumn. Even the king's own apartment was not ready when he moved into it.[22]

A high priority, however, had been given to ensuring that the palazzo was properly guarded. A detachment of Corsican guards had already arrived from Pesaro to control the gates of the city, and some Swiss guards had been sent from Rome to ensure the security of the palazzo itself. The Swiss were accommodated in the single-storey building beside the unfinished courtyard to the west of the palazzo, with a guard room immediately beside the main entrance. The Corsican guards were based in the town nearby, to guarantee a quick reinforcement in case of need.[23]

The entrances to the palazzo, then as now, were situated in a large piazza, which was surrounded on two sides by the palazzo itself, on the third side by the cathedral, and on the fourth by the buildings lining the main thoroughfare running through this part of the city. If one stood in the piazza with one's back to the road, the main entrance to the palazzo was on one's left; a second entrance, to the wing surrounding the enclosed garden, was straight in front.

Passing through the main entrance one entered the central courtyard, which had a portico extending along its entire perimeter. To the left, in a clockwise direction, one passed by the papal library and archives (north wing), the grand staircase to the floors above (situated in the

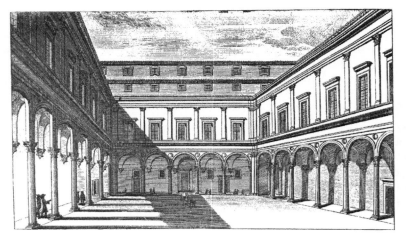

Illustration 7   The principal courtyard of the Palazzo Ducale, showing the main entrance on the north side. On the right of the entrance is one of the two doors leading into the papal library and archives, then the foot of the grand staircase in the north-east corner, and the *appartamento del Monte di Pietà* in the east wing; on the left of the entrance is one of the two doors to the guard room and the basement, then the entrance to the apartment of Lodovico Anguissola in the north-west corner, anonymous engraving published in Bernardino Baldi, *Memorie concernenti La Città di Urbino dedicate alla Sacra Real Maestà di Giacomo III, rè della Gran Brettagna etc.*, edited by Francesco Bianchini (Rome, 1724), p. 149

corner), and the *appartamento del Monte di Pietà* (east wing). Beyond that there were two covered passages, either side of a kitchen (south wing) which led through to the unfinished courtyard occupied by the Swiss guards. The south wing also contained the dressing rooms of a theatre which itself occupied the entire west wing. Beyond the theatre, in the north-west corner, was the apartment of Lodovico Anguissola, the papal vice-legate,[24] with a loggia similar to that of the Duke above, between the twin round towers. The north wing, before one returned to the main entrance, contained a passage which led to the extension around the enclosed garden, then a ramp leading down to the basements, and finally the guard room of the Swiss guards.

From this description it can be observed that the Stuart court did not occupy any of the ground floor of the palazzo – a fact which has been overlooked by all previous historians. Sharing the building with a significant group of local Italians was to influence the court's organisation and social life.

The second entrance to the palazzo, also from the piazza, led directly to the wing which extended to the north around the enclosed garden. This was divided into two main areas, separated by a small connecting room and a large staircase which was originally part of the medieval castle, and known as the *rampa del castellara*. To the left, closest to the courtyard, there was a large room dedicated to sports, and called the *sala* of the *gioco della pallacorda* (tennis court). To the right, closest to the cathedral, was the *Tribunale Civile*.[25] Thus the Jacobites were able to look down on the enclosed garden (called the *giardino pensile* because it was laid out on top of the basements), to which only the vice-legate and the lawyers of the *tribunale* enjoyed direct access.

James III occupied a large and spacious apartment on the first floor, but not the one originally created for Duke Federico, then known as the *appartamento nobile*, with the twin towers and the loggia looking out to the west. The papal authorities originally assumed that he would occupy that one.[26] But the rooms were not distributed *enfilade* in the French manner, to which he had been accustomed at Saint-Germain, so he decided that they should be retained by Alamanno Salviati, who was to continue living in the palazzo as *Presidente* of Urbino (equivalent to papal legate).[27] Instead James chose to occupy a set of rooms on the west side of the central courtyard, above the theatre, which enjoyed the same exceptional panorama.

The King's apartment consisted of a guard chamber (*anticamera*), a presence chamber (*seconda anticamera*), a privy chamber with a throne and a canopy (*stanza dell'udienza*) and a bedchamber (*stanza di letto*).

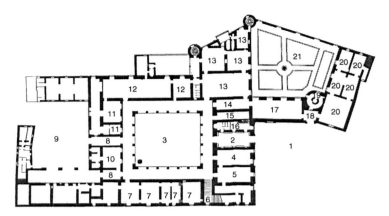

Illustration 8   The plan of the ground floor of the Palazzo Ducale, showing the position of the court theatre beneath the king's apartment, adapted from F. Arnold, *Der Herzogliche Palast von Urbino* (Leipzig, 1857), Illustration 3

The Plan of Ground Floor of the Palazzo Ducale
1. *Piazza Maggiore*
2. Entrance
3. Courtyard: *Cortile*
4. Library
5. Archives
6. Grand Staircase
7. *Appartamento del Monte de Pietà*
8. Passages to the Courtyard of the Swiss Guards
9. Courtyard of the Swiss Guards
10. Kitchen
11. Dressing Rooms
12. Theatre
13. Apartment of Lodovico Anguissola
14. Passage
15. Ramp down to the Basements
16. Guard Room
17. Tennis Court: *Sala* of the *gioco della pallacorda*
18. Second Entrance
19. Staircase: *Rampa del Castellara*
20. *Tribunale Civile*
21. Garden: *Giardino Pensile*

Beyond the bedchamber were some small cabinets (*gabinetti*) overlooking the courtyard of the Swiss guards. There was also a secret cabinet (*camera segreta*), known as the *camerino indorato*, which jutted out from the façade of the building, and which could be accessed only from the bedchamber. This was the room in which he conducted his correspondence, until it became too hot in the afternoons,[28] and which is now shown off to tourists as the *stanza del Re d'Inghilterra*, as if it was the only room occupied by the King.[29] It has a low ceiling because there is a mezzanine room above it (the *camerino di sopra*), reached by going up a small spiral staircase.[30]

In addition to the apartments occupied by the King and by Salviati, the first floor of the palazzo contained two large apartments in the east and south wings, some individual rooms in the extension from the

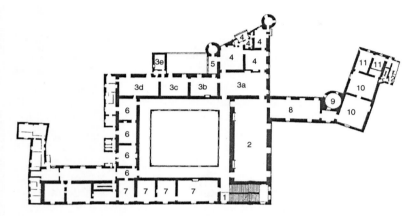

Illustration 9 The plan of the first floor of the Palazzo Ducale, showing the position of the king's apartment, adapted from an anonymous engraving published in Bernardino Baldi, *Memorie concernenti La Città di Urbino dedicate alla Sacra Real Maestà di Giacomo III, rè della Gran Brettagna etc.*, edited by Francesco Bianchini (Rome, 1724), pp. 48–49

The Plan of the First Floor of the Palazzo Ducale

1. Grand Staircase
2. *Salone/Sala Maggiore*
3. King's Apartment

    3a. Guard Chamber: *Anticamera*
    3b. Presence Chamber: *Seconda anticamera*
    3c. Privy Chamber: *Stanza dell'udienza*
    3d. Bedchamber: *Stanza di letto*
    3e. Cabinet: *Camera segreto/Camerino indorato*

4. Apartment of Alamanno Salviati
5. Corridor to the staircase down to the kitchens
6. *Appartamento della foresteria* (Dominic Sheldon; Duke of Perth)
7. *Appartamento di S. Domenico* (Duke of Mar)
8. *Sala* of the *Appartamento del Magnifico*
9. Staircase: *Rampa del Castellara*
10. *Accademia degli Assorditi*
11. Rooms leading to the inner staircase connecting the palazzo with the cathedral
12. The inner staircase leading to the Chapel of the Holy Sacrament: *Cappella dell SS. Sacramento*

south-east corner and various public rooms on the north side. One of the apartments, known as the *appartamento di S. Domenico* because it looked across the street to the church of that name, was set aside for the Duke of Mar, whenever he should return to the court.[31] The other one, known as the *appartamento della foresteria*, was available for the Duke of Ormonde, but occupied by Dominic Sheldon (Vice-Chamberlain) pending his return.[32] It is not known who occupied the other rooms. The use of the public rooms, on the other hand, is much better documented.

Above the portico, and extending around all four sides of the central courtyard, was the *soppraloggia*, a set of galleries which provided an agreeable place to walk, and which gave access to the grand staircase and the public rooms. The largest of these, occupying the entire north wing beside the grand staircase, was the *salone* or *sala maggiore*. It contained a papal throne and was regularly used by the Jacobites for their daily walks.[33] The others were collectively known as the *appartamento del Magnifico*, because Giuliano de' Medici had once stayed there in the early sixteenth century. The first room, above the large one used for the *gioco della pallacorda* (tennis court), was described as the *sala* and used for musical concerts. The remaining rooms (above the *Tribunale Civile*) had, since 1709, been occupied by a literary group known as the Academy of the Assorditi, "an institution whose members met to read the literary compositions of the academicians themselves". The first room was a waiting area for the ladies, the second was the one used by the academicians. As these were the rooms through which one had to pass when going from the main part of the palazzo to the cathedral they were not suitable for accommodation, and thus the *Accademia degli Assorditi* continued to use them throughout the period when the Stuart court was in residence, entering directly from the piazza and the *rampa del castellare*.[34]

The second floor, which was where most of the Jacobite courtiers and senior servants lived, contained two large apartments, on the south and east sides of the courtyard (occupied by Lord Edward Drummond and Lord Clermont),[35] and many small apartments and individual rooms distributed above the ones occupied by the King and Salviati, and above the *appartamento del Magnifico*. As the ceiling of the *Salone* was very high there was no space above it, so the rooms above the *appartamento del Magnifico* had to be entered via the *rampa del castellare*,[36] and were separated from those around the central courtyard. No information has survived concerning the allocation of the rooms on the second floor. It seems, however, that the palazzo was large enough to provide accommodation for virtually everyone. The only person who is known to have lived with a landlord in the town was one of the Scottish pensioners who arrived after the court had been established.[37]

We can deduce how the basements were used because they are divided into two separate parts by the *rampa di accesso* which leads down to them from the central courtyard. On the right, below the enclosed garden, the *sala* of the *gioco della pallacorda* and the *Tribune Civile*, were the stables. On the left, below the apartment of the vice-legate, were the kitchens, and beyond them, below the theatre and the single-storey extension of the Swiss guards, were the wine cellars.[38] How the Stables and the Household Below Stairs actually made use of the available space cannot be ascertained, but two conclusions can be drawn. First, the food and drink for the king's table had to pass up the spiral staircase within the tower closest to his apartment. And secondly, the Stables were situated within the palazzo itself, adjacent to the kitchens, and were thus located with the Household Below Stairs, something which had not been the case at either Saint-Germain-en-Laye or Bar-le-Duc. This was to mean, as we shall see, that it made good sense to change the organisation of the royal household and place the Stables and the Household Below Stairs under the same senior officer.

We know very little about the furniture and decoration of the palazzo while the Stuart court was there, apart from those things, notably the celebrated inlaid wood panelling in the *studiolo* of Salviati's apartment, which can still be seen. One of the Jacobites has left us a few, tantalisingly brief comments:

> The apartments are numerous and large. The stair straitly. You have his [Federico da Montefeltro's] statue on the first turn. The chimneys, windows and doors are all of hewn stone curiously cutt in diverse shapes.... theres a great sale [sic: the *salone*] a hundred and twelve foot in length and fourty five in breadth with the height proportionable. In this sale there is a statue of the present pope [Clement XI] sett up at the charges of this city. It is very well cutt and is very like.[39]

Unfortunately he gives us nothing more than this, and then proceeds to describe in considerable detail the decoration of the cathedral.

As already stated, a great deal of furniture was transferred to Urbino from both Pesaro and Rome, and the total cost of doing this, of purchasing new furniture, mattresses, blankets and hangings, and of painting and restoring the palazzo was over 2272 *scudi*.[40] The items mentioned are what one would expect in any early eighteenth-century Italian princely residence, and virtually no indication is given of where specific items were placed, apart from the canopy (*baldacchino*) in the king's privy chamber. The king's secret cabinet was painted in white and gold. Otherwise the walls of the king's apartment were hung with tapestries taken from the papal wardrobe in Rome, showing the arms of the Barberini, Borghese, Chigi and Pamphili families. The *sala*, or *anticamera* of the *appartamento del Magnifico*, was decorated with both Chigi and Pamphili tapestries.[41]

4
The Jacobite Courtiers

The Stuart court at Urbino contained approximately 80 people, just as it had at Pesaro. About 55 of these were employed as members of the royal household and received salaries.[1] The remaining 25, nearly all of whom had joined the court after the Jacobite rising of 1715–1716, received pensions.

The abolition of "fixed waiting" in the Chamber and the Bedchamber, which had already taken place at Bar-le-Duc and Pesaro, had tended to erode the distinction between the senior servants with salaries and the more important pensioners, as neither group had any specific duties to perform. Moreover, the salaries of the servants had been reduced. Thus the Gentlemen of the Bedchamber, the Vice-Chamberlain and the Scottish lords all received 200 *livres per annum*, the Grooms of the Bedchamber received 150 *livres*, and the Scottish gentlemen received 100 *livres*. At Urbino, however, with a regular papal pension,[2] James was able to increase the salaries of the servants back to their former levels. Thus the Secretary of State and the Lord Chamberlain now had an income of 471 *livres*, the Gentlemen of the Bedchamber received 353 *livres*, the Vice-Chamberlain received 314 *livres* and the Grooms of the Bedchamber received 204 *livres*. David Nairne, as Secretary of the Closet, had never had a reduction, and continued to receive 205 *livres*.[3] At Urbino, as previously at Saint-Germain and Bar-le-Duc, James attached a high priority to paying his servants as well as possible, and maintaining an impressive court. If the cost of living was lower at Urbino than it had been at Saint-Germain and Bar-le-Duc, as seems likely, then the household servants would have been better off in real terms.[4]

The pensions for the new Scottish exiles, however, were not increased, as they were free to leave the court and live elsewhere, and in the meantime were given accommodation in the Palazzo Ducale. Thus the lords continued to receive 200 *livres*, the gentlemen 100 *livres*, and below them the colonels had 60 *livres*, less than a valet and a little more than a coachman. The majors, with 45 *livres*, received the same as the king's washerwoman. The pension of James Edgar, who would one day become the king's private secretary, was the same as the salary paid to the kitchen boys.[5] The court at Urbino cannot be understood unless the contrast between the financial condition and status of the servants and that of the new pensioners is constantly borne in mind.

The departments

James III was served in his Bedchamber by a small staff of six people. He had a French Yeoman of the Robes, two valets who were also barbers, one of whom was French, the other Irish, another valet who was French, a French servant to help the valets, and an Irish washerwoman.[6] The yeoman and the valets were close to the king because of the positions they held, but the most important was Felix Bonbled, a Frenchman recruited at Avignon, who was given considerable responsibility for arranging the king's apartment, and who would continue for nearly 50 years to serve the king as one of his valets.

What had once been the Chamber was now reduced to a skeleton staff of five people. They included the Vice Chamberlain, Dominic Sheldon; the king's Irish Dominican confessor, Father John Brown; his two Protestant chaplains, the Episcopalian George Barclay and the Anglican Patrick Cowper; and his personal physician. This was Dr Lawrence Wood, who was English, succeeded by Dr Charles Maghie, who was Scottish.[7] In March 1718, when Sheldon left the court, he was replaced by the Duke of Perth, who was given the title of Lord Chamberlain, or *Maestro di Camera* – the first time the post had been filled at the king's court since 1696.[8]

The departments in the basements of the Palazzo Ducale were much larger. The Household Below Stairs was now divided into four sub-departments: the Kitchen, the Confectionary, the Bakehouse and the Wine Cellar.[9] The Clerk of the Kitchen, referred to at Urbino as the *Maestro di Casa*,[10] was Jeremiah Broomer, who had been recruited in Ireland by James II in 1689. He was supported by four cooks, three kitchen boys and his own personal servant.[11] The Yeoman Confectioner also had his own personal servant as well as an assistant, but the Baker worked by himself.[12] The Yeoman of the Wine Cellar, Charles Macarty, was another servant recruited in Ireland by James II. He had an assistant and a scourer.[13] Nearly all of these 16 people had previously served at Saint-Germain and were very experienced, most notably Broomer and Macarty. Five of them were English, three were Irish, five were French (including two recruited at Avignon), and three were Italians recruited locally, of whom the most significant was the assistant in the Wine Cellar.

The Stables, now situated in the basements on the other side of the *rampa di accesso*, originally employed 20 people, most of whom had previously served at Saint-Germain. The king had a coachman, two chairmen, six footmen and five grooms, who themselves had two helpers. There was also a Riding Purveyor and a Harbourer of the Deer.[14] The most important servants, however, were the Equerries. One was James Delattre, who had held the post since 1704 and whose wife's mother had once been the king's wet-nurse.[15] The other was John Hay, whose friendship with James III had developed during their visit to Rome. It is worth noticing that Hay was the only servant in the Stables who was Scottish and who was Protestant. All the others were English, Irish or French and Catholic. As all the servants in the Household Below Stairs were also Catholic, Hay was the odd man out in the basements, and was keen to be transferred to another post.

The secretariat

James III's political secretariat was divided at Urbino, as previously at Avignon, into two parts. There was a Secretary of State, who was Protestant, responsible for the correspondence with Great Britain and the new exiled Jacobite community abroad. And there was a Secretary of the Closet, who was Catholic, responsible for the correspondence with the Papacy, the cardinals and the Catholic princes. Both men were in contact with the Jacobites at Saint-Germain and elsewhere in France, depending on the nature of the business. The Secretary of State was the Duke of Mar, who had two under-secretaries; the Secretary of the Closet was David Nairne, who worked without assistance.[16]

When the court arrived at Urbino Mar was still in France with Robert Creagh, his Catholic under-secretary.[17] The Secretariat therefore consisted at that time of only two men, Mar's Protestant under-secretary John Paterson and David Nairne. Paterson was one of the new exiles, whereas Nairne was an old servant employed in the Secretariat since 1689. In the absence of Mar, the king used John Hay to deal with some of his personal correspondence.

The pensioners

In addition to the 55 people employed in the Departments and Sec-retariat of the royal household, there were approximately 40 other Jacobites who lived at the court of Urbino between July 1717 and November 1718. The latter group were not all there at the same time, however. The average number in attendance at any time was 25.

Most of these pensioners were Scottish. They included the Duke of Perth (who returned from Genoa, and was later appointed Lord Chamberlain), the Earl of Linlithgow (who returned from Milan with Charles Fleming) and all those who had been with the king in Rome, including the Earls of Nithsdale, Panmure and Southesk, Viscounts Kilsyth and Kingston and Alexander Maitland. The others, too numer-ous to be listed here in the text, included lairds and military officers, some of them related to the aristocrats already mentioned.[18] There was also a surgeon (James Hay) and an inn-keeper (Robert Watson). A few, like Lord Panmure and Alexander Maitland (both born in 1659), were quite old, while others, like the Duke of Perth and Lord Nithsdale (born in 1674 and 1676), were in their early forties like the Duke of Mar. But many of them were young men, even younger than the king and John Hay (born in 1688 and 1691). The younger generation included Lord Southesk and Lord Winton (both born in 1692). The Scots who had joined the rising in 1715, and then followed the king into exile, were active men and relatively young.

Some of the more important ones, including the Marquis of Seaforth, had remained in France. Others, including the Marquis of Tullibardine and the Earl Marischal, had already returned from Pesaro to France, where they were given extra money because they no longer had any accommodation and were encouraged to take service in the Spanish army.[19] But once the court had been established at Urbino, most of the Scots remained with the king. Thirteen can be identified who arrived in July 1717 and remained until October 1718.[20] Five others arrived later, and then remained.[21] Lord Southesk and Colonel Stewart of Inver-nity left the court, and did not return for several months, but very few (one of whom was Lord Panmure) left Urbino permanently.[22] Alexander Maitland, who was Southesk's uncle, had fallen ill during the visit to Rome and is the only Scot who is recorded as having died at Urbino. An inscription in a corridor of the Catholic seminary there records that he died on 7 September 1717, aged 47 years, ten months and three days.[23]

The majority of the Scottish pensioners at Urbino were Protestants, like Mar and Hay. Indeed the only Catholics among them – apart from Maitland – were the Duke of Perth, the Earl of Nithsdale, the Earl of Winton and Charles Fleming. Thus the contrast between the salaried servants of the household, who were mainly Catholic, and the pensioners in attendance, who were mainly Protestant, was still a feature of the court at Urbino, as it had been at Avignon and Pesaro.

In addition to the Scots there was a small number of other pensioners who should be mentioned. The most important was Thomas Forster, who had been one of the leaders of the unsuccessful Jacobite rising in Lancashire in the autumn of 1715, and consequently had been given the rank of general. He is described in a document in the Urbino archives as *Generale di Mare e di Terra*.[24] This document is interesting because it also testifies to the presence at Urbino of "Milord Derwentwater",[25] the four-year-old son of the 3rd Earl of Derwentwater who had been executed in 1716 for his part in the Lancashire rising. It is intriguing because it is the only evidence we have that Derwentwater was at Urbino, and raises the question of how long he stayed there and who brought him. One possibility must be his mother, the widowed Countess of Derwentwater. Another is his uncle Charles Radcliffe (later 5th Earl). But as no trace of either of them can be found in any of the archives concerning the court at Urbino, perhaps the person referred to as "Milord Derwentwater" was really Charles Radcliffe, who would later become an important member of the Stuart court in Rome.

There were also four professional military officers at Urbino, all of them Catholic Irishmen who had served in Dillon's Regiment of the French army. Major Donald Macmahon and Captain John O'Brien were promoted by James III to be, respectively, colonel and major,[26] and they remained at Urbino throughout the period that the court was there. Captain Charles Wogan left the court in August 1717 and did not return until the following April,[27] whereas Captain Sir John O'Brien was promoted by the king to the rank of colonel in October 1717 and sent on a mission to France,[28] where he later became Lord Dillon's private secretary.[29] It is likely that these Irishmen enjoyed good relations with the old servants from Saint-Germain,[30] and were not close to the new Scottish Protestant favourites. Macmahon was later to enter the service of the Grand Duke of Tuscany.[31] Wogan, as we shall see, was to become a European celebrity in the spring of 1719, after which he entered the service of the King of Spain. On the other hand, the two O'Briens, both confusingly called John, would remain with James III and eventually become permanent members of the Stuart court after it had moved to Rome.[32]

The presence of all these pensioners in the Palazzo Ducale at Urbino gave the court additional prestige, but inevitably caused problems for the king, who could give them neither the money nor the employment that they expected and deserved. It was important that the royal household should be maintained on a modest and realistic level, so that those servants actually employed should be relatively well paid. The only way in which the king could have satisfied the Scottish pensioners would have been to reintroduce formal waiting in the Chamber and the Bedchamber, and to allocate posts in both those departments, as had always been the case at Saint-Germain. Yet if he had done that at Urbino, it would have become a mock court, unable to finance itself properly, and open to ridicule by acting out a charade in an empty Presence and Privy Chamber. The terrible disappointments experienced since 1714 had left James III emotionally vulnerable, the more so because he was cut off from the world at Urbino. This was to make him liable to misjudgement in his management of men. But it is hard to criticise his decision to give priority to his household and to pay modest pensions to those exiled Jacobites who chose to live at Urbino rather than elsewhere.

5
Life at the Court

The daily life of the court at Urbino naturally revolved around the regular activities of the king. Although James spent many hours each day in his secret cabinet, dealing with his voluminous political and personal correspondence, he also joined his courtiers and provided a focus for their social life.

The dining arrangements which had been established at Avignon[1] seem to have been continued in the Palazzo Ducale. Two tables were laid each day in the king's apartment. The first was for James himself, the Gentlemen and Grooms of the Bedchamber, the Lord Chamberlain, the Vice-Chamberlain, the Secretary of State and anyone else whom the king chose to invite – and it seems that James was generous in extending invitations to the pensioners. Nairne, despite his important role as Secretary of the Closet, was never invited at Urbino: "except during one or two trips in France, and when the King was in Rome, I have never had the honour of being among those occasionally asked to sit at his table, whereas every day he invites the junior members and gentlemen of his suite".[2] Nairne ate at the second table, which was for the other senior members of the household, while the junior members were fed in the basements and given the food which remained at the end of each meal. This arrangement meant that the household servants did not need to be given board wages. The pensioners, on the other hand, when not invited by the king, were expected to feed themselves in their own rooms or in the town.[3]

It is not known what objects were placed on the king's own table, as most of his plate had been left behind at Saint-Germain. He had presumably brought with him his silver travelling plate, which consisted of various objects of state as well as others of practical necessity. Thus the king had a ewer and oval basin, and 2 salts, as well as 6 knives, forks and spoons, 12 trencher plates, 8 little dishes, 2 water pots, 6 tumblers, 4 candlesticks and various other items.[4] It was not until the autumn of 1718 that "all the plate belonging to the Scullery, Back-stairs and Pantry" was sent in two large trunks from Saint-Germain to Italy. Without the plate from the Pantry, which included both his gilt cadinet and all the gold and gilt objects placed on the royal table at Saint-Germain, including 35 large gilt plates, it would not have been possible, even if he had wanted to, to reintroduce the formal state dining to which he had once been accustomed. Moreover, as the trunks were addressed to Cardinal Gualterio in Rome the plate never reached Urbino before the court left the Palazzo Ducale for good.[5]

Plate for those who ate with the king was presumably provided by the *Camera Apostolica*, but it seems that James ordered a new set of Back-stairs plate for his own personal use. At Saint-Germain this plate, which included candlesticks, snuffers, some cups, a tankard and various other items to be used in the Bedchamber, had been valued at 1312 *livres*. The Stuart accounts mention the payment of almost exactly the same amount (1310 *livres*) to a Parisian goldsmith in December 1717 "for plate for the King".[6]

The food, chocolate and beer at Urbino would have been acquired locally, purchased from local tradesmen, with additional game and other animals brought back from hunting.[7] The wine, however, was always French, from Champagne and Burgundy, shipped from Marseilles to Leghorn, and then brought overland.[8] One typical comment of spring 1718 records that "we have excellent white and red Burgundy besides our Champagne, and good beer, small and strong".[9] When some Burgundy was spoiled by the long journey, Mar complained that "we have nothing but country wine till more come from France."[10] It was not until the end of 1718 that other French wines were tried. "Provence wine" was judged to be not "good for anything", but Côte Roti from the northern Rhone was recommended as "a clean wine", with "no other fault but being a little too strong".[11] It is clear that James III expected to provide good quality wines when dining at Urbino. A letter written from Bordeaux at the very end of 1718 (by which time the court had actually moved to Rome) records that "one hogshead of best Margaux claret and one of white wine" had been sent by river to Toulouse, to go by canal to Agde and thence by sea to Civita Vecchia or Leghorn.[12]

The king's other regular daily activity was attending mass in the cathedral beside the palazzo. His own servants and courtiers assembled in his apartment, while the local nobles of Urbino waited for him in the *sala* of the *appartamento del Magnifico*. James was then accompanied by the Jacobites through his guard chamber and the *salone* into the *sala*, where a procession was formed. The Urbino nobles stood at the front, with the Catholic Jacobites at the rear. The king stood in the middle.[13] They then all walked through the rooms used by the *Accademia degli Assorditi* to reach a little inner staircase which connected the palazzo with the cathedral. Emerging into the Chapel of the Holy Sacrament (*Cappella del SS. Sacramento*) through a little door beside the altar, they then made their way past Federico Barocci's famous *L'Ultima Cena* into the main body of the cathedral. At the end of the service they returned by the same route. The chapel was to the left of the high altar, and the little door was to the left of the altar within the chapel. Once the king had gone from there up the staircase, he would walk back through the *appartamento del Magnifico* and the *salone* into his own apartment to make plans for the rest of the day.[14]

James III was regularly accompanied to mass by the Duke of Perth, the Earl of Nithsdale, the Earl of Winton, David Nairne, James Delattre and any other Catholic Jacobites at the court: Lord Edward Drummond, Lord Clermont, Charles Booth, Roger Strickland, Dominic Sheldon and the four Irish officers from Dillon's Regiment. Presumably the king's confessor, physician and valets, and the other lesser servants joined the procession at the rear.

The Protestants, meanwhile, who had all been left behind in the *sala*, went away to hold their own daily services. Where they went is unknown, but it is very probable that a makeshift Anglican chapel was created somewhere in the palazzo.

In July 1717, when the court first arrived at Urbino, there was no Anglican chaplain. Charles Leslie had left Pesaro in May and no replacement had yet arrived.[15] The king originally hoped that Ezekiel Hamilton would return, but he was not available, having become chaplain to the Duke of Ormonde.[16] James therefore invited George Barclay and Patrick Cowper, both of whom had been at Avignon, to rejoin the court,[17] so that "his Protestant servants there might not be without some divines of the Church of England".[18] Barclay was living at Dijon, and Cowper at Rotterdam, so it took some time for them to reach the court. It seems that Barclay (a Scottish Episcopalian) arrived at the end of August, followed by Cowper during September.[19] Hay, Panmure and the many Protestants at the court (including Alan Cameron and Sir William Ellis) were therefore provided with regular services well before the return of the Duke of Mar at the end of November.[20]

It is important to emphasise that Protestant services were regularly and openly held in the Stuart court at Urbino, as they had been at Bar-le-Duc and Avignon, and as they would later be at Rome. James III argued that as King of England it was his duty to be the protector of

Protestants as well as Catholics,[21] and indeed the court at Urbino was, at the higher social level, predominantly Protestant. The Duke of Mar informed Charles Leslie in February 1718 that

> our congregation is not now very numerous there being but few with his Majesty at Urbino in comparison of what was at Avignon, and Lord Panmure's going lately for France... makes it yet thinner, but there are still a good number of us left and more than of any other profession in the family.[22]

Mar had, of course, discounted the lesser servants, all of whom were Catholic.

David Nairne did the same in his correspondence with Cardinal Gualterio. At the beginning of January 1718 he asked Gualterio to obtain a papal dispensation so that the court could eat meat on certain days during the forthcoming period of Lent, and for those not needing to do this to be allowed to drink milk and eat butter and eggs.[23] He explained that, apart from those people who for health reasons could not, and the Protestants who would not, there were actually very few people at the court who intended to keep Lent anyway.[24]

The fact that neither the Protestant pensioners nor the Protestant chaplains normally ate with the king made the arrangements for Lent easier than they might otherwise have been. It seems that the various groups already identified tended to form "clubs" to share the expense of eating.[25] In October 1718, for example, James Edgar recorded that Lord Southesk and "Mr Clephane now eat at Mr Stuart's" [i.e. in the rooms of John Stewart of Invernity].[26] Another letter written by Edgar is even more informative. It actually describes the dining arrangements immediately after the pensioners had arrived in Rome in November 1718, but it gives a good idea of what the arrangements had probably been at Urbino:

> Mr Erskine and I stay together and dine at Mr Macmahon's.... Mr Wogan and Cameron..., with ... Lord Linlithgow and Mr Fleming dine together at Lord Nithsdale's. Their meat is made ready in my lord's kitchen by a public cook and they pay so much a head. Lords Kilsyth and Kingston, Mr Menzies, Colier, Cockburn and [James] Hay have their dinner made ready by their Urbino cook at Lord Kilsyth's lodging. Clephane [and] Lord Southesk... eat together. Mr Carnegie..., I believe, will be of that club. Mr Stuart [*sic*] and Mr Mackenzie will, I fancy, make a club of themselves.

Edgar also discussed the arrangements for suppers:

> Mr Erskine and I come whiles home and take only a glass of wine and a bit of bread and sometimes go to a place like an English ordinary, where the lords and gentlemen are for the most part at night and everyone has his bottle of wine and anything he calls for and pays for it apart.[27]

Other than the daily rituals of dining and attending religious services, there was relatively little to occupy those Jacobite courtiers who were not actually employed in the Household Below Stairs and the Stables. They went riding, and they went out for short evening walks in the town. They also played cards[28] and billiards. There was a billiard table in one of the rooms on the first floor of the palazzo,[29] and in the spring of 1718 the king wrote that "we are in the middle of wind and rain, reduced to billiards and that alone".[30] However, there was also tennis and shuttlecock, the latter apparently introduced by Mar shortly after he arrived. The evidence comes in a letter that Mar sent to Stewart of Invernity in Rome: "we have been busy these two or three days about shuttlecocks or cleckings to give us some exercise, but, now they are made, we have nothing but tennis rackets and battledoors to play with. Could you send us some shuttlecocks and light rackets, which would be a great present."[31] Stewart of Invernity replied shortly afterwards that "two of the best racquets and the only 4 shuttlecocks in Rome" had been sent to Urbino with one of the Swiss guards.[32] Otherwise the Jacobites had to pass the time as best they could. Several of them turned to music, which became the most important activity, and will be discussed separately in Chapter 7. Others (including Clermont and Drummond) no doubt did a lot of reading.[33] Mar busied himself with architecture.[34] Some probably took up painting and drawing. The evidence, however, is lacking. All that we have, in the same letter sent by Mar to Stewart of Invernity in Rome, is the following brief comment: "Clephan [*sic*] wrote to you or the Earl [of Southesk] for some drawing materials, which I hope you'll send."[35] But whatever activity was adopted, life at Urbino was inevitably dull, particularly for those who could not speak Italian and mix with the local population. Mar, who could speak neither Italian nor French, wrote to Lord Panmure in February 1718: "we are going on in our old dull way, one day being as like the other as two eggs and these eaten without either pepper or salt."[36]

Some variety in the daily life of the court was brought by the arrival of British visitors on the Grand Tour. In September 1717, for example, Francis Barker and Edward Bearcroft (both of Oxford University) arrived together, en route for Venice, and stayed a few days.[37] Later the same month Theophilus Oglethorpe arrived from Venice, en route to Rome.[38] But the visitor who provided the greatest interest in the summer and autumn of 1717 was Francis Strickland (a younger brother of Roger Strickland). He arrived from Saint-Germain at the end of August with the news that the Earl of Peterborough was travelling to Italy in order to assassinate the king.

Peterborough had already made several visits to Italy,[39] and owned a property at Reggio, so his decision to travel from Paris to Bologna in the summer of 1717 should not have attracted any particular attention. But an unfounded rumour had been started in Paris that he was returning to Italy with the specific intention of assassinating James III, so Queen Mary and Lord Dillon felt that the king should be warned.[40]

The arrival of Francis Strickland created a sensation at the court. James III immediately ordered Major John Cockburne and Sir John O'Brien to go to Bologna to await Peterborough's arrival and to collect information about any strangers who were said to be travelling to Urbino.[41] James also asked Cardinal Curzio Origo, the Legate at Bologna, to arrest Peterborough the moment he arrived. On 11 September he was identified and arrested, and imprisoned at Fort Urbana (near the river Panaro).[42]

Peterborough protested his innocence, and asked to be allowed to speak to a senior member of the court at Urbino. He particularly wanted to see Dominic Sheldon,[43] who had been *aide-de-camp* to the duc de Vendôme in Spain when he himself had been the commander of the British forces there during the War of the Spanish Succession. The king agreed, and sent Sheldon to Fort Urbana at the end of September.[44] As a result of their meeting, Sheldon was convinced of Peterborough's innocence, so he was released. As a precaution, however, he was placed under temporary house arrest and then on parole in Bologna.[45]

When the British government heard what had happened it demanded his complete release, and threatened naval action against the Papal States.[46] The Pope gave way, and Peterborough was eventually given his liberty in the middle of November.[47] The whole incident, which has been only briefly summarised here,[48] provided the court at Urbino with considerable interest and anxiety. Cockburne remained in Bologna to keep watch on Peterborough's activities,[49] and did not return to the court until the latter had left for Venice at the beginning of December.[50]

O'Brien was sent to report to Queen Mary at Saint-Germain[51] and (as already stated) remained in France as Lord Dillon's private secretary.[52]

The Peterborough incident was exceptional, but it showed how very sensitive the court had to be concerning the king's security, at a time when he was still unmarried and without children. One advantage of living in such a small and remote place was that the arrival of assassins or spies could be relatively easily identified. In March 1718, James III told Gualterio that he was well aware that the Duke of Parma employed a spy at Urbino,[53] and at the end of that year a British spy, who was developing a plan "of carrying off" the king "and bringing him to England", was identified and exposed.[54]

Most visitors to the court, however, were Jacobites who were prepared to undertake the arduous journey to Urbino out of loyalty, despite the difficult roads. Peter Redmond came in December 1717 and again in March 1718.[55] Other visitors during that winter included James Oglethorpe (the younger brother of Theophilus and later the founder of the colony of Georgia)[56] and Lord Linton (son and heir to the Earl of Traquair).[57]

These visitors must have been particularly welcome at the Palazzo Ducale, where most of the courtiers could not speak Italian and could not easily socialise with the local population. The king, however, could speak Italian (though perhaps not fluently)[58] and made a point of seeing the noble families of Urbino, particularly the Staccolis, the Bonaventuras and the Albanis, and contributing to the social life of the city. He also rode out to visit the nearby religious houses, notably the church of San Bernardino, containing the mausoleum of the Dukes of Urbino (off the road to Fossombrone), and the Capuchin monastery on the other side of the city (off the road to Castel Durante, renamed Urbania by Pope Urban VIII).[59] There were also two particularly important houses within Urbino itself: the *Oratorio della Morte* and the *Oratorio di San Giuseppe*.

When the court had been at Saint-Germain, James II and David Nairne had both joined the Confraternity for a Happy Death (also known as the *Bona Mors*), which involved regular attendance to meditate on the human suffering of Christ. The services demanded of the confraternity's members were designed to prepare them against any sudden or unexpected death.[60] By chance, a branch of the confraternity had been established in Urbino, beside the archbishop's palace on the other side of the cathedral. Their little oratory consisted of two rows of benches facing each other along the lateral walls, with a large painting of *The Crucifixion with Mourners and Mary Magdalene* by Federico Barocci.[61] As a known member of the confraternity it may be assumed that David Nairne attended some of their meetings.

The king joined the Confraternity of St Joseph, which was particularly patronised by the Albani family. The purpose of the confraternity was to help the families of those condemned to death, something which no doubt had a particular appeal to James III after the failure of the rising of 1715–1716, when so many Jacobites, notably the 3rd Earl of Derwentwater, had been executed. The *Oratorio di S. Giuseppe* is situated in a little street to the left of the main road leading uphill from the principal entrance to the city (the Porta di Valbona). It consists of two chapels, the smaller of which contains a beautiful and justly famous sculpture in plaster of *The Nativity* by Federico Brandani. According to Giovanni Pucci, James was received as one of the brothers (*fratti*) of the order on 19 March 1718, on the *Festivo di S. Giuseppe*.[62] On one of the walls outside the two chapels can still be seen, within its original wooden frame, the names of the most important brothers of the confraternity, including Pope Clement XI, King James III and Alamanno Salviati. In the sacristy there is a copy of the portrait of the king painted by Antonio David in Rome the previous year. There is also a portrait of Cardinal Annibale Albani, attributed to Pier Leone Ghezzi,[63] but probably also by David.[64]

Such activities, of course, were not available to Protestants, or to the Catholic courtiers who could not speak Italian and mix with the local people. Nor would they have been available to women. But it must be emphasised that the exiled Stuart court at Urbino was almost exclusively a male community, just as it had been at Pesaro. There were virtually no women, and therefore no children – which makes the little Lord Derwentwater's presence less likely. Of course there were women of all social ranks in the town, and some of the lower ones must have been employed in the palazzo to do the necessary washing and cleaning. But for most of the time the only women permanently attached to the court were still the three who had been at Pesaro: Catherine Macane (washerwoman), her daughter Mrs Anne Prévot (in charge of mending and marking the linen) and Magdalen Rebout (scourer in the wine cellar). They were now joined by Maria Lizabetta Girelli, whose husband Francesco was taken on as an assistant in the Wine Cellar,[65] but nevertheless it was still a very unbalanced community.

Many of the servants were bachelors[66] or widowers.[67] But at least 18 of them had been told to leave their wives behind at Saint-Germain when the court had moved to Avignon.[68] The same had applied to those of the married Scottish, Irish and English pensioners: all of them without exception had come to Urbino without their wives, who had been left in Scotland or England, or even in France. The king made it clear that he was not prepared to have women at the court until such time as he himself acquired a wife.[69]

What effect this had on the behaviour and tone of the court, and on the relations between the court and the town, can only be guessed. In the summer of 1718, Nairne confided to Gualterio that Mar's valet was "thoroughly immoral".[70] He added, probably with understatement: "There are others here, some of them even the gentlemen in His Majesty's suite, whose behaviour is rather scandalous."[71] When his own teenage son Louis arrived at Urbino shortly afterwards, Nairne was worried that "some of the younger people of the court" would lead him astray,[72] and sent him away to the Palazzo Gualterio in Orvieto.[73]

There is no doubt, however, that the king did what he could to maintain discipline and good order in this sometimes rowdy masculine community. This can be seen from an incident that took place in July 1718 between Donald Macmahon and Charles Wogan, who shared the same rooms on the second floor of the palazzo. Mar recorded that they had a serious quarrel "some nights ago [when] they invited some of the gentlemen to sup with them", and then challenged each other to a duel in which they were both lightly wounded:

> They were seen by the country people, so it made a great deal of noise and their master is very angry with them. He sent and arrested them in their rooms where they still remain .... It will take them some time before they can pacify their master, and, if he allow them to see him or stay where he is, they will first have a public and severe reprimand with a certification to all his people, if any such thing happen, how severely he will use them.[74]

Under these circumstances the arrival of a woman at Urbino was regarded as very special. In November 1717 the Duke of St Andrews (Count of Castelblanco) rejoined the court with his wife (born Lady Mary Drummond, a daughter of the 1st Duke of Melfort) and the Duchess of Perth.[75] They remained over Christmas and the New Year, but in February St Andrews and his wife left for France.[76] The Duchess of Perth remained a little longer, but she also left for France at the beginning of April.[77]

The next woman to arrive was Hay's wife Marjory, who left England at the beginning of May and reached Urbino in July.[78] She was accompanied by her brother James Murray, and was allowed by the king to join the court permanently, as a special favour granted to her husband. But her presence as the only lady at the court naturally encouraged other men to ask James to extend the favour to them. Lord Nithsdale's wife had been languishing at La Flèche for several months. She was sent for by her husband in August,[79] and arrived (with George Mackenzie) at the beginning of October – bringing with her some of Queen Mary of Modena's jewellery from Saint-Germain.[80] The Duke of Mar, meanwhile, had also sent for his wife. She left England with her daughter Lady Frances in September[81] and (escorted by Charles Forbes) reached the Papal States in November,[82] though by then the court had left Urbino for Rome.

Illustration 10   Francesco Trevisani, *Marjory Hay, Countess of Inverness* (1719)

The invitations to Mrs Hay, Lady Nithsdale and the Duchess of Mar were exceptional. When David Nairne heard that Lady Nithsdale had been sent for he confided to Cardinal Gualterio how much he longed to see his daughter again.[83] But he did not dare ask the king to allow her to come for fear of a refusal. Yet he loved his daughter very much and had not seen her for several years, and was now afraid that he might die without ever seeing her.[84] Other servants must have felt the same about their wives and daughters, but by the autumn of 1718 the only ladies at the court were still Mrs Hay and Lady Nithsdale.

By then, however, the king was planning to marry Princess Maria Clementina Sobieska, and it was obvious that she would require some female attendants. This would in itself have necessitated a change of policy and brought women into the masculine community of the Stuart court. One woman, hearing the news of the king's impending marriage, decided she could wait no longer. This was Sarah Maguirk, whose husband Patrick was one of the grooms. She left Saint-Germain on her own initiative to be reunited with him – unaware that he had actually just died.[85] The other women at Saint-Germain then decided that they would follow her to Italy, and had to be stopped by William Dicconson, who refused to give them the necessary money.

The king's policy not to have women at his court would have had to change when he got married, but the news that the Emperor had arrested Princess Sobieska and her mother at Innsbruck, in an attempt to prevent his marriage taking place, precipitated events. James III sent new instructions to Dicconson at the beginning of November: "You did well to stop all the underservants coming to Urbino, but hindering wives from going to their husbands is an Imperial prerogative I do not pretend to."[86] In fact that is what he had been doing since he had arrived at Urbino. But it meant that when the Stuart court was established in Rome during 1719 it became once again a balanced community containing both wives and children.

6
Friction and Frustration

While the Jacobites were at Urbino the friction between the old servants and the new, between the Catholics and the Protestants, built up to such a point that it not only compromised the unity of the exiled court itself but also the future prospects of the entire Jacobite movement. The king was himself partly responsible for this development, because he began to show too much faith in, and favouritism towards, John Hay, the Duke of Mar, and Hay's brother-in-law James Murray, thus offending many of his supporters. The friction began in the royal household, spread to the secretariat, and even divided the Scottish pensioners.

The royal household

When the court had been at Pesaro, the king had created the new post of *Maggiordomo*. It made sense to put one man in charge of both the Household Below Stairs and the Stables because the footmen were now employed to wait at the king's table. In addition the horses were now mainly used for sending messages rather than for hunting or visiting neighbours. The arrangement of the basements at Urbino facilitated this overall coordination.

There had been six possible candidates for the new post, which was described as being in charge of "the Household Below Stairs, the Table and the Stables", and was now referred to by the Italians as *Maggiordomo e Spedizionere* [i.e. the person in charge of having messages sent].[1] They were the two Gentlemen of the Bedchamber (Lord Edward Drummond and Lord Clermont), the three remaining Grooms of the Bedchamber (Charles Booth, Roger Strickland and Alan Cameron) and the Vice-Chamberlain (Dominic Sheldon). The post had been given to Charles Booth, partly because he enjoyed the king's trust and favour, and partly because he had been a cavalry officer before being appointed Groom of the Bedchamber in 1701.[2] The appointment of one of the grooms suggests that Drummond, Clermont and Sheldon were regarded as too senior for this particular post, though Booth was given a salary increase of 100 *livres* in recognition of his new responsibilities.[3]

Immediately after the court arrived at Urbino, Hay asked James III to transfer him from the Stables and give him a post in the Bedchamber. The idea had no doubt been discussed by the two men during their journey from Rome, when they had travelled alone together, leaving Booth to travel separately. The king agreed that Hay should be given the "empty title" of Groom of the Bedchamber, with a significant increase in salary,[4] and that Booth should relinquish to him the Household Below Stairs and the Table. The king wrote on 16 July to the Duke of Mar, who was still in France, that Hay "hath my favour and he knows it, and nobody shall be able to take it from him. As for the Stables, he begged himself to have no more to do with them.... 'tis a pleasure to be attended by such a one."[5]

Booth was an old servant from Saint-Germain whereas Hay was one of the new exiles. Moreover, Booth was English and Catholic, and Hay was Scottish and Protestant. The change was therefore bound to be divisive and to create friction at the court. The king described the change as merely a transfer of posts: Booth would be transferred from the Bedchamber to the Stables, and Hay would be transferred from the Stables to the Bedchamber. But in actual fact Booth was being demoted and losing responsibility for the Table and the Household Below Stairs, whereas Hay was being promoted. To make matters worse Hay had neglected his duties and made little effort to work with the other members of the royal household, as can be seen in a letter he wrote on 23 July:

> The King on my asking it has taken away any concern I had in the Stables from me, which makes me very much easier, for I did not meddle with them, so that my having the name served only to make others neglect their business that I might have the blame.... It has always been my study to meddle as little with the King's old servants as I could.[6]

The king's obvious favouritism towards him was bound to result in bitterness and resentment.

When the king saw Booth and told him what he had decided, Booth understandably refused to accept the change, and said that he would like to take a temporary period of leave. The king's version of their conversation was then recorded in a private letter to Lord Dillon:

> I told Booth...that I found it was ridiculous he should have everything and do everything, while Hay who I was satisfied with did nothing, and I...would have them swapp their [places], which I thought most naturall Booth having already ye management of ye Stables, that I had no other end in ye change but meerly a certain decorum, for that change or no change, he and Hay would be in effect just as they were with me. He answer'd that I was master to take in whom I pleas'd, but to be degraded to the title of query was what he could not submit to, and that he had rather I should use him like Roger [Strickland] and [Alan] Cameron (who wait not at all) and then asked me leave to go to Paris for some short time to look after his own affairs.[7]

This brought the meeting to a close.

If Booth was not willing to look after the Stables only, leaving to Hay the Household Below Stairs and the Table, and if Hay was not prepared to take over all of Booth's responsibilities, the king was forced to find someone else. That person had to be senior to Hay, and thus the only available candidates were Lord Edward Drummond, Lord Clermont and Dominic Sheldon. The king chose Clermont, and then spoke to Booth again:

> I told him I would not force him to be call'd querry or quitt ye empty title of groom and that he might go to Paris when he pleas'd, but that as I had no body in his absence but Ld Clermont to look after family affairs, if I once gave him that charge on his parting I could no more take it from him, so that at his return he must be content to be under Ld Clermont, to all which he acquiesced.[8]

Booth then left Urbino a few days later, and Lord Clermont replaced him as *Maggiordomo e Spedizionere*.

The incident reveals the extent to which the king had begun to favour Hay, and perhaps suggests also that James had resented Booth's negative reactions in Rome. If Hay had been a man of more ability and better judgement, this favouritism might not have mattered, but in fact he was ambitious and unscrupulous, causing divisions within the Palazzo Ducale and turning the king against his old servants. Hay's version of what happened reveals the extent of his dishonesty. He described the change as merely "swapping places with me" and argued that this was "natural for several reasons". The first reason he gave was that "it was more proper that he who looked after the things within the house where the footmen served should look after them likewise as well as the horses, who now are mostly employed in carriages from Pesaro to this [place] of things that belonged to his household business". But, and as explained by the king, this did not make sense because Booth was already looking after them. His second reason was that "the King did not think it reasonable that I should be turned out of his service altogether, since I had done nothing that deserved being disgraced". It is hardly worth commenting that there was never any question of Hay's being "turned out" or "disgraced". His third reason was that it was not "reasonable that he should have the name of everything, and I...should have the name of nothing".[9] As Hay was already an Equerry this was no more convincing than the previous reasons. What he really disliked was being subordinate to Booth in the Stables. All he had needed was a genuine transfer to become a Groom of the Bedchamber. Although an empty title, it would have removed him from the Stables and given him titular equality with Booth.

That, however, would not in itself have struck a blow at the old servants from Saint-Germain, which seems to be what Hay really wanted to do. The king's explanation, clearly written under the influence of Hay, and indeed almost certainly dictated to him, demonstrates this all too clearly:

> I cant help making you remark how cruell it is to have to do with people who deal in such an odd manner with me.... But the evil I must bear with, and have found by experience that my goodness to certain people serves only to make them insolent, and that such as I am just to without being kind are those who give me less trouble.... As for my choice of Ld Clermont I believe I cant be disaproved nor had I indeed any choice here, for he is ye only untainted from St Germains principles I mean of St Germains people, for out of them there was a necessity of chusing at this time.[10]

Booth was away from the court until the end of November, during which time the feeling of dissatisfaction among the old servants from Saint-Germain steadily increased. In October 1717 both Roger Strickland and Dr Lawrence Wood left the court in order to return to France.[11] In November Lord Edward Drummond left for Rome, where he remained for four months.[12] Then the situation became considerably worse, for when Booth finally returned he was accompanied by the Duke of Mar, who was Hay's brother-in-law and equally hostile to the old servants.

Illustration 11　Francesco Trevisani, *John Erskine, Duke of Mar* (1718)

It did not take very long for Mar to cause trouble. At the beginning of January, we find him pretending that everything was harmonious and that there was "good agreement" among all the servants, "as there is now everywhere amongst all his people that I know of".[13] But the king's private correspondence is much more revealing. "God deliver me," he wrote on 7 January, "from such as without principles themselves can never bear to see any honest people about me that they cannot govern; I thank God Urbino is pretty well purged now, may it long continue so."[14] But Mar was systematically poisoning the king's mind still further against his old servants, whether they had stayed at Urbino or had left. He told James that he should have "the liberty of employing such as he pleases", and that "making emulation and discord...is the old St. G[ermai]ns way".[15] This seems to be what the king wanted to hear. He confided soon afterwards that in Mar "I have found a probity quite unknown in most of the people from Saint-Germain".[16] At the beginning of March, we find him writing that "I will be master in my own business, and that I both must and will show that I cannot be imposed by tricks and that honest men alone can thrive with me". The honest men were, of course, Hay and Mar. Those who tried to impose themselves on the king by tricks were people like Booth and Clermont. "I must confess", the king added,

> that, though I never much admired St. Germain's proceedings, I am now quite surprised of them, and that...I do not desire to have any more to do with them; their principles and notions and mine are very different...; so that I am not at all fond of the ways of those I have so long lived with.[17]

Mar's success may clearly be seen in the following comment made by the king shortly afterwards: "as to Mar I must say I never yet found...anybody more unwilling to hurt anybody with me".[18]

During this period Booth resumed his management of the household, under the supervision of Lord Clermont. There is a document in the Stuart Papers which describes Booth discussing the catering arrangements at the beginning of the day with Jeremiah Broomer, then inviting colleagues to join him for a cup of tea, and then walking around the *salone* with Lord Clermont.[19] But the situation was bound to come to a head sooner or later, and it finally did so in the middle of April.

The precise circumstances remain obscure, but what resulted is clear enough: more of the old servants left Urbino to return to Saint-Germain. Mar's private secretary wrote on the 14th that "a day or two ago some enquiry was made into the management of our domestic affairs and...but little to...Lord Clermont's satisfaction".[20] The king himself wrote two days earlier to Mar, who had gone off to visit Rome:

> at your return you may find my family either under very good discipline or diminished, for I gave some orders to-day with calm words but grating circumstances, which I will have obeyed, for with people that have no right sense of their duty, that are incapable of friendship,

or personal attachment, and not very susceptible of shame, one must take a very particular way to work.[21]

It is difficult to imagine James writing in this way a few years earlier about the son and heir of Lord Middleton.[22] This letter, however, was dictated to Hay and survives as a file copy in his handwriting.[23]

The result was not surprising: the court was again diminished. Lord Clermont left for Saint-Germain, followed by his brother-in-law, Lord Edward Drummond, who had recently returned from Rome. Dominic Sheldon had already left in March, and Booth left for good in May.[24] Hay was thus left supreme, in charge of the Household Below Stairs, the Table and the Stables, and indeed of all the royal household except the ceremonial in the Chamber, controlled when necessary by the Duke of Perth, and the Secretariat. At the beginning of October the king even created him Earl of Inverness.[25]

The only person who maintained a degree of independence was the Treasurer, Sir William Ellis, who had previously been one of the Commissioners of the Household at Saint-Germain. It was he who received the quarterly papal pension of 2500 *scudi* from Belloni, the king's banker, and effectively acted as the keeper of the king's purse within the palazzo. Assisted by a young man whose father had been a cook for many years,[26] it was also his responsibility to pay the salaries of all the servants and the pensions of all the new exiles. The Stuart Papers contain many documents produced by Ellis for the king while the court was at Urbino, showing exactly how much money the king had in his bank account, and how much money Ellis had received.[27] It was perhaps significant that in August 1718, when Hay had taken charge of the household, Ellis was suddenly asked to provide full details of all his accounts.[28]

The secretariat

David Nairne was an old servant and a friend of Booth. It is not, therefore, surprising that he disliked Hay and disapproved of the changes which took place in the management of the household. He had also served for many years under Lord Middleton, at Saint-Germain and Bar-le-Duc, and felt a loyalty towards his son. His extensive correspondence reflects the opinion of the old servants towards the new prominence achieved by Hay, and reveals the extent to which the secretariat, conducting the king's important political correspondence, now also became divided.

Illustration 12   Alexis-Simon Belle, *David Nairne* (1714)

A few weeks before Mar returned to the court in November, Nairne expressed his feelings in the following private letter:

> I allways admird My Ld Mid's disinterestedness.... I have writt to Mr Dillon [*sic*].... he writes so obligingly to me [from Paris] that I can do no less than correspond on my side as gratefully as I can. And I would do the same with Martel [i.e. Mar] if he us'd me as I think I ought to be, but I never writt a scrape of a pen to him all the time he has been absent tho' I am not at all ignorant of his ex[traordina]ry favour.... I love old tryd friends, and cannot bring my self to admire some new great men so extraordinarily.... I had rather...be sincere than be a flatterer.[29]

Once Mar had arrived at Urbino it was inevitable that the relations within the Secretariat should become increasingly strained. In fact Mar and Hay would no doubt have persuaded the king to dismiss Nairne if they had been able to. But as neither Mar nor Paterson could write French,[30] and Creagh could not yet understand Italian, Nairne was considered by the king to be indispensable. Moreover, Nairne had developed a close friendship with Filippo Gualterio, now the Cardinal Protector of England. So the tension within the Secretariat steadily increased during the winter and the spring of 1718.

A letter written by Nairne to Gualterio at the end of March illustrates this point. The king had decided to give a warrant to Antonio David, appointing him to be his official portrait painter,[31] and had told Mar to produce the necessary document. But Mar disliked David's portrait of the king, and thought it was "by no means a good picture",[32] so he deliberately delayed producing the document. Nairne reassured David "that he can count on the warrant since His Majesty has promised it",[33] but asked Gualterio to tell him to be patient: "The Duke of Mar has recently been so occupied with other more important matters that he has had no time to think about it."[34] When the warrant was finally ready it was given Nairne for him to send to Gualterio, to be handed over to David. In his letter Nairne apologised for the poor quality of the Latin, saying that he had had nothing to do with it, and that he had merely reminded the king about it from time to time, "without troubling to provide a model for the office of the Protestant Secretary of State, where I have never had any business, nor ever will, God willing (but I am only saying this in confidence to Y[our] E[xcellency]".[35] He confided to a friend that

> I must say without vanity I labour as much and as usefully in my post as the great man in his, and I see no great doings of his either as to advising or writing but what I could make a shift to compass perhaps as well as he if supported as he is, whilst what I do I am sure he could not do.[36]

The event which particularly offended the old servants was the king's decision, prompted by Mar, abruptly to dismiss Lewis Innes from his post as Lord Almoner to Queen Mary of Modena at Saint-Germain.[37] Nairne wrote to Innes' brother in May that "I cannot yet overcome the impression which the sudden resolution taken about your brother has made upon me, it sticks with me still". By then Lord Clermont had been reprimanded by the king for his management of the household, and Nairne added that "many other things I have remarkd of late and do

remark dayly make me wish heartily I had my quietus". So he decided
to write to Lewis Innes himself, and to show his letter to the king before
sending it off:

> I had the satisfaction at the least ... to shew him under my own hand
> what my sentiments were both as to himself and to my friend, and
> that I was silent out of respect yet I was far from approving certain
> things. I believe I have not made my Court by it, but I cannot help
> that. I am perhaps a little usefull, and for that reason more than incli-
> nation I continue still to be trusted and imployd, but I shall not be
> surprisd if my turn comes as well as others.[38]

During July 1718, Nairne started a secret correspondence with
Cardinal Gualterio, which the two men conducted in parallel, on paper
of a different size to distinguish it from their official correspondence
which had to be shown to the king.[39] From these secret letters we discover that Mar tried to reorganise the Secretariat by taking control of all
the correspondence, thereby making Nairne his subordinate:

> as for the Duke of Mar, we are getting on fairly well at the moment.
> He saw that the King did me the honour of coming to see me several
> times when I was indisposed, and came himself to visit me. Having
> seen, as did the King, that I was not going to take orders from him,
> now when we work together he shows more civility towards me. So
> I have kept my independence and I think that the situation for the
> present is that neither he nor the King will treat me like a clerk.[40]

It was fortunate for Nairne that this had been established, because
there was more trouble on the way. During the summer of 1718 the
court was joined by two people who were closely related to Mar and
Hay, and who were soon also to become favourites of the king. The
first was Hay's wife Marjory; the second was Marjory's brother, James
Murray. The latter, described at Urbino as the king's *Confidentissimo*,[41]
combined extreme ambition with a rudeness and lack of tact which had
already offended several important Jacobites.[42] Murray was determined
to play a leading political role at the court, even if this meant eventually
supplanting Mar himself.

A letter which Nairne sent to Cardinal Gualterio, and which he specifically asked him to burn, reveals the unsatisfactory situation in the
palazzo ducale by the beginning of August:

The King continues to treat me with confidence and ... consideration, but by love and inclination he has put a deeper and exclusive trust in someone else. Mâtre [i.e. Mar] is the oracle and Mr Hays [*sic*], who is a young man of only average merit and capabilities, is all-powerful in the household with nothing concealed from him. Lord Clermont and poor Mr Booth have been pushed aside to make room for him, though he certainly has neither their experience nor their intelligence, but it is not always real merit that governs inclination .... Mr Murray, who has real aptitude and genius for business but who is still very young, thinks himself more capable than he actually is and gives himself the airs of a Minister. He too enjoys full confidence, being Mr Hays' brother-in-law and also totally devoted to Lord Mar. This is how I see things.

The Secretariat was now divided in a way which it had never previously been. Nairne continued,

I keep myself to myself and only go to the King when he asks for me, and get on with my own work .... It is true that in important matters he seems to be completely open with me, and has the kindness to ask my opinion often, and when ... Lord Mar talks to me, we discuss things together with great ease but I never ask him to confide in me .... He certainly favours neither the Catholic nor the old servants' side, having got rid of a large part of the latter, and I do not know how I have not suffered the same fate before now. But I imagine my turn will come .... I am pained by many things, not for myself but for the good of His Majesty's service .... I only speak so openly to Y[our] E[xcellency] .... I hope you will be good enough to burn this letter.[43]

As the summer went on, Nairne felt increasingly dissatisfied. He told Gualterio that the only way anyone could have good relations with Mar was by flattery and by pandering to his self-importance. He even allowed himself to criticise the king in a way he had never done before:

he believes me to be philosophical enough not to notice those things which affect me .... Every day he distributes favour to others and tells me about them, but that is the only part in it he allows me to have, and I say nothing, which does not mean that I do not have an opinion. In fact I see everyone rewarded and every newcomer promoted over my head.[44]

Nairne continued to criticise Mar, "the favourite" [Hay], "his wife" and "the brother-in-law" [Murray] in his secret letters to Gualterio.[45] He wanted to retire but could not afford to, so (as he wrote in October) "I take the line of respectful silence".[46] The king, of course, noticed this, and commented that Nairne, "an old and faithful servant", seemed "a bit put out".[47] But the fact was that James had surrounded himself with new and unpopular advisers, to whom he was showing too much favouritism. Nairne noted that Murray in particular was now given "every imaginable honour" by the king.[48]

Of course the new favourites saw things differently, as can be seen from a private letter written by the Duke of Mar at almost exactly the same time:

> There are indeed some of those who have long been of the King's family, who have left him some time ago, so very few of them are now with him and perhaps not very likely to be in haste again, but they are only those of St. Germains who have contrived it so that the King could no longer endure their ways, since he had others to make choice of.[49]

Whatever the truth of the matter, the fact is that the household at Urbino had become very divided, between the old servants who were Catholic and the new servants who were Protestant. Because the old servants were virtually all English, Irish, French and Italian, whereas the new servants were all Scottish, the rift was therefore national as well as religious.

The Scottish pensioners

The rivalry between the two groups was to be magnified because the great majority of the other Jacobites at the Stuart court were also Scottish and Protestant. That did not mean, however, that the new Scottish exiles formed a united group, and it soon became apparent that they were divided into various factions. Many were no doubt non-aligned, and the membership of the factions probably changed as time went by. Nevertheless certain generalisations can and should be made.

It was natural that Hay, Mar and Murray, as the most influential members of the court, should command the support of a significant group. It included Colonel William Clephane, James Edgar (who would later become the king's private secretary) and William Erskine (a relation of the Duke of Mar). A second group, including Colonel John Stewart of

Invernity, gathered around the Earl of Southesk. They seem to have enjoyed good relations with Mar, but above all they disliked the old servants from Saint-Germain.

Even before the end of July 1717, Southesk was said to be dissatisfied with the organisation of the court at Urbino.[50] By November he could stand it no longer, and left for Rome with Stewart of Invernity.[51] Once he had arrived there he gave vent to his feelings of resentment towards the old servants in a letter to Mar's under-secretary. He particularly disliked the fact that their salaries had been increased back to their former levels, while the pensions given to the Scottish peers and gentlemen had remained the same:

> they now give themselves their great St. Germains airs and esteem themselves the only sufferers for the King, while they have been growing rich by him these nine and twenty years, and are in better circumstances than they could ever hope for, had he been on his throne.... there is not an Italian but believes they [the household servants] are the only people who are favoured by the King, and the only ones worthy of his favour, and that is come to such a height that they think even little Nairne a greater man than any that followed the King in our late affair.[52]

The Scottish lords had persuaded the pope while they were in Rome that they were not the equivalent of Italian *conti*, but the people in provincial Urbino are unlikely to have appreciated this point – one reason, no doubt, why Southesk had returned to the papal city. And since none of the Scottish pensioners could speak Italian, they had little opportunity to make the local Italians understand just how important some of them were in their own country.

It is certainly true that the Italians, including Cardinal Gualterio, did have a higher opinion of Nairne than of Hay, if only because he *could* speak their language and because he was a Catholic. But by then the king's preference for his new Scottish favourites was becoming ever more obvious, so when Mar returned to the court an attempt was made to persuade Southesk to come back. He refused to do so in February,[53] but Mar did not give up and made a second attempt in March, when the king had just dismissed Lewis Innes from his post at Saint-Germain. He wrote to Stewart of Invernity: "Pray tell Lord Southesk that ere long he will hear of a convincing proof of those people he used not to like having much meddling, having less than ever, and next to none at all."[54] Southesk still held out, but finally agreed to return to Urbino in October.[55]

Like Lord Southesk, the Earl of Panmure also resented the fact that he had nothing to do at Urbino and received only a relatively modest pension. He had already complained about this at Pesaro. But unlike Southesk he disliked both the old servants *and* the favour shown by the king towards Hay and Mar. As a much older man – he was actually Mar's uncle – he not only believed that he should be brought into the royal household and given a formal court appointment,[56] but also that he should be regularly consulted by the king on political questions.[57] When James still refused to do either, Panmure left the court in February 1718 and went to live in Paris, taking with him his physician and friend, Dr John Blair.[58] Having arrived there he asked to be allowed to succeed Dillon as the king's representative in Paris,[59] but his request was ignored.[60] Not surprisingly Panmure went to complain to the queen at Saint-Germain,[61] where he had some relations,[62] making Mar believe that he might "now fall in with those of St. Germains, with whom he used to be so angry".[63]

Lord Panmure was by no means the only Scottish exile who resented the influence of Mar and Hay. Some important Jacobites revealed their feelings by remaining in France and never going to Urbino. Among these were the Earl Marischal and the Marquis of Seaforth, both of whom were Catholic.

Marischal was the nephew of the 2nd Duke of Perth, of Lord Edward Drummond and of Lord Clermont's sister. Although he had been at Pesaro, he did not accompany the king to Rome, and went instead to Paris, where James III allowed him to remain to make himself "master of the French" language.[64] Seaforth's sister was married to John Caryll, whose cousin (also called John Caryll) was a gentleman usher of the queen's privy chamber at Saint-Germain, so Seaforth was thus also in contact with the old servants whom Mar disliked and mistreated. The latter was warned in October 1718:

> beware of Seaforth, for he swore most bitterly before me, that he would put a spoke in [your] wheel, if ever it lay in his way, and on my saying I believed Marischal had taken some disgust or other, he answered, who the devil would not be disgusted at Mar's conduct?[65]

Another letter, written from Saint-Germain, informed Mar of a further conversation with Lord Seaforth:

> He told me that the Earl Marischal and he had been together several times.... He found in the plainest terms by the Earl Marischal there

never would be a reconciliation...betwixt him and Mar.... Seaforth
mentioned a picquish letter or two that had passed of late betwixt
him and Mar....[66] All that can be said for Seaforth is that nothing has been left undone by the Earl Marischal and his emissaries
to make an irreconcilable break betwixt Seaforth and Mar, having
endeavoured to persuade him that Mar was in all things his real
enemy.[67]

Alarmed by the open hostility of two such important peers, particularly when Seaforth wrote to complain to the king,[68] Mar realised that
he would have to do something to limit the damage he was doing to the
Jacobite cause, and perhaps his own position. He sent what amounted
to an apology to Lord Seaforth,[69] but by the same post wrote a letter
to his informant in which he sneered at the 25-year-old Lord Marischal
as "that boy".[70] The profound hostility provoked in the Earl Marischal
by the behaviour of Mar (and Hay and Murray) at the court of Urbino
would have long-term consequences for the Stuart court after it had
been transferred to Rome, when Marischal would eventually become
one of the most eminent men in Europe.

Religion was certainly an important factor in determining the attitudes of the Scottish pensioners, because the three men at Urbino who
enjoyed the best relations with the old servants were all Catholics.
Marischal's uncle, the Duke of Perth, was the Master of the Horse to
the queen at Saint-Germain,[71] as well as the half-brother of Lord Edward
Drummond, and there is evidence that his relations with both Mar and
Hay were strained by the spring of 1718.[72] The Earl of Nithsdale was
married to one of the daughters of the 1st Duke of Powis, who had been
the Lord Chamberlain at Saint-Germain. There is no evidence of friction
between Nithsdale and the household servants. Finally the 5th Earl of
Winton is reported by Mar as having given "a regal" in February 1718
"to old Dominic [Sheldon], Sir William [Ellis], N.n [Nairne], B.h [Booth]
and De L.r [Delattre]".[73] By that time these men were (with the single
exception of Lord Clermont) the only remaining senior servants from
Saint-Germain who were still at Urbino, and Winton must surely have
been making a deliberate point in inviting them all to eat with him. It
is difficult to imagine Hay, Mar, Southesk or Panmure doing the same.

It is not possible or even necessary to speculate what the attitudes
were of the other Scottish pensioners, including the Earl of Linlithgow,
Viscount Kilsyth and Viscount Kingston, but it is probable that they
would have fallen within one or other of the factions already described.

What matters is that there was not only friction between the old servants and many of the new Scottish exiles, but also within the latter group. We should, however, be careful not to exaggerate. If a small number of people both caused and expressed resentment and hostility for personal reasons, the fact remains that all the Jacobites were conscious of a shared political loyalty and of a common British identity within a foreign country.

7
The Music of the Court

Many of the Jacobites at Urbino also shared an appreciation of music, which was by far the most important form of entertainment provided for James III and his courtiers while they were in the city. Some music was organised and even performed by the Jacobites themselves. Some was provided by the more important noble families of the town. Although there was disagreement over musical taste, it did not necessarily coincide with the rivalries between the old and the new servants. Indeed a common love of music was one thing which managed to bring together some of the Jacobites who were otherwise divided. For a short time during 1718 Urbino became one of the most significant musical centres in the Papal States, a fact which has escaped the attention of previous historians.

The most important families in Urbino when the Stuart court arrived there were the Albanis, the Staccolis and the Bonaventuras. Pope Clement XI's younger brother, Orazio Albani, had died in 1712 leaving three sons, Annibale, Carlo and Alessandro. Annibale (born in 1682) had been created a cardinal by his uncle and lived in Rome. Carlo (born in 1687) also lived in Rome, where he had married Teresa Borromeo, but he had been instructed by the Pope to keep in contact with James III, and he visited the Stuart court for an extended period during 1718. Alessandro (born in 1692) was a priest in Rome and would later become a particularly influential cardinal. Although the Albanis were no longer actually living in their palazzo in Urbino, they provided both James III and the people of the town with a direct channel of communication to Clement XI.

The Staccoli family was related to the Albanis by marriage,[1] and was resident in Urbino throughout the period that the Stuart court was there. Camillo Staccoli's wife Lucrezia was the leading hostess of the town, and held regular *conversazioni* (musical evenings) in the Palazzo Staccoli. His sister Giulia had been married to Cardinal Gualterio's brother, created Earl of Dundee by James III,[2] and his wife's niece would later be employed at the Stuart court in Rome.[3]

There were four Bonaventura brothers. Guido was the Governor of Ferrara, Giovanni Bernardino was the Governor of the prison-fortress of San Leo (situated on a rocky hill-top near Urbino), Sebastiano was the Bishop of Corneto and Montefiascone, and Giovanni Battista was the Archdeacon of Urbino. They lived in a palazzo immediately beside the south side of the Palazzo Ducale, and often entertained the king, who would later repay their hospitality by selecting Sebastiano Bonaventura to baptise his elder son.

At some point during the autumn of 1717 Guido Bonventura, the head of the family, returned from Ferrara in order to entertain James III and his courtiers. Giovanni Pucci noted that he provided them with "molte conversazioni", during which the lords and gentlemen of the court had the opportunity to meet and dance with the ladies of the town:

> It started with singing and playing by many musicians and virtuoso performers brought in for the occasion and other kinds of entertainment for His Royal Highness' pleasure. The King then stood to leave and with impeccable politeness bowed to all the Ladies, just as he did when he arrived, not wanting the Gentlemen of Urbino to move but to remain seated and attend the Ladies. Once the *conversazione* accompaniment had finished, the Lords and Gentlemen provided some popular entertainment of games and then danced with the Ladies. The Gentlemen of the town renewed their pleas that the King should stay, saying his departure would greatly offend their host, the *Cavaliere Castellano* Guido Bonaventura.[4]

During the autumn of 1717 concerts were also organised within the Palazzo Ducale itself.[5] They probably took place in one of the rooms of the king's apartment or in the *sala* of the *appartamento del Magnifico,* though no details about them have survived. Music could also be performed in the large theatre, on the west side of the central courtyard, and the Jacobite courtiers hoped that this might be used for the performance of opera.

This theatre, which was on the ground floor, had for many years been occupied by a company called the *Accademia Pascolini*, but was only used for putting on plays, especially during each carnival season.[6] It was, however, also suitable for opera, and in October 1717 James asked Don Carlo Albani to obtain permission from his uncle for some works to be presented the following winter. He specified that he would like the company at Pesaro to come to Urbino and give four performances of each of their operas, preferably with "a few fine female voices".[7] For reasons which are not clear, the Pope refused,[8] which meant that anyone who wanted to see a staged opera had to go elsewhere, to Fano or Pesaro or even further afield.

This did not mean, however, that operatic music could not be heard at the Stuart court, and when the Duke of Mar arrived in the second half of November there was a sharp increase in musical activity. He brought with him a large quantity of new music in manuscript from Venice and Bologna, which he had acquired *en route*, and then set about building up a large music library at the court. More manuscripts were ordered from Venice and Bologna. Others came from Fano, Milan and Rome. The music consisted of arias from the latest operas of Tomaso Albinoni, Antonio Maria Bononcini, Francesco Gasparini, Antonio Lotti, Francesco Mancini, Giuseppe Maria Orlandini, Carlo Francesco Pollarolo, Nicola Porpora, Giovanni Porta, Domenico Scarlatti and Antonio Vivaldi.[9]

The operas from which the arias were extracted have nearly all been identified. Even some of the original manuscripts have survived from the music library in the Palazzo Ducale. Lord Panmure took away with him two arias, one of them from Orlandini's *La Merope*. They are now in the National Library of Scotland (NLS.).[10] Forty-six others (with a sinfonia and three cantatas) were recently discovered at Berkeley Castle, among them some arias from Vivaldi's *La costanza trionfante* which are not extant in any other source.[11]

This repertory calls for some comment, because it was essentially Venetian, or in what was recognised as the new Venetian style. The Stuart court at Saint-Germain had once been an important musical centre which had introduced and helped popularise Italian music in the Paris area during the 1690s.[12] That music, however, had been from Rome, not Venice, and was already being regarded in northern Italy as a little out of date. Moreover, the operatic music at Saint-Germain, on which James III had been particularly keen, had all been French. Mar's new music library consequently represented, whether he intended it or not, a direct challenge to the musical taste which had hitherto prevailed at the exiled court. The Jacobites waited to see how the king would react. He had already heard a great deal of new Italian music during his recent visit to Rome, and he was now regularly attending the *conversazioni* in the Palazzo Bonaventura, but his operatic taste had apparently remained French – as Don Carlo Albani had assumed when he commissioned Domenico Scarlatti to compose his cantata for the king at Castel Gandolfo. The antagonism between the old servants from Saint-Germain and the new Scottish exiles thus took on a musical dimension. Would James turn away from French music, just as he had begun to reject other aspects of his Saint-Germain background?

Immediately after his arrival, Mar began to organise regular concerts in his large *appartamento di S. Domenico*. On 9 December he wrote to the famous castrato Nicoloni that "I have got a little concert made up here of such voices and instruments as the place affords, some of which are not bad, and they perform in my room thrice a week."[13] By early January these concerts were well established: "I have music in my rooms thrice a week, a voice tolerably good, an excellent violin, one that plays well on the harpsichord and sometimes Painter [Colonel William Clephane] plays on the bass fiddle and Mitchell's Jack [Sir John Preston] on the flute." Mar added with some satisfaction that "the King looks in often when they are at it, and is really come to like it."[14] In another letter Mar referred to "some pretty good voices and excellent instruments", but again it was the king's reaction that was really important: "our Master looks in and is come to be a convert to the Italian music."[15] The king confirmed this shortly afterwards, writing that "we have virtually no company or entertainment here, except a little Italian music, which I am beginning to enjoy very much."[16]

The Duke of Mar's best singer was a castrato called Paolo Mariani, generally called Paulino and nicknamed "the golden" by some of the Jacobites.[17] In January 1718 he left Urbino to take part in the new opera season offered by the Teatro della Fortuna at Fano. The first work was a pasticcio setting of *La constanza in trionfo*, with an unspecified intermezzo starring Mariani, now described as "virtuoso del duca di Mar".[18] The lesser quality of his voice compared to those of the other singers was noticed by the Jacobites who went to Fano to attend some of the performances:

> I left Urbino at 12 and got to Fano before 6, where I went to the opera, that lasted till 12. 'Twas, I think, the finest I have seen anywhere, a noble theatre, spacious, regular and well lighted, with a great variety of regular and noble scenes, and several of the best voices, I believe, in the world. Paulin [*sic*], that sang for the Duke of Mar, was among them, but can hardly pretend to be a sixth rate in comparison of others there.[19]

Other enthusiastic reports about the operas at Fano were soon received,[20] and the message was clear. Anyone who had enjoyed Mar's concerts at Urbino would be overwhelmed by the quality of the performances at Fano. Or, as the Duke of St Andrews put it to David Nairne: "I am persuaded that after hearing the operas of Fano, you will not be able to bring yourself to hear the concerts of Urbino."[21]

Not surprisingly the king decided that he would himself like to go to Fano, particularly when he was told that the weather there was very much better.[22] But before he could go he had to attend two plays which had been specially prepared in his honour by the *Accademia Pascolini*. They were *L'Agrippa* and *La Griselda*, both of them to be presented in the theatre of the Palazzo Ducale with the same intermezzi entitled *La Forze di Ercole*. Performing these plays for the king, however, posed a problem, because the theatre did not contain boxes, and it was not considered proper for the king to sit among the rest of the audience. Alamanno Salviati therefore had a large box especially constructed at the front of the auditorium: "For the use of His Royal Highness and his courtiers, a large box was constructed at the foot of the theatre stalls, paid for by the *Camera Apostolica*."[23] The king attended the first performances of each play on 20 and 21 February with his courtiers, who presumably found them difficult to understand. On the following day he left for Fano, where he stayed in the palazzo of Marchese Claudio Gabuccini.

James' visit lasted from 22 February to 2 March and was an enormous success. In addition to the opera already mentioned, the king and his courtiers saw performances of *Il tradimento traditor di se stesso* by Antonio Lotti, with Tomaso Albinoni's celebrated *Il Pimpinone* as an intermezzo. Numerous letters in the Stuart Papers, as well as some *relazioni* in Italian, testify to the success of the visit and to the king's enthusiastic response to what he saw and heard.[24] As Mar put it, there were "two fine operas acted by some of the best singers in Italy, with balls, where he danced, and conversations, their word for assemblées, where the people of the opera sang, as they did every day to the King at his own lodgings, he having become a great liker of the Italian music".[25] It was not only the king and Mar who were pleased, because Nairne wrote to Gualterio to tell him how much he also had enjoyed the operas.[26]

This visit to Fano was to have an important influence on the music of the Stuart court during the rest of 1718, as James III determined that some of the singers he had heard at Fano should be invited to perform at Urbino. The Stuart accounts are very revealing. James spent 202 *livres* on the various performances of the two operas which he attended at the Teatro della Fortuna, but he spent an additional 335 *livres* on hiring the singers to perform privately for his court.[27] The singers who now agreed to come to Urbino were Pietro Sbaraglia, called *il Pesciattino*, who promised to come in March, and Carlo Cristini, who was to come in April.[28]

Back at Urbino, James III attended some more performances of *L'Agrippa* and *La Griselda*, and the intermezzi of *Le Forze di Ercole*, while waiting for the singers to arrive.[29] Meanwhile Alamanno Salviati began to make plans for two oratorios to be performed in the theatre. As Cristini was not yet available, Salviati persuaded Domenico Tempesti, who had been singing in Rome, to come to Urbino to sing with Sbaraglia and, presumably, Mariani. The first oratorio was planned for 26 March, the second for 6 April (in the week before Easter), and Salviati ordered that the libretti should be printed in advance by a local printer named Angelo-Antonio Monticelli.[30]

Sbaraglia had arrived by 17 April,[31] and on 21 April was given a formal warrant to be the king's *virtuoso*.[32] Tempesti arrived shortly afterwards. While waiting for the first of Salviati's oratorios, the Jacobites had some musical evenings at the Palazzo Staccoli. Nairne informed Gualterio that

> there was a little conversation at Madame Staccoli's the other evening, where that lady sang herself, and very well. His Majesty heard there for the first time a famous musician called Tempesti who had been brought in specially by the President. This man remained for quite a time to please His Majesty, who is beginning to develop a taste for Italian music.[33]

The first oratorio, which Mar described as "a kind of sacred opera",[34] was performed as planned on 26 March and entitled *San Romoaldo*. The printed libretto does not give the name of the composer, but it was probably Giovanni Clari or Antonio Lotti.[35] Pucci noted, "Exceptionally, since His Majesty was present with some brothers [of the Confraternity of St Joseph] in his box, it was Sbaraglia and Tempesta [*sic*] who sang for both the Ladies and Gentlemen of the City and the foreigners."[36]

While the second oratorio was being prepared, a little incident took place which caused a stir at Urbino and upset Salviati. The Duke of Mar had persuaded the king to let him visit Rome for a few weeks, and he left early on the morning of 28 March, without bothering to wait for the oratorio. At the last moment both the king and Hay decided to accompany him as far as Pesaro, and then to make a short visit to Forli, without telling anyone what they were doing. This caused consternation at the court, among both the household servants and the pensioners, because it was assumed that the king had left to embark on a restoration attempt without telling anyone. Some of them were simply angry, others were hurt and offended. Mar and Hay claimed to find it all very amusing, but Salviati was not amused,[37] partly because he felt he should have been informed, and partly because he had made detailed arrangements for the second oratorio.

Il Sepolcro di Cristo fabbricato dagli angeli, with music by Francesco Mancini, was performed in the theatre of the Palazzo Ducale on Wednesday, 6 April. The king described it as "very pretty both in words and music".[38] It lasted two hours and Paterson informed Mar, by then in Rome, that "our virtuosi here approved of the music, and give it the preference to that which you heard before you left us". It was also another occasion for James to invite "the whole ladies of the town".[39] Pucci recorded that "His Majesty went to his appointed place in the Theatre with the President and his courtiers, while the Ladies and Gentlemen of Urbino were placed in the stalls in order of their social rank."[40]

On the following day Tempesti left Urbino, having been paid 83 *livres* by the king for his private performances,[41] and having promised to return for Easter.[42] As there is no reference in the accounts at this time to any payment for Sbaraglia, and his name is not mentioned in the Stuart Papers after this point, it is impossible to say how long he remained in Urbino.

Easter week, which began on Wednesday, 13 April, put a stop to the concerts arranged by the Jacobites themselves, but provided music in the cathedral instead. On the first two days there were "Lamentations [*Leçons de Ténèbres*] in close harmony with harpsichord and other instruments, newly composed by Gabrielle Balami",[43] the *maestro di cappella*, and sung by Tempesti.[44] He sang again in the cathedral on Easter Sunday, provoking James to tell Mar that "Tempesti did wonders".[45] On the following day there was a sung mass in the cathedral for the soul of Princess Louise Marie, James' sister, to mark the sixth anniversary of her death. It was organised by Archdeacon Giovanni Battista Bonaventura "with music sumptuous enough to persuade the famous musicians brought in by Alamanno Salviati to stay on in the city". Pucci noted James' extreme gratitude to Bonaventura for arranging this.[46]

In the weeks which followed, until the middle of May, the musical life of the court continued unabated. There were concerts in the Palazzo Ducale and *conversazioni* in the town, both in the Palazzo Staccoli[47] and in the Palazzo Bonaventura. Tempesti had remained at Urbino, and he sang at most of these concerts, being joined at the beginning of May by Cristini.[48] The sensation of the season, however, was the arrival of a soprano from Bologna called Signora Innocenza. She was the daughter of the *Commissario* (or Doge) of the little republic of San Marino, and had been invited by Giovanni Bernardino Bonaventura. Her first performance at the Palazzo Bonaventura on 26 April was described by Pucci: "with the excellence of her singing and the mastery of her lute playing, she added a touch of exquisite beauty to such a noble meeting, and His Britannic Majesty repeatedly sang her praises".[49] Several letters testify to the impact she made on her audience. The king told Mar that her voice would "drive" the men of the court "into her garret",[50] and Hay added that Creagh was "touched...so much that he says he would marry her".[51] The best description, however, was provided by Paterson:

> Some few days ago arrived here a young lady of Bologna, who, they say, is pretty enough and sings to a miracle, as I am told by our virtuosos. She sang at a conversatione at Signor Bonaventura's the night before last, where the King was present and all his subjects except Sir W. Ellis and myself, and lucky it was for us. Never any lady, I believe, made a more universal conquest. Not a single man escaped her, I mean of a subject, for such as were not killed dead on the spot came home mortally wounded, and still there is nothing talked of but her amongst those that have life enough to speak at all. Of the wounded Nairne and Creagh seem to be in the most desperate condition.[52]

When Paterson did hear her perform he too was "wounded". In letters which he later received from Nairne, the latter referred to her as "your beloved",[53] and even jokingly as "your future wife".[54]

The concerts given by Tempesti and Innocenza were abruptly interrupted when the news of the death of Mary of Modena was received at Urbino on 18 May.[55] The court immediately went into mourning,[56] and Tempesti was paid off.[57] Nevertheless there was still music to be heard. The Archbishop of Urbino (Tomaso Marelli) provided a requiem mass for the queen in the cathedral, with a setting of *Libera me Domine* which was described as "with sumptuous music".[58] A few days later Salviati organised a memorial service for the queen in the church of S. Domenico "with a sung Mass and a celebration of a *Messe basse* [Low Mass], as was the custom in France".[59] Many other services took place, culminating in another requiem mass with a motet in the cathedral at the end of May.[60]

The concerts in the Palazzo Ducale seem to have been resumed during July, when Don Carlo Albani arrived with his wife Donna Teresa to spend several months in the Palazzo Albani. A letter from the Duke of

Mar gives a good description of the important role played by music in the entertainment of the court:

> They [the Albanis] dined with the King yesterday. After dinner and reposing for an hour or two as their custom is, we had cards and music and, the day being wet, which prevented going abroad in the evening, it continued till 8. We had three voices and several instruments, which performed excellent music that we had a collection of from all places. It was too soon by the rules to have this in the King's own rooms, so it was in Mar's, but he got the Duke of Perth [as Lord Chamberlain] to do the ceremony. There was a lady of the place [Lucrezia Staccoli?] and Mrs Hay of the company, a neighbouring Abbé and his brother, ... and your friend the President [Salviati].[61]

Once the concerts had resumed, both Tempesti and Innocenza were summoned to return to Urbino,[62] where they performed throughout the late summer and early autumn, accompanied by Agostino Tinazzoli, described by Nairne as "one of the best players on the harpsichord and ablest masters of music in Italy".[63] Innocenza was accommodated in one of the convents (probably Santa Chiara), and in one of his letters Nairne describes how he and Erskine (Mar's cousin) went to hear her sing there and then, "after Salut", spoke with her through the convent "grate".[64] The last description we have of her comes in the middle of October when "she sang ... and played on the lute most charmingly to Lady Nithsdale and had the applause, vivats and benissimos of all the company".[65]

It is frustrating that we do not know exactly what she and the others sang on each occasion. We cannot say what the balance was between vocal and instrumental music, nor do we have any information about what instrumental works were performed. It would be fascinating to know if any musical manuscripts had been brought to Urbino from France, and if the recent publications of Venetian music (notably Vivaldi's Opus I–IV) had supplanted the Roman music (notably Corelli's Opus I–V) which had been favoured at Saint-Germain. It was clearly the singers, rather than the composers, instrumentalists and specific works, which the Jacobites mentioned in their correspondence. But there can be no doubt that music played a very significant role while the Stuart court was at Urbino.

It obviously provided an extremely important and necessary form of entertainment, but it did much more than that. It was a force both for division and unity. The new Scottish exiles, Mar, Hay and all the pensioners, had only ever experienced Italian opera before following James III into exile. Converting the king to Italian music was therefore regarded by them as an important factor in their struggle against the old servants from Saint-Germain. Yet some of the old servants, most notably David Nairne, were just as enthusiastic about the new Italian operas as were the new favourites and pensioners. Music also fulfilled another very important function at the Stuart court. It brought a feminine element into the otherwise masculine community. Whether it was Innocenza, or Lucrezia Staccoli singing and entertaining at her *conversazioni*, the ladies of the Bonaventura family, the other ladies of the town with whom the Jacobites could dance, or the ladies who attended the performances of Salviati's oratorios, music provided the occasion for some mixing of the sexes. The very last reference to music at the court comes from a letter written by the Duke of Mar in the middle of October. By then James III was expecting to be able to move his court from Urbino to Castel Gandolfo, and Mar emphasised to Nairne how important it was to retain the services of Innocenza and prevent her from returning to Bologna or San Marino: "I hope you'll get Signora Innocenza to remove to a convent at Castello [Castel Gandolfo] or Albano."[66] Here at least was a subject on which Mar and Nairne could both agree.

8
James III and the Papacy

As an exiled king living in a foreign country, James III was dependent on the goodwill of the local ruler. At Saint-Germain and Bar-le-Duc this had meant Louis XIV of France and Duke Leopold of Lorraine, both of whom were very well disposed towards him, and with both of whom he had regular contact. Once he entered the Papal States, however, James was faced with a much more complicated political situation. The Pope was in Rome, yet the Stuart court was based far away, at Avignon, then Pesaro and then Urbino. Pope Clement XI was an old man with no personal dynastic links with the Stuarts, who would sooner or later be succeeded by one of the cardinals. It was therefore essential for James to cultivate good relations with the cardinals as well as the Pope, and to encourage the existing pro-Jacobite faction among the leading families of Roman society.

Opinion in Rome and among the Italian princes always had been pro-Jacobite. But it was one thing to support the Stuart king when he had been living elsewhere and no practical help had been required. It was altogether another when he was living within the Papal States and requiring both financial assistance and social recognition. With the Austrian Habsburgs now ruling Naples, and enjoying good relations with King George I, there was bound to be an Imperialist faction at Rome which opposed the interests of the Stuarts. It thus became important for James to have a group of supporters who would protect his interests in Rome and elsewhere in Italy as actively as possible.

He had made a start while he was in Avignon. There he had met Alamanno Salviati, who had followed him to Pesaro and Urbino. He had also met two influential ladies, who visited the city while he was there. They were the Principessa di Piombino (a relation of Salviati) and the Marchesa di Cavailla (a relation of Archbishop Gontieri). The former returned to Rome, the latter to Turin and James made a point of keeping in touch with both of them.

At Pesaro and Urbino James had established good relations with the local prelates. They included Cardinal Davia and Cardinal Ruffo (the Legate and Vice-Legate of the Romagna), Cardinal Origo and Cardinal Buoncampagni (the Legate and Archbishop of Bologna), Cardinal Gozzadini (Archbishop of Imola), Cardinal Spada (Bishop of Pesaro) and the various priests at Urbino, one of whom, Domenico Riviera, would later become a cardinal. But the influence of these men tended to be restricted to the northern parts of the Papal States. What James needed was a group of active supporters in Rome itself, and notably (during the lifetime of Clement XI) within the Albani family.

The king took advantage of his visit to Rome from May to July 1717 to cultivate good relations with the Pope, the Albanis and as many people as possible. The actively Jacobite group of cardinals included Gualterio, Sacripanti and Imperiali (the Protectors of England, Scotland and Ireland), Acquaviva (the Spanish ambassador), Barberini, Colonna and D'Adda, the last of whom (now Bishop of Albano) had been the Papal Nuncio in England during the reign of James II. Cardinal Ottoboni (the Protector of France) was also a supporter, as was Cardinal Paulucci (the Secretary of State). Backed up by Cardinal Annibale Albani, and even more by Don Carlo Albani, these men formed an influential group to support James III in his dealings with the Pope.

Among the princely families of Rome James also enjoyed good relations with the Ruspolis,[1] and with the Principessa di Piombino, with whom he renewed the close friendship he had started at Avignon. But at this time he was particularly associated with the Colonnas, who were his cousins.[2] The head of the family was Prince Fabrizio Colonna, known as the Constable, then only 17 years old. He, with his mother Diana, his uncle Cardinal Carlo and numerous influential relations, provided James with strong support from their palazzo in the Piazza dei SS. Apostoli.

The king encouraged this influential group by giving them his portrait. As we have seen above, while James had been in Rome he had commissioned Antonio David to paint a new three-quarter length portrait, showing him with a closed crown as well as both the Garter and the Thistle. This portrait was intended for Queen Mary of Modena at Saint-Germain, but James decided that numerous copies should be made before it was sent away. These copies, all of them busts, were to be given as diplomatic presents to the leading members of the pro-Jacobite faction.

Illustration 13 Antonio David (from left to right) *Cardinals Imperiali, Sacripanti and Gualterio (the Protectors of Ireland, Scotland and England) standing behind Cardinal Albani (nephew of Pope Clement XI)*, a detail from *The Baptism of Charles, Prince of Wales, 31 December 1720* (1725)

Illustration 14 Antonio David (from left to right) *Cardinals Aquaviva, Barberini, Paulucci and Ottoboni standing behind Don Carlo Albani (nephew of Pope Clement XI)*, a detail from *The Baptism of Charles, Prince of Wales, 31 December 1720* (1725)

Immediately after arriving at Urbino, David Nairne entered into a lengthy correspondence with Cardinal Gualterio, then in Rome, to decide who should be given a copy of the new portrait. It was Gualterio's task to deal with the painter, and to make sure he worked as quickly as possible.

James wanted one copy for himself and two miniatures (one of which was also for his mother at Saint-Germain), in addition to the copies to be given away. He eventually ordered nine other copies, for Cardinals Gualterio, Sacripanti, Imperiali, Acquaviva and Barberini, and for Don Carlo Albani, Principessa Colonna, the Principessa di Piombino and the Marchesa di Cavailla.[3]

It would take David some time to produce these ten copies. James had received the two miniatures by October and entrusted the one for the queen to Francis Strickland to be taken back to Saint-Germain.[4] But then David fell ill for two months during which time he was unable to work,[5] and it was not until February that the ten copies were all finished.[6] They were then given to all the recipients in Rome,[7] with one sent to the king at Urbino, another to the Marchesa di Cavailla at Turin and the three-quarter length to the queen at Saint-Germain. To make up for the delay David gave an additional (eleventh) copy to Nairne as a personal present,[8] which was then sent to his daughter in Paris in the package containing the original for the queen.[9]

Once these portraits had been finished the king ordered another copy for Cardinal D'Adda,[10] thus making 12 in all in addition to the original. Several copies have survived, some of them in private collections with a provenance which suggests that David also made some copies which were not commissioned by the king.[11] One additional copy was definitely ordered by Redmond and sent to Madrid.[12] David seems to have employed assistants, because the copies which have survived are not all of the same quality, and it is to be noted that David actually specified that he had himself painted the entirety of the portrait sent to the king at Urbino.[13]

These portraits were intended to inspire the loyalty of the pro-Jacobite faction, by being prominently displayed as a constant reminder that the exiled Stuart king was only biding his time in far away and remote Urbino. In April 1718 Nairne passed on to Gualterio a letter he had received from the Marchese di Cavailla at Turin:

Y[our] E[xcellency] will see from the attached letter from the Marchese de Cavailla that the portrait of the King you sent for his wife has arrived safely and was received with great pleasure. Mr David has been much complimented on his painting at the court of Turin, where the Queen herself has admired and praised it.[14]

The distribution of portraits was not the only way in which James III sought to strengthen his political position in Rome. He also promoted an important marriage, which took place in July 1718,[15] between Prince Fabrizio Colonna and Salviati's niece Catterina Teresa.[16] James made no secret of the interest he took in what he termed the "illustrious house" of Colonna,[17] but he now promoted the interests of the Salviatis as well. On 1 June he wrote to the Pope to ask him to grant to the Salviati family the honours enjoyed by princes of the first rank at the papal court.[18] The Colonna–Salviati marriage was intended to strengthen James' position in Florence as well as Rome.[19]

James was also keen to strengthen his position with the Italian princes. Grand Duke Cosimo of Tuscany was friendly, as was Duke Rinaldo of Modena (though not friendly enough to let James marry his daughter). Duke Francesco of Parma was particularly worth cultivating because he was the uncle of the influential Queen of Spain. In June 1718 James discovered that the duke expected to be addressed in their correspondence as *Celsitudo* (*Altesse* or Serene Highness), because that was the way he was now addressed by the King of Spain, the Emperor and King George.[20] Nairne immediately wrote to the duke's secretary to offer the king's apologies "for the ceremonial of which he was not sufficiently aware to be able to put it into practice immediately, especially as it involves changing a style adhered to until now by his predecessors in their correspondence with his uncle the Duke of Modena and His Serene Highness".[21] James could not afford to alienate Duke Francesco, and was keen to retain his support, even though it meant addressing him in a way to which he had never previously been entitled. As Nairne tactfully put it to Gualterio, "We were in ignorance of true English ceremonial at Saint-Germain, and therefore believed it sensible to practice that of France. Indeed in all the last thirty years, the protocol adopted in the King's Secretariat has always been that prescribed by Monsieur de Torcy."[22] If the French did not address the duke as *Celsitudo*, there was no reason why James should, but the duke's influence in both Rome and Madrid counted for more than questions of protocol. There was, however, another reason why James III was keen to appease the Duke of Parma. By June 1718 he had decided to marry one of his nieces.

In the winter of 1717–1718 James had sent Captain Charles Wogan, one of the Irish pensioners at Urbino, on a tour of the European courts to find a suitable princess whom he could marry. By June 1718 he had selected Maria Clementina, then only 16 years old, the youngest of the three unmarried daughters of Prince James Sobieski.[23] On 24 June the king sent James Murray, recently arrived from England, to Ohlau in Silesia to ask Sobieski for the hand of his daughter.

If the primary purpose of the proposed marriage was to secure the Stuart succession to the thrones of England, Scotland and Ireland, the secondary and more immediate aim was to strengthen James' diplomatic position. Prince James Sobieski was very wealthy and enjoyed the enormous prestige of being the son of King John III of Poland, who had saved Vienna from the Turks in 1683. His sister Thérèse Cunégonde had married the Elector of Bavaria, whom James III had known when they were both living in exile outside Paris during the War of the Spanish Succession. James already knew, and was friendly with, their three sons.

Through her mother, Elizabeth of Neuburg, Maria Clementina Sobieska was related to several of the ruling houses of Europe. Her aunts had married Duke Francesco of Parma (as already mentioned), the Emperor Leopold I, King Peter II of Portugal and King Charles II of Spain. One of her uncles was the Elector of the Palatinate, another was the Archbishop–Elector of Mainz and another was the Prince Bishop of Augsburg. Queen Elizabeth Farnese of Spain, the Emperor Charles VI and King John V of Portugal were her first cousins. Through her paternal grandmother she was related to some of the leading noble families in both Poland and France. Even allowing for political divisions within her family, the connections which the Sobieskis would bring to the dynastically isolated Stuart king would be enormously important.

The marriage contract was signed at Ohlau on 22 July. As a dowry James III was to receive 600,000 *livres* of *rentes* which Prince Sobieski had invested in the Hôtel de Ville in Paris; the estate of Szawle, on the borders of Courland, Livonia, Sweden and Muscovy, worth 800,000 French *livres*, "of which estate the King may take possession at his pleasure", and 250,000 *livres* which were owed to Prince Sobieski by King Augustus I of Poland.[24] It was agreed that Maria Clementina would travel from Ohlau with her mother to a place in northern Italy, where she would marry James III during October.

It was recognised that the marriage, which was so obviously beneficial to the Jacobite cause, would be opposed by the supporters of King George. Moreover the Emperor Charles VI had just become an ally of King George by joining the Quadruple Alliance, so the Imperialist faction in Rome would bring pressure to bear on the Pope to try to prevent it taking place. This, then, was the moment when James would need the support of the carefully cultivated pro-Jacobite faction. His proposed marriage also brought to a head two other matters which required support. The king had no desire to remain at Urbino for another winter and was determined that his new bride should live somewhere which was both less remote and less cold. He was also impatient to take renewed steps to effect his own restoration to England, particularly as the political situation there seemed increasingly favourable. Neither of these aims could be achieved without active papal support: he needed to be given an alternative palace near Rome as a more suitable temporary home for his court, and he needed to be given a substantial sum of money with which to finance a military expedition. Both necessitated the backing of the Albani family and the pro-Jacobite cardinals in Rome.

During James' visit to Rome in 1717 the Pope had promised to give him 300,000 *scudi*, in addition to his annual pension of 10,000 *scudi*, to help him prepare an expedition to England,[25] but since then Clement had had second thoughts, perhaps because of the British threats during the Peterborough affair. In February 1718, when he had still received nothing, James wrote to Cardinal Gualterio from Fano, asking him to concert with Cardinals Paulucci, Albani and Imperiali to persuade the Pope to give him what had been promised.[26] At first it seemed that this pressure would be successful,[27] but as time went by and no money was forthcoming the king became increasingly pessimistic about ever receiving it.[28] On 24 April he sent a tactful letter to Cardinal Albani, saying how sorry he was that the Pope had not been able to give him the money promised, but that he was confident of receiving it at some later date.[29] The matter was then dropped for the time being.

Meanwhile the king began to think of moving away from Urbino. At one point he thought of going to Lucca, and even made a tentative approach to the senators of the city, but the idea was dropped because the small republic was too dependent on the Emperor's goodwill.[30] James stated that he did not particularly mind where he went ("I am such an Urbinist…, that after Rome and Bologna the rest is hang choice"),[31] but the prospect of marrying Maria Clementina Sobieska made him more than ever determined to get away.[32] By the beginning of July he hoped that his new residence would be the papal palace at Castel Gandolfo, overlooking Lake Albano, where he had stayed the previous year.

It was the arrival of Don Carlo Albani and his wife during that July which encouraged the king to ask the Pope for Castel Gandolfo and to renew his request for money.[33] James and Don Carlo agreed that they should start by getting the Pope's agreement to the change of residence. Thanks to Don Carlo's influence at the Quirinale, the first objective was fairly quickly achieved and it was agreed that the Stuart court should move to Castel Gandolfo in November, immediately after the king's marriage.[34] James sent a polite letter of thanks to Cardinal Albani in Rome:

> I beg you to help me thank his Holiness for the loan he has made me of his palace at Castello. My future wife will have the chief obligation to him, when she sees herself thereby delivered from the snows and mountains of Urbino, which make it a real prison in winter.[35]

But a letter of the same day to Cardinal Gualterio shows how much opposition had had to be overcome, and how reluctant the Pope had now become to offend the Emperor and King George:

> You have made a vivid picture of fear, meanness and perplexity by simply narrating the Pope's words. All this seems to me worthy of contempt. Taking with a good grace what has been given me with a bad, I shall dissemble everything and shall content myself with having obtained my request.[36]

By this time the king and Don Carlo Albani had already revived the question of a papal subsidy to finance a Stuart restoration. In a long letter dated 7 August, James both reminded the Pope of the 300,000 *scudi* he had been promised and informed him of his impending marriage to Maria Clementina Sobieska. He recognised the difficulty the Pope might have in giving him so much money secretly, and then came to the point. Perhaps the money might be given him as a wedding present, ostensibly for the maintenance of his new queen.[37]

When no reply had been received from Rome for two and a half weeks, James wrote again. The Vatican Archives contain a further long letter dated 24 August, written by the king himself, another of 25 August in the handwriting of David Nairne, and three long memoranda also in Nairne's handwriting, all urging the Pope to give James as a wedding present the 300,000 *scudi* which he had been promised.[38] Despite the support of Don Carlo Albani, who was still at Urbino, the Pope could not be persuaded to hand over the money. Given his reluctance to let James have Castel Gandolfo, perhaps it is not surprising that he was not willing to give him the money as well. But the main reason must clearly have been the Battle of Cap Passaro, which was fought at the beginning of that month. It is hard to know exactly what role was played by Cardinal Albani, to whom the king wrote on 15 September: "Your brother has explained to me the reason of your silence about the money. I well know you are not in fault."[39] By the beginning of October, James was obliged to accept that he would not get the money in the forseeable future. As he wrote to Gualterio, "the money affair remains as it was, my new demands [to have it as a wedding present] have been refused and God knows when the old ones will be executed."[40]

In the weeks which followed, James therefore concentrated on the preparations for his marriage and on the transfer of the court from Urbino to Castel Gandolfo.

9
The Planned Move to Castel Gandolfo

By the autumn of 1718 it was agreed with the Pope that the Stuart court would leave Urbino and move south to Castel Gandolfo. The king would marry Maria Clementina Sobieska, and take her with him to his new residence, and thus the court would be transformed by the presence of a queen and her ladies. The only uncertainty seemed to be how long the Jacobites would remain at their new home, because the king now had hopes of obtaining military and financial assistance from Spain for a restoration attempt.

The months of September and October were a period of planning and preparation. There was much to be done. The details of the marriage had to be arranged, the new queen had to be provided with a team of servants, the possessions of Mary of Modena had to be transported from Saint-Germain to be given to Maria Clementina, and the palazzo at Castel Gandolfo had to be made ready.

At the beginning of September the king entrusted his two new Protestant favourites with the task of arranging his Catholic marriage. Hay was sent to visit Prince Sobieski at Ohlau in Silesia and to accompany his daughter over the Alps to Italy;[1] Murray was given a warrant to marry Maria Clementina by proxy if that should prove necessary.[2] Hay and Sobieski agreed that the best place for the marriage would be Ferrara, and that the princess should be accompanied there by her mother and a staff of about 20.[3] The king approved of this idea, particularly as Guido Bonaventura would be on the spot to help with the preparations, assuring Hay that "my true and solid kindness to you is unalterable".[4] The precise date was to be selected by Maria Clementina and her mother, but Hay told James that they expected to reach Ferrara on about 11 October.[5]

When the Jacobites heard the news that the king was to be married there was speculation as to the nature of his wife's future household.

It was hoped by some that James might reverse his decision and reintroduce "fixed waiting" in her Chamber and Bedchamber at Castel Gandolfo. Even if he did not, it was assumed that he would at least provide the queen with her own household of ladies, women and gentlemen, perhaps financed by her large dowry. Several people applied to the king in the hope of obtaining a position at court.

In fact they were all to be disappointed, as James had already decided that he would not give a separate household to his wife, who was only 16 years old, and that he would therefore employ as few women as possible. In the long run this was to become the most divisive issue at the exiled Stuart court and would eventually cause Maria Clementina to separate from her husband.

The first person to ask for a post, as a Lady of the Bedchamber, was Lady Nithsdale. She had applied as early as January 1718, before James had selected his bride,[6] and been given an outright refusal. There was to be no "fixed waiting" in the Bedchamber or the Chamber of the queen, just as there was none in his own.[7] The same reply was given to Anne, Lady Murray, who had been one of the Bedchamber Women to Princess Louise Marie at Saint-Germain. She was told by Mar in September that "as to...your being employed about our Queen, when we shall have one, the King says it will be time enough to think about that when the thing happens, but at present he has resolved that nobody shall have the name of any post about his Queen".[8] In October, Olive Trant sent a long letter asking for a post,[9] and Lady Nithsdale (recently arrived at Urbino) renewed her request to be made a Lady of the Bedchamber, but both were refused.[10] Even the Stricklands were given a negative reply. Roger's mother Bridget (previously a Bedchamber Woman to Mary of Modena, and widow of her Vice-Chamberlain) asked the king to give a post to her daughter Teresa (herself a former Bedchamber woman and widow of her father's successor, John Stafford). Mar wrote in December:

> I spoke...to the King of what Mrs Strickland wrote to me concerning your sister.... He ordered me to tell Mrs Strickland that, were people to be employed about the Queen...in such places, there is nobody he would sooner choose than Mrs Stafford, but that he has resolved that nobody should have the name of a place about her.[11]

The king also received three applications from people who had actually been formally promised a post. In July, Sir George Colgrave asked to be appointed one of the queen's gentlemen ushers, and enclosed with his letter three certificates of December 1705, signed by Father Sandars, the king's confessor at Saint-Germain. They recorded the promise he had then been given of receiving a post with the new queen whenever the king should get married.[12] The king's reply was categorical: "I remember the promise to Sir George Colgrave.... No new servants to be taken in."[13] John Caryll sent an equally unsuccessful request at the end of September:

> The late Queen's promises of recommending me to the King that I might be made Vice-Chamberlain to the Queen, whenever he should marry, besides his own promises to me, make me hope, after having spent seventeen years and my fortune in his service, I might be thought worthy of that station, which is a gradual rise from my post about the late Queen, and which I hope I may deserve in consideration of Lord Caryll's services and sufferings, which he counted on would entitle me to the King's favour, and therefore left me nothing but his death-bed recommendation to their Majesties.[14]

The most difficult request to refuse came from the eldest daughter of Mary of Modena's Bedchamber Woman and personal friend, Contessa Veronica Molza. She had married the queen's Equerry, John Nugent, in 1711, and wrote from Saint-Germain to remind the king of the promise which he had written in his own hand in the articles of her marriage: "We do moreover promise the said Margaret Molza that, whenever we have a Queen Consort, she shall be one of her Bedchamber Women."[15] This letter reached the king while he was at Bologna, where he was visited for several days by Contessa Molza.[16] But even this request was refused, James merely writing to Dillon that "I have a very good opinion of Jack Nugent, my servant, to whom I shall always be as kind as I can, as I promised his mother-in-law when I saw her."[17]

The rejection of these applications is particularly revealing about the nature of the exiled Stuart court after it had spent over a year at Urbino. The king not only broke several promises – and there might have been others of which we have no record. He also turned away household servants who had proved their loyalty in the past and who would probably have made ideal servants for the new queen. Margaret Nugent, moreover, had the advantage of being an anglicised Italian. Some of these people might, after all, have been allowed to join the court without being given formal petitions, as Lady Murray pointed out after receiving her rejection.[18] But James had turned away so thoroughly from his Saint-Germain background, and come to rely so totally on his new Scottish favourites, that he was not prepared to give way and allow

Maria Clementina to have a proper household made up of people from Saint-Germain.

Yet the new queen had to be given some female servants to provide her with company in what would otherwise be, at the higher level, an exclusively male court. If all these people, including even Lady Nithsdale, were to be turned away, who could these female servants possibly be? By the autumn of 1718 the answer had become clear. The only ladies who would gain access to the new queen would be the wives of Hay and Mar.

David Nairne came to realise this as early as July, as he explained in one of his secret letters to Cardinal Gualterio:

> I confess to Y[our] E[xcellency], from whom I can keep nothing hidden, that I find it impossible to close my eyes to what I see distributed around me every day not only in compliments but in actual benefits to other new favourites.... Y[our] E[xcellency] will see that when we are fortunate enough to have a Queen, these men's wives, relatives and friends will be put above everyone, and not even the smallest position will be given to my elder daughter, though she is the King's god-daughter and brought up quite well enough to have a post like Madame Molza once had or to be a Maid of Honour, if the former post is to be filled by married women only.[19]

Shortly afterwards, when the news of the king's marriage contract reached Urbino, Nairne told Gualterio in confidence: "Mr Hay's wife has been promised a place close to the Queen when we have one, and the Duchess of Mar to be a Lady of the Bedchamber when she arrives."[20] In other words, the new queen would after all be given some servants, whatever titles they had, but they would not be Catholics with a Saint-Germain connection, but the Protestant wives of the king's Scottish favourites. It was certain to cause serious trouble sooner or later.

Maria Clementina was to be given all the jewellery and other personal items which had belonged to Mary of Modena at Saint-Germain. Detailed inventories had been drawn up in June and July[21] and arrangements made for transporting to Italy everything which belonged to James III and his mother – except for the paintings which were to remain in the château there.[22] Lady Nithsdale, as we have seen, brought a selection of the jewellery, consisting of "three pearl necklaces, the diamond earrings and a diamond buckle for a girdle".[23] Everything else was sent to Rome at the end of September in five large wooden cases and a large strong box.[24] The first two cases contained the plate belonging to the

Scullery, Backstairs and Pantry. The remaining three were mainly filled with items for Maria Clementina, of which the most important were Mary of Modena's two "toilettes", one of which was described as the "Japan Toilette". There was also "an old picture of our Lady, a little Japan box with five or six Mignatures, [and] a box with forty small silver Etuis to putt gold in". There were also some important items for James III, notably the collar of the Order of the Garter, with its "diamond George", "the great seals" and "a Cellar inlay'd with Silver which belong'd to K[ing] Ch[arles] 2d".[25]

The strong box contained a large number of relatively small items: 19 miniatures, including the one by David of the king "which was sent from Italy"; six medallions; nine medals; James II's gold watch; Mary of Modena's two seals; a looking glass; two jewels of the Order of the Garter (lesser St Georges); samples of the blood and hair of James II and Princess Louise Marie; the "gold ring with a great Ruby, sett about w.th small Rubies" which James II had worn at his coronation; another one with the arms of the Prince of Wales; a golden crucifix; and "a box with a Cross and Chain found in St. Edward's tomb in ye year 1685". Many of these objects, including the ruby ring, but mainly the miniature family portraits, were to be given to Maria Clementina as soon as she arrived,[26] and the Stuart Papers contain four inventories (three in English and one in French) showing the "Pieces taken out of the Kings Strong Box by Mr Murray for the Queen".[27]

The king had meanwhile sent Felix Bonbled, one of his *valets de chambre* who spoke Italian, to inspect the palazzo at Castel Gandolfo, to make recommendations about how the apartments should be allocated and furnished, and to identify what building works would be necessary to make it suitable as a winter residence for the court. Cardinal Albani wrote to assure the king that "all possible assistance" would be given him.[28]

The palazzo contained three storeys, the third of which, described as the "principale floor" or *piano nobile*, was reserved for the king and queen. The king's apartment, previously occupied by the Pope, was to contain a *sala* and three antechambers, a formal Bedchamber, an Eating Room (*stanza dove mangia M[aesta] S[ua]*) and a *Stanza dal Udienza*. There was also a private chapel, a closet and a "Room of Backstairs" with "a bed in it for a valet de chamber and a bed in the next room for a footman". The queen was to have both a winter and a summer apartment, the second of which was described as "the Great apartment", but no details have survived concerning them, except that there was to be a "dressing room", with "a bed in it for a fame de chamber and a bed for a footman in the passage room".

The second storey below contained eight apartments, which were allocated to the Duke of Mar, the Duchess of Mar, the Duke of Perth, John Hay, Marjory Hay, David Nairne, James Murray and Father John Brown. Mar's apartment was to include a room for John Paterson.

The first storey contained three apartments, which were allocated to Sir William Ellis, Dr Charles Maghie and Dominic Sheldon (in case he should return from France). It also contained a hall for the footmen and an eating room for the second table. Bonbled was then "to dispose of the lodgings for the other servants and kitchings for the King's". The other servants included Alan Cameron (Groom of the Bedchamber), James Rodez (Yeoman of the King's Robes), the king's valets, the Anglican chaplains, Robert Creagh (Mar's other under-secretary) and all the servants in the Household Below Stairs and the Stables.

This list is noteworthy because no accommodation was provided for any of the Scottish pensioners, who were presumably expected to find their own lodgings in the town. It also confirms that the only ladies of quality who would be at the court, and able to serve the queen, would be the Duchess of Mar and Mrs Hay. There was no accommodation for Lady Nithsdale or for any of the others who had applied for posts with the queen. Finally the list shows that the senior courtiers were expected to have their own servants. Mar, Perth, Hay and Mrs Hay would have two each, the Duchess of Mar and her daughter would have three and the others would have one.[29]

When Bonbled inspected the papal palace at Castel Gandolfo, he became conscious that it had been built as a summer residence only and had never been occupied by the popes during the winter months. For that reason it had hardly any fireplaces and chimneys. When therefore Bonbled delivered his report on 14 September, identifying all the things that would need to be done to prepare the building for James III and his court, he recommended that as many as 37 new fireplaces would be needed.[30] Prompted by Mar, the king wrote to Cardinal Albani to give full support to all of Bonbled's recommendations:

"I conjure you to hasten the fireplaces at Castel Gandolfo. There is no hurry about the stairs, but, if one of the fireplaces is wanting, I must stay at Rome till it is finished, which is the course I shall take if the villegiatura of his Holiness prevents, as is reasonable, their working at those of his apartment, which is to be mine."[31]

The Pope's extended stay was bound to delay the beginning of the building works recommended by Bonbled, and thus doubts began to be felt about the prospect of the court's being able to move to Castel Gandolfo at the beginning of November,[32] though Mar remained optimistic.[33] Then, in the second half of September, it became clear that the Pope was definitely placing obstacles in the way of James' moving to Castel Gandolfo, just as he had refused to give him the money he had promised for a restoration attempt. A letter was received at Urbino from Don Alessandro Albani which raised objections to the proposed move, and which was regarded as "impertinent". The king determined to speak to Don Alessandro's elder brother Don Carlo, who was fortunately still at Urbino. A document in Mar's handwriting, dated 25 September, records what he thought James should say:

> As to the politic part, it is not seen what inconveniences his being at Castello can bring on the Pope from other princes more than his being at Urbino or Pesaro, and, those places being found bad for his health, he is resolved not to continue at either this winter.

> He is persuaded he will find Castello every way convenient if those small alterations proposed on the plan were made, the objections to which are so fully answered by Signor [Francesco] Bianchini [of the *Camera Apostolica*] that it is needless to say more. Even without these he is resolved to go to Castello about the end of October or beginning of November, since the Pope is so good as to let him have the use of it and make the best shift he can for this winter, preferring that to living either at Rome or Viterbo. The palace of Albano could not contain his family and wants more repairs than that of Castello, so he cannot think of it. When the Pope shall wish to go to Castello either in spring or autumn, the King will for that time see to dispose of himself and his family somewhere else.

> The furniture asked by Bonbled for Castello is such a trifle that it is not worth mentioning.[34]

It seems that James and Don Carlo agreed that Bonbled and Mar had asked for too much, and that some compromise was unavoidable. Some of the chimneys would have to be eliminated, otherwise it might not be possible to stick to the original plan of going to Castel Gandolfo in November. Mar explained to Bonbled that "the house being made after this maner will be habitable tho in winter and pretty comod tho we northern people would think it much better had it more chimenies".[35]

Time, however, was beginning to run out, and the date of the king's marriage was fast approaching. James wrote to Gualterio on 3 October:

> I leave this on Thursday to go to Bologna and thence to Ferrara, where my marriage is to be celebrated very secretly. We shall afterwards return here and at the beginning of the month set out for Rome, and shall stay with you there, if you find it good, while waiting till Castel Gandolfo is ready. The Pope does all he can underhand to hinder my going there, but, as he does not retract his promise, I always persist in going there, and Don Carlo hopes that my firmness will succeed in getting more chimneys at least.[36]

During the weeks which followed Bonbled did what he could to persuade the papal authorities to begin the necessary work at Castel Gandolfo, but it became increasingly clear that they did not intend to cooperate.[37] On 9 November, by which time the court had originally hoped to be able to move in, Bonbled reported that only one fireplace had been built, "in one of the servants' rooms". Castel Gandolfo, he told Nairne, "is in the same condition as I have seen it these 15 years".[38] The plan to move the court to the palace had been effectively sabotaged.

That did not mean, however, that the king was prepared to remain where he was. His personal goods had been despatched from Urbino to the Palazzo Gualterio in Rome on 11 October,[39] and as far as he was concerned new accommodation would have to be found for him. James told Nairne frankly that, "as to Castello, I have no more to say. We must get what we can of conveniency there, but, though we get nothing, I'll still go to Rome."[40]

10
The King's Second Visit to Rome

Before James III could move to Castel Gandolfo or Rome he had to travel to meet and marry his bride. At the end of September 1718 preparations were set in hand for the king's journey. The plan was that James and a small party would go to Bologna, and wait there until Maria Clementina had arrived at Ferrara and everything was ready for the marriage to take place.

It was necessary to send off two advance parties to warn the Papal Legates at Bologna and Ferrara of what was being planned. One party had the less important task of seeing Cardinal Origo in Bologna and informing him of the king's imminent arrival. The other had the more important and certainly more prestigious task of seeing Cardinal Patrizi in Ferrara, of getting everything ready, and greeting Maria Clementina Sobieska and her mother when they arrived with John Hay. The king decided to send the Duke of Perth to Bologna[1] and to send James Murray to Ferrara.[2] Nairne's opinion was that Perth, as Lord Chamberlain and a duke, should definitely have been sent to Ferrara and that it was extremely good of him to accept the lesser assignment. Nairne himself was not invited to attend the marriage.[3]

On 3 October Murray left Urbino. He took with him a valet named Michele Vezzosi (who had previously worked for Lord Nithsdale and replaced Bonbled, absent in Rome), one of the cooks (Matthew Creagh) and a footman. He also took with him his sister Mrs Hay, who was to be the only lady given the privilege of meeting the king's bride. Hay had specifically asked James to let her attend: "If my wife be to have the honour to meet her mistress, as you told me before I came away, would it not be proper that she be at Ferrara when they come?"[4] The king had, of course, agreed, but had refused Lady Nithsdale's request to be included: "Madame Nidsdale [sic], who has recently arrived and who is Catholic, being the daughter of the late Duke of Powis, pleaded to have the honour of going with them, but the King did not want it, so that now it is only Madame Hay who has this advantage."[5] Murray and his sister were to stay at Ferrara in the house of Guido Bonaventura.[6]

Two days later, on 5 October, Perth left Urbino with Thomas Forster, who was the only one of the pensioners invited to attend the wedding.[7] Forster's presence was essential, because without him there would not be a single Englishman to witness the marriage of the King of England. On the following day, the 6th, James III himself left Urbino with the Duke of Mar, his senior *valet de chambre* (Thomas Saint-Paul), a cook (Richard Bains) and two others described as valets (probably James Rodez, the Yeoman of the Robes, and a footman). They were followed on the 7th by Dr Charles Maghie and Mar's secretary John Paterson, and on the 8th by the king's confessor, Father John Brown.[8]

The king spent two nights en route, and reached Bologna on the evening of the 8th.[9] He and his small party were accommodated in the Casa Belloni.[10] Murray then reported on the 12th that everything had been made ready at Ferrara, and even that Father Brown had come over and sorted out certain details with Cardinal Patrizi.[11] There was only one problem. The Sobieskis and Hay had still not arrived.

And so Murray waited at Ferrara, and the king waited at Bologna. There were three more days of suspense, and then, on the 15th, bad news arrived from Innsbruck. Maria Clementina and her mother had been stopped and placed under house arrest on the orders of the Emperor. It seemed that King George had brought pressure to bear and that the Emperor had agreed to prevent the marriage by not letting the Sobieski party proceed south over the Alps into Italy.[12] The king had little choice but to remain at Bologna, hoping to get news from Hay that the Sobieskis had been released. But he quickly made an important decision. He would never go back to Urbino:

> We are to return no more to our old quarters but are to go straight to Rome, when we see any end, one way or another, to what keeps us, and the King has now sent orders to his family and people and things to go there immediately, before the roads be broke.[13]

For three more days the king did nothing, hoping against hope that he would get some positive news, and summoned Murray and Mrs Hay to join him from Ferrara.[14] Meanwhile the court at Urbino remained in ignorance of what had happened. There is a letter written by David Nairne at precisely this time which captures his mood, having been deliberately excluded from the king's marriage. It is dated Thursday, 20 October: "I am not so vain as to believe myself indispensable to the King, and Mar's young friend [i.e. Murray] is perfectly capable of fulfilling my duties. He will then be rewarded and rejoice in every imaginable honour that I myself was only granted in part."[15] Within two days of writing this letter his life was to be transformed, and he was to realise just how necessary he was to the king.

The news that something had gone seriously wrong first reached Urbino on Tuesday, 18 October. On that day Charles Macarty (the Yeoman of the Wine Cellar) returned from a trip to Pesaro with a story he had heard from one of the Pope's couriers, to the effect that the princess had been stopped at Innsbruck. Then, later the same day, Don Carlo Albani "told publicly at table" the same story. But there were contrary rumours, and so the court remained optimistic.[16] It was not until Saturday, 22 October that the news was officially confirmed from Bologna. And, as we have seen, it was dramatic. The princess had been arrested, the marriage had been postponed, the king was never returning to the Palazzo Ducale and the servants and pensioners were to go to Rome immediately.[17] They had no accommodation prepared for them in Rome, nor even at Castel Gandolfo, but they were nevertheless to leave Urbino without delay.

The king had written a letter to David Nairne, dated 18 October, enclosing others for Don Carlo Albani, the Pope and Sir William Ellis. In effect, Nairne was instructed to obtain the backing of the Pope against the Emperor by activating the support of the Albani family and the pro-Jacobite faction among the cardinals:

> I would have you go immediately to Rome..., but you must...speak to the two nephews [Don Carlo and Cardinal Annibale Albani] in my name, giving Don Carlo the letter I here send you and showing them both that you have here for the Pope, which you must deliver with your own hand.... You must also make my compliments to Don Alexander [i.e. Don Alessandro Albani]...and ask his good offices. I would have you also see Cardinals Paulucci, Imperiali and Sacripanti. In fine your business is to make all the clamour and noise you can, and to move heaven and earth for remedy and in speaking of it call everything by its own name. You must not mention a word of money, chimneys or any thing without other people begin with you and restrict yourself wholly to the great point.... you must stay there till further orders to solicit and press as much as you can.... my business is to make all the noise I can.

Nairne was of course to contact Cardinal Gualterio, who was in the country, and he should also sound out Cardinal Acquaviva. And before leaving he should see Alamanno Salviati, Archbishop Marelli, Archdeacon Bonaventura and Lucrezia Staccoli, and tell them that the king would not be returning.[18]

The king's letter to Don Carlo, who was still at Urbino, pointed out that it was now "16 days since her arrest without our getting any information except what is public knowledge, and without a single letter either from Mr Hay or from the Princesses or anyone else in their suite". It asked for Don Carlo's support at the Quirinale and stated that the king regarded him and his brother the cardinal as his best friends.[19] The one to the Pope begged him "to listen favourably to the bearer [Nairne], who is not unknown to you".[20]

Nairne left Urbino early on the morning of Monday, 24 October, taking with him one of the footmen (James Kerby), and travelled down the Via Flaminia to Rome as fast as he could. He carried the king's letter to the Pope, and another one from Don Carlo to his brother Annibale. At Foligno he stopped off to see Cardinal Imperiali and obtained from him a letter of support to Cardinal Paulucci. At Soriano (the Albani estate near Viterbo) he saw Cardinal Albani and obtained another letter to Paulucci and one to Don Alessandro Albani, who was looking after the family's interests in Rome. He finally reached the Porta del Popolo late at night on Thursday, 27 October, and went straight to the Palazzo Gualterio on the Corso.

In the days which followed, Nairne did what he could to bring pressure on the Pope. His aim was to secure from Clement XI a letter to the Emperor which condemned the arrest of Maria Clementina and her mother, and called for them to be released so that they could continue their journey. Between Sunday, 23 October and Wednesday, 9 November he sent ten very long letters to Bologna, five for the king and five for Mar, outlining in detail everything he did.[21] He saw Cardinal Paulucci repeatedly, and had three audiences with the Pope. He also saw Cardinal Sacripanti, had secret dealings with Cardinal Acquaviva via Gualterio's private secretary (Cavaliere Lucci), and even saw Bishop Sebastiano Bonaventura, who "cried downright" when he heard the news. Nairne showed energy and tact, and stimulated support for the king among the officials of the papal court, assisted by the nephew of Cardinal Imperiali. By 5 November he had succeeded. The Pope sent a strongly worded letter to the Emperor, and also confirmed that he had done so in a personal letter to James III.[22]

While he was in Rome, Nairne received five letters from the king, keeping him up to date with developments at Innsbruck and Bologna.[23] The king's letter of 3 November assured him that he approved of "all you have said and done", but Nairne was pessimistic – rightly – that the Pope's letter would make any difference at Vienna. The king also wanted Nairne to keep up the pressure: "it is our business still to make all the noise we can, for that may do good, and can do not hurt".[24] But Nairne was not so sure:

> As for making all the noise I can here and teasing the Pope etc, about this affair, though I be naturally the unfittest person in the world for either one or t'other, yet as far as I can judge it to be in your intention and interest, I have done it hitherto, but to rail or be too importune I thought would not be altogether so proper, but I encourage and excite others to exclaim as much as I can.[25]

While Nairne was negotiating in Rome, and the king remained in Bologna with Mar, Murray and Mrs Hay, or Lady Inverness as she now was, the Jacobites had been leaving Urbino. "The King's Orders to Sir W. Ellis", enclosed with the letter telling Nairne to go to Rome, effectively marked the end of the Stuart court at Urbino:

> The family and all the goods to go to Rome as soon as conveniently can be and remain there till further orders. My French post chair to be lent to Lord Southesk. The berlin and saddle horses must also go to Rome and [James] Delatre [Equerry] with them and, if Sir William has a mind, he may go in it with the money, which he will take care should go safely. As I do not return to Urbino, none of my goods must be left there and [Gerald] Fitzgerald [*valet de chambre*] must take great care of the two miniatures [presumably of Maria Clementina] that no wet comes near them. Sir William is to offer to all the lords and gentlemen an advance of two months, if they please, for their journey, for as to Delatre, [John] Sheridan [Riding Purveyor], [Robert] Creagh [under-secretary] and himself he must defray their journey as well as for all the under servants. Sir William must look for a proper place at Rome to put the goods in and hire rooms for himself and such servants as I lodge .... Sir William must give 10 Spanish pistoles to Don Francesco [Soanti], the concierge, and 5 to the poor Clare nuns and agree with Nairne what small matter should be given to the two or three young clergymen, who used to serve my Mass and he'll take care to give any other little present that's fit.[26]

Mar added an extra instruction in a letter to Nairne:

> I cannot order my papers and things which are in my cabinet and in Paterson's rooms to be sent away, till I send Paterson to pack them up, so good care must be taken of them where they are till Paterson's arrival, but everything else belonging to the King cannot be sent too soon.[27]

The Stuart court left Urbino between Sunday 23 and Saturday 29 October.[28] First to leave, on the 23rd, were Southesk, Erskine, Macmahon, Wogan and Edgar. As we have seen, Nairne left on the following morning, having packed up all his papers and visited all the people the king had instructed him to see. The other pensioners then left in small groups during the days which followed. They were all given an advance payment of two months' pension (for November and December) to cover the expenses of the journey and finding accommodation in Rome. Last to leave was Lord Nithsdale, who had to be given extra money because his wife did not yet have a separate pension.[29] It took much longer for the household servants to pack everything up, but Ellis reported on Friday, 28 October that "I have got all things ready and hope to part on Saturday, if I can get a sufficient number of voitures for the goods and servants". Ellis found what he needed, and did leave as planned. By the end of Saturday, 29 October the apartments and the basements of the Palazzo Ducale were deserted. All that remained were the papers and possessions of the Duke of Mar, locked up in the *appartamento di S. Domenico*.[30]

The Jacobites travelled by different routes and at different speeds, some going directly down the Via Flaminia from Acqualagna, others going by Fano, Ancona and Loreto, and joining the main road north of Foligno. Apart from Nairne who went as quickly as possible and reached Rome after only four days, they all journeyed for more than a week. The pensioners and servants, making up a combined party of at least 70 people, then all arrived in Rome between Saturday, 29 October and Thursday, 10 November.[31] Nairne reported to the king on 8 November that "the mules with all the equipage arrived here yesterday, and Sir William [Ellis] this afternoon with Mr Delatre, Mr Creagh and the saddlehorses".[32] Apart from those who were with the king at Bologna, and those still stranded at Ferrara, the only person who had not yet arrived was Lord Winton, who had been away from Urbino when the king's orders had been received. A letter written by James Edgar on

9 November effectively announced that the exiled Stuart court was now in Rome rather than Urbino:

> Mr. Erskine and the company I came in were first here after Lord Southesk and Mr. Nairne, next came Lord Linlithgow and Mr. Cockburn, then Mr. Colier, Mr. Menzies and James Hay, a day after Mr. Carnegie and Sir John [Preston] and Mr. Grahame and brother Allan [Cameron] and a day after them Lord and Lady Nithsdale and Lord Kilsyth. Lord Kingston and Mr. Fleming came together. Sheridan, McCarty and Bromae [*sic*] came here on Monday and Sir William, Delatre and Creagh in the King's berlin yesternight. Dr. Barclay came also yesternight and says Dr. Coupar will be here to-morrow. We expect Mr. Stuart [*sic*], Clephane and Mackenzie to-night, but have no account what way Lord Winton comes.[33]

Temporary lodgings had to be found for all these people, and Nairne, still negotiating with the Pope, gave "Bonbled the list of the persons and horses" so that he could obtain what was necessary.[34] The household servants were lodged either in the Palazzo Gualterio or in the surrounding area. As the cardinal was still in the country he told Nairne that "the King should make use of his palace and coaches as entirely his own".[35] Not everyone, however, could be fitted into Gualterio's palazzo, and the five packing cases had now arrived from Saint-Germain. Nairne reported that the servants are "all lodged hereabouts as well as could be and the plate and other goods are either in the Cardinal's palace or Mr. Lucci's house, all safe".[36]

The sudden and unexpected arrival of the Stuart court, while the king was still at Bologna, raised a very important question, which in the first instance had to be dealt with by Nairne. Did the king still intend to spend the winter at Castel Gandolfo, despite the lack of progress in building the necessary fireplaces? If so, the court would be in Rome only very temporarily, as originally planned. Or was the king now to spend the winter in Rome? If that was the case, then Nairne would have to find an available palazzo into which the court could move.

Nairne himself had absolutely no doubt as to what should be done. The king should definitely spend the winter in Rome, and should leave Bologna and join his court as soon as possible, without giving the Pope advance warning. In his letters to James III and to Mar he advocated this as strongly as he could, partly because he was afraid that "if the English and the Emperor had a mind, there is nothing so easy as to send in a night a sufficient body to carry off the King" from Castel Gandolfo, and partly because he was afraid that the Emperor might send a message to the Pope ordering him not to allow James to live in Rome.[37] While waiting for a decision from the king he opened negotiations with the Pope and the *Camera Apostolica* to find a suitable palazzo.

During these days when the court had moved to Rome, and when Nairne was continuing negotiations, the king had remained in Bologna with Mar, Murray and Lady Inverness. On 23 October he sent a letter, via a secret agent, to Lord Inverness at Innsbruck:

> I am in an inconceivable and inconsolable condition, since I had the news of your arrest.... I wait impatiently for news of them [Maria Clementina and her mother] and shall have no rest till I receive it, and, if possible, I wish you would be the bearer yourself. You are of no use to them at present, and I want you here.[38]

To his surprise the imperial authorities allowed Inverness to leave: "Inverness escaped worse usage by being treated only as a follower of the Queen's and 'tis not known or not minded that he belongs to me."[39]

The arrival of news that Inverness had been released, and was travelling to Bologna, coincided with more news that the Duchess of Mar, who was travelling to join her husband at Bologna, had been taken ill at Vercelli (between Turin and Milan).[40] Mar therefore felt obliged to leave Bologna and escort her and Lady Frances Erskine for the last stage of their journey.[41] It was while he was away that the king received Nairne's letters urging him to come to Rome as quickly as possible. James was quickly convinced by what he read and remained at Bologna just long enough for Inverness to arrive (on Sunday, 6 November).[42]

Nairne had therefore succeeded in everything he had tried to do. He had persuaded the Pope to send a strongly worded letter to the Emperor, and he had persuaded the king to come to Rome. Letters had to be sent to the Duke of Mar apologising that he would find the king gone when he returned. Murray explained,

> He [the King] understood ... by what Nairne and others wrote that, if he did not arrive there very soon, a command might come from the Emperor to the Pope in a manner to order him not to come. After such a thing had been intimated, a journey to Rome would have been flying directly in the Pope's face, whereas he cannot take his going ill at this time and far less turn him out of Rome, when he is once there. Some letters say that in the present strange conjuncture of affairs the King's person cannot be safe at Castello.[43]

James left Bologna on Wednesday, 9 November with Inverness and the servants, and travelled as fast as he could via Florence. He arrived late at night on Monday, 14 November after a journey of six days, which he described as "the most fatiguing journey I ever made". Nairne had been right about a speedy arrival, and the king promptly gave up the idea of going to Castel Gandolfo:

> I find every moment the more necessity there was of my coming here, out of which all the world agrees my liberty might not be secure. The Palazzo [Quirinale] are in a terrible puzzle on my coming here, before they so much as knew I had left Bologna, but here I am and here I'll stay and the Pope, I am sure, will never make me go out.[44]

When the king saw Don Alessandro Albani later the same day, the latter "could not easily conceal from me his master's apprehensions on my coming here".[45] Nevertheless, Clement XI agreed that James and his court would have to be allowed to remain.[46]

The court, however, was not yet complete. Murray and Lady Inverness, with the Duke of Perth and Thomas Forster, left Bologna on Friday, 11 November and travelled via Florence much more slowly.[47] They presumably arrived about a week and a half later. The Duke and Duchess of Mar then left on Tuesday, 15 November, accompanied by Paterson and Dr Maghie, and also by Lord Pitsligo who had arrived from Vienna.[48] They went to Pesaro, and remained there for two days while Paterson made the journey to the deserted Palazzo Ducale at Urbino to collect all Mar's papers and possessions, and arrange for them to be sent to Rome.[49] They then continued via Fano and Loreto, and finally arrived at the Palazzo Gualterio on Thursday, 24 November.[50]

It was under these totally unexpected circumstances that the Stuart court hastily left Urbino and moved to Rome in October and November 1718. The servants and pensioners had known that they were to move before the onset of winter, but they had expected to greet the new queen in the Palazzo Ducale, and then accompany her to the papal palace at Castel Gandolfo, stopping briefly in Rome *en route*. Now all that had changed. They found themselves living in temporary accommodation while a palazzo was sought in Rome into which the court could move, at least until James could achieve a restoration.

James III remained in the Palazzo Gualterio from November 1718 until February 1719 and used the apartment of the cardinal, who stayed

Illustration 15   Giuseppe Vasi, detail from an engraving showing the Palazzo Gualterio beside the *Palazzo Ruspoli sul Corso*, published in *Delle Magnificenze di Roma Antica e Moderna*, vol. 4 (Rome, 1754), no.68. The property was rented by Gualterio from the family of Cardinal Ottoboni. The façade of the building on the Corso had been heavily damaged when it was aligned with the Palazzo Ruspoli to allow the street to be straightened. It had two asymmetrical ends, a glass-covered balcony overlooking the street, and a belvedere tower on the roof

away in the country. Apartments and rooms were also provided for the Duke and Duchess of Mar, Lord and Lady Inverness, James Murray and some of the servants, but many of them, including even David Nairne[51] and John Paterson,[52] had to move into lodgings elsewhere. This placed a great strain on the king's finances, so that major economies became necessary until all the servants could be accommodated in a single building provided by the Pope.[53]

These economies mainly affected the people who were not living with the king in the Palazzo Gualterio. Nairne, for example, had to dismiss his servant because he could no longer afford to employ him. But he noted that the man then found employment with Murray who, like the other new favourites, seemed to be as well off as before.[54] He wrote on 10 January:

> since I arrived in Rome my allowance for food, heating and lighting has been reduced so that I have only about 20 *livres* a month ..., and I don't know if the cuts will stop there. What I do know is that the new favourites controlling the family will do as they wish.[55]

Despite this the court reestablished itself socially as best it could under difficult circumstances. Lord Southesk requested that Protestant services should be resumed[56] – a request that was apparently granted because both Barclay and Cowper, the Anglican chaplains, remained at the court. The Duke of Mar also began arranging regular concerts. In the middle of December he wrote to Lord Panmure's brother, who played the viol:

> My friend [the Duchess] makes you her compliments, and wishes you were here just now to assist at a kind of concerto she and some others are busy at here by me, viz, Sir John P[resto]n on the treble and C[le]p[ha]n bassing them with all his might. There's another virtuoso too ... who plays on the violin and Lord P[itslig]o and two or three others standing by.[57]

And meanwhile the Jacobites began to explore the city. As one of them put it, "go where we please we meet something wonderful and, I believe, I'll wear [out] a pair of shoes here in a fortnight".[58]

There was already a Jacobite community in Rome, based on the English, Scottish and Irish colleges, and this also provided the court with entertainment. Nairne noted that the king attended performances at the English College, where the music was particularly good.[59] Then, on 7 January, the three opera houses opened for the new carnival season.[60] The king went to see several performances of *Astianatte* by Francesco Gasparini at the Teatro Aliberti, of *Marco Attilio Regolo* by Alessandro Scarlatti at the Teatro Capranica and of *Erminia* by Giovanni Bononcini at the Teatro della Pace,[61] sometimes accompanied by Don Carlo Albani. Nairne, who was invited by Gualterio's brother, the Earl of Dundee, and by Prince Vaini, noted that the king "prefers the one at the Aliberti, as does most of Rome".[62] The Duchess of Mar, on the other hand, seems to have preferred the Pace. Her husband commissioned Francesco Trevisani to paint a double portrait of her and their daughter Lady Frances, seated beside a harpsichord on which can be seen an aria from *Erminia*.[63]

Illustration 16 Francesco Trevisani, *Frances, Duchess of Mar and her daughter Lady Frances Erskine* (1719)

Some time during December 1718 and January 1719 Trevisani also painted a new half-length portrait showing James III in his Garter robes, with the closed crown of a king. It was hoped that the Emperor would

Illustration 17   Francesco Trevisani, *James III* (1719)

soon be obliged to let Maria Clementina Sobieska and her mother leave Innsbruck and come to Rome, and the portrait was intended to be given to her as a present on her arrival.[64] This decision was itself of considerable significance, carrying as it did the implication that James might not be there to greet her. Although he was hoping that his court would soon be able to leave the Palazzo Gualterio and move into another palazzo in Rome, James had no intention of settling there himself. In fact he had reason to hope that he would be restored to his kingdoms during 1719, and was thus expecting to be in England when Maria Clementina finally arrived in Rome.

11
The Palazzo Del Re

When David Nairne first opened negotiations with the Pope and the *Camera Apostolica* to find a suitable palazzo in Rome to house the Stuart court, he had to bear in mind three important points. It had to be large enough to provide accommodation for the entire household, it had to be close enough to the Quirinale to provide easy access to the Pope; and, if at all possible, it had to have a garden. The Duke of Mar was pessimistic and told James that "I much doubt if you will easily find a house at Rome, which could lodge all your people that were in the house of Urbino."[1]

The Palazzo Riario was briefly considered because it had been occupied by Queen Christina of Sweden, but it was quickly ruled out because it was in Trastevere and therefore too far away from the Quirinale. An ideal location seemed to be the Piazza dei SS. Apostoli, which contained the Palazzo Colonna. On 2 November Nairne discovered that the Palazzo Cibo, immediately opposite the Palazzo Colonna and beside the Palazzo Chigi, would probably be available, so he wrote to the king to ask for instructions:

> It stands in the Piazza Santi Apostoli in a very fine situation and looks noble without, but it has no garden and I cannot tell what conveniency it has within, but Prince Ruspoli and his lady and all his family lodged there, and 'tis furnished with Monsignor [Cibo]'s furniture, but that could only serve, as Cardinal Davia's did at Pesaro, till the Pope give other furniture.

Nairne pointed out that the Pope would be prepared to rent and furnish the palazzo for him: "If the King likes it, said he, I am willing."[2]

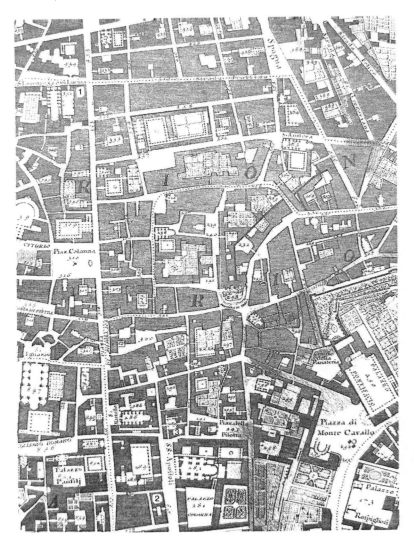

Illustration 18   Giovan Battista Nolli, *Pianta di Roma*, a detail showing the location of the Palazzo Gualterio on the Corso [1], and of both the Palazzo Cibo [2] and the Palazzo del Re [3] in the Piazza dei SS. Apostoli (1748)

Nairne therefore went to inspect the Palazzo Cibo. He wrote again on 5 November that "the fine appartement is very nobly furnished" and that "there is a good deal of lodging in it". There were apparently "few or no chimneys, but these Bonbled says can soon be made".[3]

Nothing more was done until James III arrived in Rome late at night on the 15th, but he then agreed that the Palazzo Cibo would be suitable.[4] All that was necessary to finalise arrangements was to persuade Cibo to allow the *Camera Apostolica* to rent the palazzo, which he agreed to do. The Stuart court thus expected to leave the Palazzo Gualterio and move into its new home before the end of the year.[5]

Then Cibo suddenly changed his mind and said that he was not prepared to make his palazzo available after all.[6] Two weeks had been wasted, and the court had to remain where it was into the New Year. But this disappointment turned out to be useful in the long run, because a much more suitable palazzo now became available. It belonged to the Marchese Giovanni Battista Muti and was situated very nearby, at the north end of the Piazza dei SS. Apostoli. It contained much more accommodation and, of particular importance, had a garden. Nairne was able to give Gualterio the good news on 7 December.[7]

The next few weeks were a period of waiting. As Mar put it on the 13th, "we are still in a very uneasy way here and shall be so, till we get into a house of our own, which we shall not, I fear, till some time next month, they going here bel bello in everything".[8] He was right. It was not until the 18th that Marchese Muti gave his formal agreement,[9] and not until the 22nd that the contract was drawn up and signed by Muti and the *Camera Apostolica*.[10] Only then could the necessary work begin to get the building ready for the court.

Nairne kept Gualterio informed of the progress, because the cardinal could not return to his own palazzo until it had been vacated by the Jacobites. On 31 December Nairne wrote that "they are working on the King's new residence but the works are progressing as things do in this country – *piano*" [slowly].[11] He hoped the work would be finished by the middle of January,[12] because the first instalment of rent was due to be paid by the *Camera Apostolica* on the 15th.[13] The trouble was that much of the work could not be carried out until the building was empty, and Muti had no intention of leaving before he had to.[14] So everything was delayed and the work progressed slowly.

Once it had been decided that the Stuart court should move into the Palazzo Muti, the building was renamed the Palazzo del Re.[15] Mar wrote that "the house is a very convenient though not a very magnificent one, and, I believe, will lodge as many as the palace where we were last winter".[16] This was also Nairne's opinion. The palazzo, "although not very impressive, will be very convenient".[17] These contemporary views are important because there has been considerable misunderstanding about the Palazzo del Re. It did not have a magnificent façade, as did many other palazzi which nevertheless had relatively little accommodation behind. But it was ideally situated, it had plenty of room for all the household servants and it had a private garden. It was also occupied exclusively by the court, and it did not contain a series of shops around most of the ground floor, as the larger palazzi tended to have. The fact that it contained plenty of accommodation was observed by Lady Nithsdale on 3 January 1719, in a letter in which she regretted that the Scottish and other pensioners were not to be given accommodation in the palazzo:

> I am kept at as great a distance from my Master as can well be, as much industry used to let me have none of his ear as they can; and tho' he is going to a house that his family can scarce fill, I could not obtain to be admitted under his roof.[18]

The papal archives contain very full details of all the work done, and of the furniture and decoration provided, to make the Palazzo del Re ready for James III and his court. The general building work, including repairs and painting, and the creation of a new gallery for the king, was supervised by the architect Alessandro Specchi[19] and finished on 11 February. Most of the furniture was then delivered during March, April and May, by which time the *Camera Apostolica* had spent 13,678 *scudi*.[20]

The household servants moved into the Palazzo as soon as they could, even while the painting and decoration were still going on, but it was not until these were virtually complete that the king's plate was brought from the Palazzo Gualterio.[21] The last people to arrive were the Duchess of Mar and Lady Inverness, on 11 February. Nairne then wrote to tell Gualterio that as all of the king's family had moved into the Palazzo del Re he could at last return from the country and occupy his own palazzo.[22]

The Palazzo del Re occupied a plot of land surrounded by the Piazza dei SS. Apostoli on the south side, the via di S. Marcello on the west, the via dell'Archetto on the east, and the little vicolo dell'Archetto on the north. A bridge across the *vicolo* gave access to both the garden and other buildings which were also rented for the court. The palazzo did not contain any basements, so the Household Below Stairs and the Stables, which had been situated together below the Palazzo Ducale at Urbino, had to be accommodated elsewhere. The Stables moved into two adjacent houses, which were specifically rented by the *Camera Apostolica* for that purpose. The Kitchen, the Confectionary, the Bakehouse and the Wine Cellar all occupied the ground floor of the palazzo itself. Because the pre-existing kitchen was much too small both to feed the king and to provide food for the two tables he decided to keep, a new and much larger one had to be built by reducing the size of the central courtyard on the east side.[23]

The apartments of the king and queen were situated in the south-west corner of the palazzo, overlooking the via di S. Marcello and the Piazza dei SS. Apostoli. The queen's was on the second floor and was for the present left unfurnished because Maria Clementina was still under house arrest at Innsbruck. The king's was on the first floor immediately below and was richly decorated and furnished. But James had no intention of occupying it. When the Stuart court moved into the Palazzo del Re James III was no longer even in Rome.

12
Changes at the Court During the Nineteen

In December 1718, while James III was living in the Palazzo Gualterio, the news reached Rome that Great Britain had declared war on Spain. The Duke of Ormonde and the Earl Marischal had both gone to Madrid, and the Spanish government was preparing to send a large force to invade England and thereby restore the Stuart king. The invasion would be commanded by the Duke of Ormonde, but a diversionary force would also be sent to Scotland under the Earl Marischal.[1] In a letter dated 22 December, Ormonde informed James that "it is the King of Spain's desire that you should come away immediately and as privately as possible and not to bring above two or three persons at most". Cardinal Alberoni, the chief minister to Philip V, would make available a Spanish ship and had suggested with Ormonde's agreement that "you ought to disguise yourself, even in a livery if it be necessary". Cardinal Acquaviva, the Spanish ambassador, should not be informed: "Alberoni insists on the strictest secrecy, all depending on it."[2] During January 1719, therefore, while he was attending the operas and ostensibly waiting to move into the Palazzo del Re, the king was making secret plans to leave Rome and travel by sea to Spain.

The only people at the court who knew what the king intended were Mar, Inverness, Murray, Nairne, Paterson and perhaps also Perth. The plans were laid for the king to board a small Spanish ship, commanded by a Jacobite officer, at Nettuno on 8 February. He would take with him only four people: Inverness, Thomas Saint-Paul (*valet de chambre* and barber), Peter Jolly de Falvie (Harbourer of the Deer) and Richard Bains (cook). All the other household servants would be left behind in the Palazzo del Re, to be summoned to rejoin the king in England once the invasion had succeeded.[3]

In case anyone might suspect that the king was planning to leave Rome, it was agreed that the Duke of Mar should leave the day before,

7 February, and travel north to Genoa, and then make his way through France to join the invasion force when it landed in England. He was to travel with the Duke of Perth, and with John Paterson disguised as the king. By travelling north immediately before James travelled south to Nettuno, it was hoped that their departure would serve to conceal the true plan.[4]

The sudden disappearance of the king, Inverness, Mar and Perth was bound to have serious implications for the management of the court, which was moving into the Palazzo del Re at precisely this time. The king had to decide who was to be left in charge during his absence.

The Secretariat, as we have seen, was divided into two parts. The Catholic correspondence, including dealings with the Pope, had been entrusted to David Nairne; and all the rest of the correspondence had been controlled by the Duke of Mar as Secretary of State. Both Nairne and Mar reported directly to the king. The royal household had been managed by Inverness, who also reported directly to the king. The departure of Mar and Inverness, and of the king himself, would therefore upset the entire command structure of the court. Who was to be left in charge? The king made an unfortunate decision. Nairne would continue to handle the Catholic correspondence, but would work closely with Gualterio and do nothing without his agreement. Mar would be replaced as acting Secretary of State by James Murray, assisted by his under-secretary Robert Creagh. And Inverness would be replaced by Sir William Ellis, the Treasurer. But the king's position as head of the court would be assumed by Murray, who would thus be placed above Ellis and, in effect, above Nairne. And if Murray was in this way to be given responsibility for managing the entire court, he was by extension to be in charge of the Scottish and other pensioners as well. Trouble was certain to ensue, because virtually everyone disliked Murray.[5]

The king had received repeated warnings that Murray should not be given too much responsibility, because he was rude and arrogant and, as one person put it, gave himself grander airs than even Alexander the Great and Cardinal Richelieu![6] But Mar had consistently defended him[7] and allowed him to establish considerable influence with the king. What Mar had apparently not realised is that Murray was keen to make himself the king's sole adviser, which would mean pushing aside not only Nairne but even Mar himself. When the latter had left Bologna to meet his wife and daughter, Murray had assumed responsibility for all his correspondence, albeit only temporarily, and moved one step closer to achieving his ambition.

Illustration 19　Francesco Trevisani, *James Murray* (1719 or 1720)

It is probable that Mar had finally begun to realise this during the weeks that the court was based at the Palazzo Gualterio. On 4 February he wrote a letter to the king in which he advised him to appoint a new Secretary of State, once he and Ormonde had landed in England, and asked that he himself should be allowed to remain one of the Gentlemen of the Bedchamber when "fixed waiting" was reintroduced at the restored Stuart court:

> as for the seals..., you may very freely without any apprehension of giving me a mortification dispose of them as soon as you land in England.... my ambition is to have the honour... of being near your

person. You have been pleased already to give me a post, wh entitles me to that.

Mar then specifically advised the king to appoint his new Secretaries of State from among those Jacobites who had remained in Great Britain.[8] This, intentionally or not, would effectively have blocked Murray's ambitions.

Mar was worried about leaving his wife in Rome, particularly as she had only just arrived and had not been told of his imminent departure. He therefore entrusted her to Lord Pitsligo, who was his first cousin, in a letter dated 7 February, the day that he set out.[9] The Duchess of Mar and Lady Inverness would be the only ladies in the Palazzo del Re, and Murray would obviously be taking care of his own sister.

The king meanwhile recorded as clearly as possible his instructions for the running of the court. On 2 February Murray was given a formal warrant empowering him to open and answer all the letters addressed to the king which arrived during the latter's absence, and also those addressed to Mar as Secretary of State.[10] The king then dictated another paper to Nairne entitled "Directions for Sir William Ellis", which gave specific instructions for the household servants who were lodged in the Palazzo del Re. It is to be noted that Lord and Lady Inverness were referred to as Mr and Mrs Hay:

> The family and pensions are to be payd as usuall. The Dutchess of Mar and Mrs Hay are to have a small quantity of plate and linning till their own things come up.
>
> My Lady Mar, My Lady Nidsdale and Mrs Hay are to have the use of the King's Coach or Coaches, providing they use them discreetly, and do not spoil the horses. Butler is orderd to drive them. The Ladys must send to Sir Will. Ellis to desire him to order the Coach for them, and he is to give it equally amongst them when they do not go out together. . . .
>
> Such servants as had board wages at St Germains beside their sallary when they did not eat in the house are to have it now.
>
> The servants in general are to obey Sir Will. Ellis, Mr Delatre and Sheridan [in the Stables] to be comprehended.
>
> Care must be taken to keep the house in order without taking in new servants, the gates shutt at a reasonable hour and opend to none of the underservants, and great order kept.

If any of the servants be found drunk Sir Will. Ellis is to diduct five livres of their pension [*sic*] for each time, and if they be guilty of any misdemeanour, has full power to turn them out.

Having laid down these rules, the king then came to the most significant part of the paper:

In general Sir William Ellis is to follow Mr Murray's directions whither in mony matters or others.

This was the key instruction which meant that Murray had not only replaced Mar as Secretary of State but had assumed the overall coordination previously exercised only by the king himself.

The rest of the paper dealt with "mony matters". Lady Inverness was to receive her husband's salary of 200 *livres* a month. Murray was also to receive 200 *livres* a month. The Duchess of Mar and Lady Nithsdale were now to be given their own independent pensions, of 400 *livres* and 200 *livres* a month respectively, though these were only to start in March. And finally three more women were to be allowed to live at the court. Sarah Maguirk, who had arrived from Saint-Germain to find that her husband had died at Urbino, was to be given a pension of 15 *livres* a month, and the wives of Fitzgerald and Vezzosi (the two *valets de chambre*) were to be allowed to join their husbands and "be lodged in the house".[11]

Before he left, James then wrote and dictated five letters, three dated 7 February and two dated 8 February. The first was to tell Cardinal Gualterio that he would be leaving very early the following morning:

I have left with Nairne a kind of letter of accreditation for him to the Pope.... I recommend to you this old and faithful servant who will keep you fully informed of what he does.[12]

The second letter was the one for Nairne, who was created a baronet, to give to Clement XI. It asked the Pope to regard Nairne as James's official representative in the absence of Cardinal Gualterio, "our Minister and Protector of our Kingdom of England". Nairne was described as "our old and faithful subject Sir David Nairne, Secretary of the Closet and of our Privy Council". The king also emphasised the fact that Nairne, unlike his new favourites, was a Catholic: "We beg Your Holiness to receive him and listen to him with favour, and to regard him as one of our oldest and most loyal Catholic subjects and servants in whom Your Holiness can have complete confidence."[13]

The king's next two letters were also addressed to the Pope. The first was a letter of apology, regretting that he had not been able to tell him of his intended departure. It asked the Pope to look after Maria Clementina if she should arrive in Rome during his absence. And then, in a postscript, it referred to the Palazzo del Re:

> I beg Your Holiness to allow my family to remain in the residence he had the goodness to give me in this city, until I am in a position to send further instructions and to inform Your Holiness of my future plans.[14]

The fourth letter contained another apology, and was post-dated 8 February, by which time James had actually left Rome.[15]

This last letter was dictated to be signed by Nairne, and then given to the Pope by him after he had presented his "lettre de créance". The long letter began by referring to the many things for which the king wished to thank the Pope and his three nephews, adding that the king looked forward to the day when he would be able to reward all three of them properly. It continued by asking the Pope to find a way of giving Gualterio some financial recompense for accommodating the court in his palazzo, perhaps by giving him an abbey. It then recommended to the Pope several Jacobites and all the people in the Papal States who had been particularly helpful since his arrival at Pesaro.[16]

There was one thing that none of these letters mentioned, and which was known by only a very small group. This was that Charles Wogan had been sent to plan Maria Clementina's escape from Innsbruck.[17] Nairne was told by the king to keep asking the Pope to put pressure on the Emperor to release the princess and let her come to Rome, but meanwhile Wogan was planning a spectacular escape in case these long drawn out negotiations failed. This was a secret which no one else in Rome, with the single exception of Gualterio, was allowed to know. Nairne told the cardinal about it in his letter of 21 January, and noted that it was too secret to be mentioned even in his own file copy.[18] In thanking him, Gualterio commented that "when matters remain between you and me only, His Majesty can be assured of secrecy".[19] But Murray, of course, was also privy to the secret. The warrant which the king gave him on 2 February authorised him to solemnise the marriage to Maria

Clementina if she were to be released by the Emperor, or rescued by Wogan, while he was in Spain or England.[20]

By 9 February it was known in Rome that the king, Mar and Perth had left the city. That afternoon Nairne went to see the Pope and present the letters which he had been given by the king. He told Gualterio, who was still in the country, that he had been very well received, and that the Pope had taken care not to ask him why James had left Rome so suddenly, or where he was going. In the same letter he warned Gualterio that all their official correspondence would now be read by Murray, and reminded him that all personal comments should be restricted to their secret letters.[21]

Gualterio returned to Rome in the middle of February, once he knew that the court had evacuated his palazzo,[22] and he and Nairne then collaborated successfully together. Nairne had some more audiences with the Pope to discuss Maria Clementina's release,[23] but he did nothing without Gualterio's support and agreement.[24] He always travelled to see the Pope at the Quirinale in Gualterio's coach,[25] and it is clear from their secret correspondence that the two men now consolidated their warm friendship.[26] Meanwhile the personal relationships between Murray, the household servants and the pensioners became increasingly acrimonious.

As early as 11 February, only three days after the king's departure, Murray sent Mar a letter in which he referred to what he described as "the discontented club". It included Lord Pitsligo, James Edgar, George Mackenzie, William Erskine and John Paterson, all of them, significantly, friends and supporters of Mar himself.[27] Trouble came to a head a few days later when Edgar sent a letter to Paterson, then travelling with Mar, complaining that Murray had been extremely rude to him. Edgar was afraid that Murray might misrepresent to the king what had happened and asked Paterson to obtain for him Mar's protection.[28] Unfortunately for Edgar, Murray opened this letter before it could be sent,[29] and was furious. He actually despatched it to the king, who was by then still travelling to Spain, with the comment that "from this, your Majesty will see what a situation I am in".[30] In a second letter to the king he likened Lord Pitsligo and Mar's friends to the old servants from Saint-Germain: "You'll be pleased to know that those lately arrived at your Court act upon the same principles and notions with which your friends at Paris were formerly infected, in conjunction with one or two they found here of the same sentiments." The news had just come through that Inverness' elder brother, like Murray's own elder brother, had taken the oaths of loyalty to King George, which inevitably raised doubts about the loyalty of the new favourites among the Scottish pensioners. This Murray interpreted to the king as "their constant pee-vish discourses, finding fault with everybody and everything".[31] A few days later, as Murray became more aggressive and authoritarian, Nairne wrote to Gualterio of his "intention to put myself always under Y[our] E[xcellency]'s care and protection".[32]

Meanwhile important events were happening elsewhere. James III landed at La Rosas in northern Catalonia on 7 March and travelled south to Barcelona.[33] He then made a formal state entry to Madrid on 27 March,[34] and was lodged by Philip V in the Buen Retiro palace. Meanwhile Mar, Perth and Paterson travelled north via Pesaro, Rimini, Bologna, Modena and Parma to Piacenza, whence they entered Savoy intending to go to Voghera and then south into the Republic of Genoa. But their presence was discovered by the imperial authorities who had them arrested at Voghera and imprisoned at Milan.[35]

This had unfortunate consequences for the court because Mar and Perth were released in March and escorted back to the Papal States. As a result they unexpectedly returned to the Palazzo del Re to find the court in turmoil because of Murray's overbearing behaviour. And who was now to be in charge of the correspondence and the court, Murray or Mar?

The two men had a major row shortly after Mar's return, and Murray quickly sent off a letter to the king on 17 March to defend himself.[36] Mar too sent off a very long letter to the king, who by then was travelling from Barcelona to Madrid, in which he gave an account of the quarrels between Murray and the other members of the court, and complained of Murray's behaviour.[37] The relations between the two men were so bad that Mar even had a minor reconciliation with Nairne. The latter wrote to Gualterio on 18 March that "I have only seen the Duke of Mar once since he arrived and he behaved towards me with great decency." But Mar was unlikely to remain in Rome for very long, and Nairne was clearly worried as to what Murray might do next. He repeated his request for Gualterio's protection, saying that he did not want to live "like an ordinary person or a dismissed or disgraced servant".[38]

On the same day Nairne wrote a long letter to inform the king about the meetings he had been having with the Pope, but he did not go into details, merely remarking that "I suppose Mr Murray has given the sub-stance of it, for I informed him exactly of all that past." He reminded the king of his excellent relations with Gualterio:

> for my part I...behave myself towards him with such deference and
> circumspection, and cordiality that he having allways been the best
> of friends to me and professing still to be the same I am confident

I shall make him very easy for I am sure I love him, and I know he loves the King from the bottom of his heart.[39]

Mar and Perth remained at the Palazzo del Re for about a month, until the middle of April, and the situation was permanently tense. Further evidence of the reconciliation between Mar and Nairne can be found in a letter which the latter wrote to the king on 1 April:

I must do him [Mar] the justice to say that since his return hither I have been truly edify'd with the effectual measurs he took on his side to keep peace and prevent any eclat that might have been prejudicial to the King's service in a certain tracasserie of which he assurd me his intention was not to have mentiond a word even to the King himself not to give him the least trouble or uneasiness at this time with little malentendus of this kind, if he had not been prevented [by Murray's writing to the King], and so obliged to relate also the fact on his side afterward.[40]

Throughout this period the members of the court remained confident that James III would shortly be joining the Spanish fleet, that his restoration was imminent and that they would soon be able to leave the Palazzo del Re. For the time being, therefore, Murray's arrogance and rudeness just had to be accepted. But the situation inevitably became worse when Mar and Perth left again, this time separately and without Paterson. Mar got as far as Geneva, where he was again discovered and arrested, and not released.[41] Perth managed to evade capture, and eventually reached Spain via France, but not until August.[42]

In fact, unknown to the court, disaster had struck the Spanish fleet. It had sailed from Cadiz, intending to collect the king at Corunna, but had run into a terrible storm off Cape Finisterre. After 12 days of battering, some ships had been sunk, and others had returned to port unfit to make the journey to England. When James arrived at Corunna on 17 April, he was given the appalling news. He withdrew to Lugo in Galicia for three long months,[43] hoping that something might yet be achieved by the diversionary force sent to Scotland. But when the news was received in July that the Earl Marischal had been defeated at Glenshiel James realised that he had no choice but to return to Italy.

The court in Rome did not discover the news from Corunna until the end of April, nor the news from Scotland until July. It was during this period that Charles Wogan brought off a spectacular coup and managed to rescue Maria Clementina from Innsbruck. Helped by three other Irish officers from Dillon's Regiment, Major Gaydon, Captain Misset and Ensign O'Toole, and also by Misset's wife Eleanor, the princess escaped on 27 April and reached Bologna during the first week of May.[44] Murray then travelled up to Bologna with Lady Inverness to greet her, accompanied by Lawrence Mayes, the Agent of the English Catholic Clergy in Rome. On 9 May, using the power given him by the king, Murray had a proxy marriage ceremony performed by Mayes.[45] The king later said that "the ceremony that was performed at Bollonia having been to serve politick ends" was "in reality... no mariage by procuration".[46] But at the time the marriage was regarded as genuine and binding. For a very brief moment, before the extent of the disaster at Cape Finisterre became apparent, it had looked as though luck had finally turned in favour of the exiled Stuart court.

Maria Clementina, now given the title of the Queen of England, arrived in Rome on 16 May and was given accommodation by the Pope in the Ursuline convent, partly because her apartment in the Palazzo del Re had not yet been furnished.[47] But her arrival turned out to be a mixed blessing, because Murray now became ever more overbearing. As Lord Pitsligo put it, "he carried higher every day, even before he executed the Proxie, but that affair made him quite forget himself".[48] In particular Murray refused to allow any of the servants or pensioners to meet their new queen. The Duchess of Mar and Lady Nithsdale were given very limited access. Otherwise the only people who were allowed to meet her, and obtain her favour, were himself and his sister, Wogan and Eleanor Misset.

By the middle of June, Lord Pitsligo decided he had had enough, and wrote a letter of complaint to the king (then at Lugo):

> I think it absolutely for your Mat.'s honour and interest to acquaint you that the person in whose hands you left your affairs has managed them in the manner least agreeable in the world to your people here and I am afraid to the inhabitants who know anything of them .... it was observed very soon after your Mat. left Rome, that Mr Murray put on more airs than before.

Pitsligo told the king that Murray had prevented the Scottish lords and gentlemen from being properly introduced to the queen, and had refused to allow them to wait on her, monopolising her himself. Even

Illustration 20   After Francesco Trevisani, *Queen Maria Clementina* (1719)

the Duchess of Mar and Lady Nithsdale were kept away as much as possible. Pitsligo added one more damning complaint: that Murray was repeatedly rude to the Duchess in public.[49] Mindful of what had happened to Edgar's letter in February, Pitsligo entrusted his letter to Nairne, who promised to send it with Cardinal Acquaviva's packet to Spain.[50]

By this time Nairne was only too keen to oblige, as his own relations with Murray had steadily deteriorated. This is very clear in the long letters he sent to the king during April, May and June. On 22 April he was openly sarcastic:

Mr Murray is so capable so active and so diligent that while he is here there is little left for me either to do or say, so I look upon the most part of the exercise of my employment in this place to be suspended as long as another dos so willingly and heartily alone all that is needful.

The letter then went on to describe his negotiations with the Pope, in collaboration with Cardinal Gualterio.[51] And his next letter quotes Gualterio as saying that "he had and always would have an intire confidence in communicating everything to me".[52]

But it was true that Murray was gradually pushing Nairne aside, and telling Gualterio and others in Rome that Nairne was no longer trusted by the king. By keeping him away from the queen, and by bullying him into a position of subordination, Murray was establishing dictatorial powers over all aspects of the court, and the letters which arrived from James supported him in everything he did.[53] Under these circumstances the bad news from Spain, which implied that the court would have to remain in the Palazzo del Re for longer than originally hoped, was particularly depressing. Nairne wrote to Gualterio on 12 June that "it is true that I am no longer of use in the King's service". He described himself as "old, useless and a bad courtier".[54] Three days before he was given Pitsligo's letter, he hinted to the king that the atmosphere at the court was now very strained:

I live as retirdly as I possibly can, I wait on the Card.l from time to time to ask if he has any orders for me, and what letters I receive of news or other things I communicat regularly to his Em.ce and to Mr Murray which last shows them to the Queen when there is anything worth her knowledge .... As for visits to our people in town I make none, and if there be any disgusts among them, I thank God I have no hand in them, and am far from encouraging them either, directly or indirectly.[55]

Despite this Nairne did use his position to help Lord Pitsligo by forwarding his letter. He wrote to the king that he was enclosing a

letter from My Lord Pitsligo who brought it me last night and told me only it was about some privat affairs of his own, so that he would be glad it should come streight into your own hands. I inquird no further only assurd him I should forward it with care."[56]

Given the bad relations at the court, of which Nairne was well aware, it is hard to believe that he did not know what Pitsligo's letter was likely to contain.

James III later claimed that he never received Pitsligo's letter, though Nairne's covering letter is in the Stuart Papers. Whatever the truth of the matter, Pitsligo and his friends waited in vain for a reaction from the king. And so the weeks slipped by and the atmosphere in the Palazzo del Re became even worse.

During June and July 1719 the *Camera Apostolica* began to prepare the queen's apartment in the Palazzo del Re, so that Maria Clementina could move there from the Ursuline convent.[57] In the meantime she did not understand why her husband's servants and pensioners were not coming to see her. She was visited by all the cardinals and by the leading ladies of Rome, such as the Principessa di Piombino, and on 17 July a cantata specially composed by Giovanni Giorgi was performed in honour of her 17th birthday.[58] But the Jacobites were all kept away. When the king heard about this he wrote to Wogan, to quote Pitsligo, "in pretty harsh terms against his subjects in Rome who had been misrepresented to him as guilty of very wrong things", notably of being rude and unfriendly to the queen by refusing to be introduced to her.[59]

Murray now realised that some compromise would have to be made, and in August decided that, exceptionally, Nairne should be allowed to meet Maria Clementina for the first time. In an extremely frank letter to the king, dated 12 August, Nairne recorded what happened:

> I was agreeably surprisd when I had in the afternoon a message sent me from the Queen by Mr Wogan (upon what new motive or reflexion I know not) to be at the Convent at night where her Ma.ty would speak with me after she had given audience to the Card.l [Gualterio]. Accordingly I waited on her Ma.ty and ... she was pleased to tell me that she was very glad to see me, and that I might come hereafter when ever I pleasd, and yt she would allways see me willingly.

But Nairne implied that the other courtiers should be allowed to meet her:

> The next time I met Mr Murray I ... thankd him for the honour he had procurd me of an audience of her Ma.ty unasked, which I supposd to have been an effect of his advice or insinuation; he told me I might have seen her sooner if I had askd it and spoken to him but

I told him... that I pretended to no distinction but just to make my Court as all the rest of yr Ma.ties subjects do.... He told me... I was too nice and ceremonious, that as I was imployd in yr Ma.ties affaires my case was different from others.... I confess I thought so my self in the beginning, but afterward finding such a combination of reservedness and discouragement I was easily rebufed, and so at last took the party which I thought would be lik'd best, for peaces sake. Nor would I for the same reason so much as take notice to Mr Mur[ray] that I had some reason to think I was at least neglected if not distrusted.

No reply had yet been received from the king to Lord Pitsligo's letter, so Nairne emphasised that "I have kept myself free hitherto" from "any indiscreet factions divisions or discontents amongst friends". Yet he told the king frankly that Murray had completely undermined his position with Gualterio.[60]

The situation had become so bad by the summer of 1719 that even the tensions at Urbino now seemed minor by comparison. In August Nairne received through the post a pamphlet which had been published in London: "I know not by whom or by whose order" it was sent. It was entitled *A Letter from a Gentleman in R[ome] dated 15 September 1718. To a friend at London*. It "accused Mar of monopolising the king, surrounding him with a small group of Scottish favourites, [and] insulting and abusing the best of his own countrymen (including the Earl Marischal)"[61] – all of which had been completely true at Urbino, but was now out of date. Nairne reported this to the king with the comment that, "tho I be perswaded that Martel is wrongd", people would believe what they read: "what is plain from this is that Martel must have enemys and very malicious ones".[62]

By the middle of August it was clear that the king would have to leave Spain and return to Italy – in fact he embarked with Inverness from Vinaros (between Tarragona and Valencia) on the 14th. This filled the courtiers with hope that their grievances would at last be redressed and that Murray would be brought down. At the same time the young queen insisted on seeing all the Jacobites, and forced a reluctant Murray to give way. On 11 August she received the senior servants and pensioners at the convent.[63] A few days later she visited the Palazzo del Re for the first time, and saw the king's apartment, "and that above which was design'd for herself".[64]

The courtiers were naturally delighted to meet and be visited by their new queen. They were also very proud of her when she made her first public appearances. She was invited by Cardinal Acquaviva to join him on the balcony which was specially erected every summer outside the Spanish church in the Piazza Navona. Nairne described the scene:

> [Acquaviva] has now for two Sundays consecutively invited her to see the great concours of Coaches in Piazza Navona which is all coverd with water all the Sundays of this month, and in some parts comes up to the horses bellys. The Queen was seated in a balcony under a canapy very richly furnishd with red damask and gold fringes, where her Ma.ty made a very glorious appearance, and drew the chief attention of all the spectators.... She had...with her three Ladys, and the gentlemen who have the honour to be her only constant attendants.... I had the pleasure to go in a coach of purpose to see the shew from the piazza, and was truly delighted with it.[65]

Murray was evidently less delighted. The three ladies and the gentlemen, having been sent by Prince James Sobieski, had accompanied Maria Clementina to Innsbruck,[66] and then joined her in Rome. Murray was determined to get rid of them, and wrote to the king on 26 August that

> if we are to remain here for any considerable time I take the liberty to represent to you that the method we are now in of keeping table for the Gentlemen who came with [the Queen] is not only the most expensive but is a very great constraint upon Mrs Hay [*sic*] and me.[67]

Things had reached such a point that Murray not only believed that his own convenience should count for more than the wishes of the queen, but also was prepared to admit it openly in a letter to the king.

On the following day James landed at Leghorn and began his journey to Rome.

13
The King's Marriage at Montefiascone

When news of the king's return reached Rome, arrangements were immediately made for his marriage. Murray and Gualterio decided that James should be met by Maria Clementina on his way south from Leghorn, before he reached the capital. As the Via Aurelia (the coast road) would involve travelling through Austrian territory, James had to take the Via Cassia, which passed through Tuscany and then south via Viterbo. Just to the north of Viterbo on the Via Cassia lies the hill-top town of Montefiascone, overlooking Lake Bolsena. The meeting place of the king and the queen was chosen because Sebastiano Bonaventura, whom James had known and liked at Urbino, was the bishop there. It was also only a few miles from Don Carlo Albani's estate at Soriano. At the end of August the Pope sent Bonaventura a post-dated warrant (it is merely dated September 1719) authorising him to marry James and Clementina.[1]

Murray, meanwhile, was to make the arrangements to escort the queen to Montefiascone and, of particular importance, to decide who should be invited to go with her. The Jacobites naturally wanted to see the king as soon as possible, but they could not go to Montefiascone without Murray's permission, and Murray decided to keep numbers to an absolute minimum. Apart from himself, some grooms and the coachman (Edmund Butler), only four men and three women were allowed to travel north with the queen. They were Sir David Nairne, Charles Wogan, Colonel Sir John O'Brien (Wogan's superior officer in Dillon's Regiment, and now returned from France), Father John Brown (the king's confessor), his own sister Lady Inverness, and two chambermaids (Sir John Misset's wife Eleanor and Gerald Fitzgerald's wife Mary). The Duchess of Mar, Lady Nithsdale, the Scottish lords (Linlithgow,

Nithsdale, Winton, Kilsyth and Pitsligo) and even Thomas Forster were excluded.

The king and the queen met at Montefiascone on 1 September, and were married by Bonaventura at midnight in the private chapel of his palazzo opposite the cathedral.[2] The marriage contract was formally witnessed by Lord Inverness, James Murray, Charles Wogan, Sir John O'Brien, the local vicar-general (Sebastiano Antonini) and Father John Brown.[3] Sir David Nairne was presumably also present. In the painting (attributed to Agostino Masucci) which records the scene, the 31-year-old king and the 17-year-old queen are shown with the three closed crowns of England, Scotland and Ireland, kneeling in front of Bishop Bonaventura and his five chaplains. Immediately behind the royal couple Lady Inverness can be seen standing in attendance on the queen. Behind her there are three gentlemen kneeling (Murray, Wogan and O'Brien), and behind them three gentlemen and three ladies standing (the attendants sent by Prince James Sobieski). Father John Brown can be seen in his Dominican robes standing beside the chaplains, while on the right-hand side of the picture Don Carlo Albani stands with the vicar-general and Lord Inverness.[4] There is no Englishman shown in the painting, and indeed there was no Englishman present at the ceremony.

The king and the queen then remained at Montefiascone for two months, during which time they were visited by Cardinal Albani and the Principessa di Piombino, and were entertained by the celebrated castrato Pascolino Tiepoli.[5] They did not leave until 28 October. One reason for the delay was uncertainty about where they would live. The court had left Urbino the previous autumn in order to pass the cold winter months elsewhere. Yet the king had never slept even one night in the apartment prepared for him in the Palazzo del Re, and it was possible that the Pope might now suggest an alternative winter residence. While James enjoyed his honeymoon at Montefiascone, he had to face the very real prospect that he might have to travel north to Urbino, and not south to Rome. He himself had told Don Carlo Albani the previous September that he wished "to have the liberty of returning to Urbino next summer, if the Pope pleases and he shall then so incline".[6] With his position now weakened by the turn of events in Spain, there was a strong possibility that the court might have to go back to Urbino whether James liked it or not.

The people of Urbino were naturally keen that the court should return, and Murray had advised James not to live in Rome. In a letter of 28 August he argued that the Pope would not furnish the queen's apartment properly, that Rome would be too expensive and that therefore he should live elsewhere.[7] Nairne strongly disagreed, and advised the

Illustration 21   Agostino Masucci, *The Marriage of James III and Maria Clementina Sobieska at Montefiascone, 1 September 1719 (1735)*

king not to go back to Urbino if he could possibly avoid it: "it would be a very melancholy winter sejour for your Ma.ty and yet more for a young Queen.... I hope at least you'l have a year full liberty to live here [Rome]... without being confind to the top of a desert mountain".[8]

The king agreed in this instance with Nairne and not Murray. In a letter drafted by Nairne, and sent from Montefiascone the day after his marriage, James told Cardinal Gualterio:

> I spoke to Murray about my return to Rome and I confess that I find all the reasons in favour of return stronger than I do any against. Therefore I pray you to hasten the furnishing of the house, and to press the Pope ceaselessly on this matter. It is surely not possible that His Holiness will refuse to give us what is necessary at such a time.[9]

The fate of the Stuart court then hung in the balance. When he had still not received an answer, James wrote again on 8 September: "in the end, nothing short of an outright prohibition from His Holiness will prevent us coming to Rome, and I cannot believe that he would do us such a great wrong in the eyes of the world as to treat us so harshly".[10]

In the event the Pope decided to allow James and Maria Clementina to occupy the Palazzo del Re,[11] and instructed the *Camera Apostolica* to clean, decorate and furnish the queen's apartment as quickly as possible. The work was resumed in September, and all of the queen's furniture was transferred to the palazzo from the Ursuline convent. More furniture was brought from the palazzo of the Congregation of Propaganda Fide. The papal archives show that everything was ready by 28 October,[12] which is why the king and the queen left Montefiascone on that day.

While James III was at Montefiascone he had to resolve, one way or another, the problems created during his absence by Murray's high-handed behaviour. The Jacobites in Rome understood that there was limited accommodation at Montefiascone, but they wanted to be allowed to go there and pay their respects to the king and the queen. Murray, now supported by Inverness, was keen to keep them away. The Duchess of Mar and Lady Nithsdale were particularly affronted that they were not allowed to attend the queen, and on 13 September Lord Nithsdale wrote that "we have had thes som moneths past severall mortifications.... All this affaier has been occasioned by a hote-heeded young man.... You may gues how I mean."[13] On the same day the Duchess wrote to tell the king that she would like to leave the court and join her husband in his imprisonment at Geneva.[14]

There then took place an episode which demonstrates how far the king was prepared to allow Murray to go. Colonel Clephane and Lord Nithsdale had both written to the king to ask permission to visit him. The replies which they received were signed by Nairne, and sent as though he had written them himself. In fact they were written by Murray, who now humiliated Nairne by forcing him to pretend they were his own. The letter to Clephane was brief, and set the scene for the snub which was to follow: "his Majesty desires to see you here, and therefore you may sett out in order to receive his Majesty's commands, as soon as you can conveniently".[15] Lord Nithsdale, who as a Catholic peer would have outranked both Murray and Inverness, was then told in no uncertain terms that he was not welcome:

> as to any of the King's subjects coming here, I know it was his Majesty's intention from the beginning, that during his retreat in this place nobody should come from Rome, but such as he sends for, which is all the light I am able to give your L[ordshi]p in this matter.[16]

The courtiers in Rome could not believe that things were now so bad. Lady Nithsdale's reaction sums up the situation:

> My companion [the Duchess of Mar] is going to her husband, and I feare neither he nor she intends to return, so that I am the only one now left of my station: and shall in all appearance be yet more trampl'd on than we were both in our Master's absence. At his return we hoped for some redress, but now we have reason to believe we are to expect none, for everything is approved that was done in his absence.[17]

Yet there was worse to come. George Mackenzie, a friend of the Duke of Mar and Lord Pitsligo, wrote a letter of complaint to Sir David Nairne, which the latter then showed to the king. The result was a major humiliation for Nairne, who was forced to copy and sign the following reply drafted by Murray:

> I received by the last post yours of the 9th, and as it contained expressions of your duty to the King, I thought myself obliged to shew it to him. His Majesty received graciously your own particular good wishes, but as to the duty and affection of his subjects who are att

present in Rome (in whos name you take upon you to speak) he ordered me to tell you that he is too well assured of both, to want to have his opinion in that respect confirmed by your authority, and that therefore you might have spared yourself the trouble of answering for them upon this occasion. What you mean by impressions of misrepresentation and aspersion I'm att a loss to imagine. All who have the honour to know his Majesty must be perswaded that if there were any persons so vile as to endeavour to misrepresent any of his people to him such an attempt would be as certain a way to incur his displeasure as to behave with disrespect to himself or those immediately imployed by him, and it is indeed in some degree injurious to his Majesty to think otherwise; wherefore Sir I must believe that these termes have slipt inadvertently from your pen. However, I earnestly intreat of you for the future not to make choice of me for a canal to communicate letters of this strain to the King, for fear His Majesty may thereby receive impressions of us both to neither of our advantage.[18]

This letter was greeted with incredulity and outrage by the Jacobites in Rome, and provoked Lord Pitsligo to ask Nairne if he had ever sent on to the king the private letter which he had written in June. Nairne showed this letter also to the king, who denied that he had ever received the earlier one, but said that Pitsligo "might when you think fitt aquaint him with the contents of it".[19] As Pitsligo had kept a copy, he then transcribed it and sent it to Montefiascone.[20]

The king's reaction was not at all what Pitsligo expected, because James once again completely supported Murray and wrote an extremely angry reply. In it Pitsligo was ordered to make sure he had left Rome before the king returned.[21] But this exchange also undermined Nairne's position with the king, because it was he who had passed on the letter. Murray persuaded James that Nairne should effectively be demoted, and that he (Murray) should now handle all the king's correspondence, Catholic as well as Protestant.

At the beginning of October, Cardinal Gualterio came to visit the king and the queen for a few days at Montefiascone.[22] Just before he left he was informed that, once the king had returned to Rome, his dealings with the court would be with Murray instead of Nairne. The latter had not yet been informed, but Murray had the pleasure of employing him as the messenger. He wrote to Gualterio on 10 October: "I have reason to believe that in his letter to Y[our] E[xcellency], the King has gone into some detail and I therefore take the liberty to beg Y[our] E[xcellency] most humbly not to communicate the contents to Mr Nairne even though he has brought the message to you."[23] Unaware of what had been decided, Nairne wrote to tell Gualterio how sorry he was that he had left, adding that "as for myself I am able to let some rather disagreeable things pass so as not to upset anyone, but it does not mean that I do not feel them keenly".[24]

Murray's triumph was complete. When even Mar wrote to complain that his wife had not been invited to Montefiascone, and that Murray had been rude to her, the king wrote back to defend everything that his favourite had done.[25] When Mar supported Pitsligo, the king replied by criticising Pitsligo and defending Murray, "who was used as I believe no man ever was who was vested with my authority".[26] Their correspondence continued through October, November and December, but nothing that Mar wrote could persuade the king that Murray had done anything inappropriate.[27]

As for Pitsligo, he wrote to Nairne to defend himself, but promised to leave Rome before the king and the queen arrived. In a passage which he actually omitted from his letter, he wrote again of Murray's extreme rudeness: "I have seen the Dss. of Mar in tears, another time ready to faint in the streets. And any that knows her will think there must have been some remarkable mortification."[28] Both Pitsligo and the Duchess left Rome during October, the latter taking Paterson with her.[29] So also did several of the Scottish pensioners, including George Mackenzie, William Erskine, John Stewart of Invernity, Sir John Preston, Lord Kingston and Lord Southesk. Lady Nithsdale wrote of the king that "his company he used to have about him is much diminish'd: many are gone, and more is going daily". Her husband wanted to leave, but she persuaded him to stay because they had no money other than the pensions they received from the king.[30]

The same also applied to Sir David Nairne, who told Gualterio while he was still at Montefiascone that he knew that he was no longer in the "bonnes graces" of the king: "I shall be very pleased and content to leave both the Court and this Life whenever providence should wish .... I now have very little credit, and perhaps have shown too clearly that I cannot approve of everything I see, and therefore have become slightly suspect."[31] Gualterio wrote back to reassure him that "you are entirely in His Majesty's good graces and have his confidence",[32] but of course he knew it was no longer true and that Nairne would be replaced by Murray the moment the king arrived at the Palazzo del Re. He also knew that Nairne's salary had been reduced by a half, from 240 to 120 *livres* each month.[33]

The king, however, was satisfied that he had done the right thing in supporting Murray. He sent copies of the Pitsligo correspondence to Dillon in Paris, and described the letters as "some papers relating to what has given me a great deal of trouble of late". But he added that "the comfort of doing ones duty, is what no malice can deprive one of".[34]

By this time the news had reached Montefiascone that the queen's apartment had been prepared and furnished, and that everything was now ready for her. Murray, who had been reluctant to go back to Rome, wrote to Gualterio on 27 October that they would leave the following morning, and arrive in Rome on Sunday evening, 1 November, "even though in the end the Queen will find her apartment still without furniture, after all that has happened".[35] Not only was the queen's apartment properly furnished by the *Camera Apostolica*, but it had been filled with all the plate previously used by Mary of Modena at Saint-Germain, as shown by various receipts, and a long inventory in the Stuart Papers entitled "Pieces of Plate and other things deliverd for ye Queen".[36] Nairne, who had been sent back to Rome early, informed Gualterio that "the Queen found her apartment quite well furnished, and the King's is very fine and one can say that Their Majesties are suitably and commodiously installed".[37]

Thus James III and Maria Clementina prepared to move permanently into the Palazzo del Re in Rome, and the Stuart court could look forward to a more settled future than it had experienced during the transitional period at Urbino. The former senior servants had returned to Saint-Germain, and Nairne had been humiliated and demoted.[38] The Duke of Mar, once so powerful and influential, was imprisoned at Geneva, and replaced in the affections of the king by Murray and his sister, Lady Inverness. John Hay, now Lord Inverness, had succeeded in maintaining his position, so that the court was now dominated by the Scottish Protestant triumvirate of Murray, his sister and his brother-in-law.

It is impossible to assess the sense of isolation felt by James III following the numerous disappointments he had experienced: the failure to land in Scotland in 1708, the sudden death of Queen Anne while he was in Lorraine in 1714, the death of Louis XIV and the defeat of the Jacobite rising in 1715–1716, and now – worst of all – the destruction of the Spanish fleet and the invasion force in 1719. Raised as a legitimate king at Saint-Germain and Versailles, with every reason to believe that he would soon be restored to his kingdoms, it must have been unbearable to have been left for three long months, with only a few attendants, in an obscure town in Galicia, and now to have to accept another prolonged period of exile, housed this time by a reluctant Pope in Rome. Yet it is hard to understand why James placed so much confidence in Murray and the Hays, against the unanimous advice he received from Jacobites who disagreed on so many other things. It would be tempting to say that he now placed his trust entirely in the Scottish Jacobites, but that would be completely wide of the mark. The favourites were all Scottish, yet so too were the Duke of Mar, Sir David Nairne, and the great majority of the pensioners who were thoroughly dissatisfied and bitterly hostile to the triumvirate. It is most likely that James now wanted the company of confident people of his own age, optimistic that a restoration would one day be achieved.

Yet there were clear signs that there might be trouble in the years to come. The king might have placed his trust entirely in the hands of his three Protestant favourites, but there was no reason why his young Catholic queen should do the same. In November 1719 she was only 17 years old, but she already felt very resentful towards Murray and his sister because of their high-handed behaviour since her arrival in Rome.[39] According to Sir Charles Wogan, the queen "was not only angry with Mr Murray but despised him".[40] In retrospect it seems obvious that there would be clashes in the years to come, when the queen would mature, have children and ask to have control of her own separate household.

The changes which took place at the exiled court during the transitional period at Urbino can thus be seen to have had long-term consequences for the Jacobite movement. Once in Rome, the courtiers remained divided between those who accepted and those who resented the favour shown to Murray and the Hays. The influential Jacobite community in France, soon to be joined by the Duke of Mar, remained suspicious and even hostile towards the king's principal advisers. Jacobites in England and Scotland were deterred from going abroad to join the exiled court. Back in 1693 the Earl of Middleton had left England to become the Secretary of State at Saint-Germain. In the early 1720s even those Jacobites who were already in exile declined to join the court in Rome because of the favour shown to the Scottish triumvirate. This, in turn, had the effect of making James III regard the latter as indispensable.

Although the story of the Stuart court in Rome lies beyond the scope of this book, it may be stated here, and without exaggeration, that the problems it encountered during the 1720s, and the difficulties which were later experienced in the upbringing of James III and Maria Clementina's two sons, were directly caused by the presence and behaviour of Murray, his sister and Hay. The favour shown to the Hays alienated the young queen. The decision to entrust the upbringing of her elder son, Prince Charles, to Murray resulted in her separating from the king for nearly two years, with catastrophic consequences for the Jacobite movement at home and abroad. And the hostility felt towards Murray by the young prince was to drive that fatal wedge between father and son which has been fully described by all Stuart biographers. If things had developed differently during the years of transition at Urbino – if Murray had remained in England or France, and James III had not shown such a lack of judgment in his choice of favourites and advisers – then the story of the exiled Stuarts, and perhaps even their chances of achieving a restoration, must have developed differently.

Yet the period of transition was not entirely negative for the exiled court. Its departmental structure and organisation were modified to take account of the altered circumstances. Religious toleration became an accepted part of its daily life. Finances were placed on a relatively sound footing. A more suitable building was acquired in a much more convenient location, with easy access to painters and engravers, and the opportunity was opened to participate in and influence the rich musical and operatic life of the papal city.

Most important of all, the court acquired a new queen, bringing the hope that Stuart dynastic prospects would no longer rest solely on the continued good health of the king himself. In 1717, James III had transferred his court from Avignon via Pesaro to Urbino, all of them far removed from any centre of power and influence. The Stuart queen, Mary of Modena, had presided over the remnants of the old court at Saint-Germain. Now, at the end of 1719 the new Stuart queen, Maria Clementina, was with James at Rome at the head of a consolidated and streamlined court, in regular contact with the Pope himself and his closest advisers, and within sight of the Quirinale. The successful cultivation of a strong and predominant pro-Jacobite faction among the cardinals resident at the papal court, maintained by the presence in their midst of the popular king and his young, attractive and well-connected queen, was not the least among the positive developments which emerged while the exiled Stuart court experienced its years of transition.

Appendix I: The King's Household at Pesaro

Bedchamber

Earl Marischal	(Gentleman)
Lord Edward Drummond	(Gentleman)
Lord Clermont	(Gentleman)
Charles Booth	(Groom)
Roger Strickland	(Groom)
Alan Cameron	(Groom)
James Rodez	(Yeoman of the Robes)
Catherine Macane	(Washerwoman)
Gerald Fitzgerald	(*Valet de Chambre* and Barber)
Thomas Saint-Paul	(*Valet de Chambre* and Barber)
Felix Bonbled	(*Valet de Chambre*)
Jean Legrand	(Servant to the Pages)

Chamber

Dominic Sheldon	(Vice-Chamberlain)
Rev Charles Leslie	(Anglican Chaplain)
Rev Ezekiel Hamilton	(Anglican Chaplain)
Dr Lawrence Wood	(Physician)
Dr John Blair	(Physician)

Secretariat

John Paterson	(Under-Secretary)
David Nairne	(Secretary of the Closet)

Household Below Stairs, the Table and the Stables

Charles Booth	(*Maggiordomo*)

Household Below Stairs

Sir William Ellis	(Controller, and Treasurer)
Joseph Martinash	(Assistant)
Charles Macarty	(Yeoman of the Wine Cellar)
Magdalen Rebout	(Scourer)
Jeremiah Broomer	(Clerk of the Kitchen)
Richard Bains	(Cook)
Matthew Creagh	(Cook)
Théophile Lesserteur	(Cook)
James Miner	(Cook)
Pierre Pecquet	(Yeoman Confectioner)
Antonio Seiro	(his servant)
Henry Read	(Confectioner)
Jean Bouzier	(Baker)
Richard Conway	(Kitchen Boys)
Marco Cartolari	
Ignace Faure	

The Stables

James Delattre	(Equerry)
John Hay	(Equerry)
John Sheridan	(Riding Purveyor)
Edmund Butler	(Coachman)
Two	(Postillions)
Henry Kerby	(Chairman)
Antoine Brun	(Chairman)
Andrew Simms	(Footmen)
John Morice	
Nicolas Prévot	
Jacques Catillon	
James Kerby	
Francesco Mesi	
Patrick Maguirk	(Grooms)
Nicholas Clark	
Frank Ridge	
Mark Manning	
Roger Ryan	
John Coghlan	(Helpers)
Laurence Doyle	
Peter Jolly de Falvie	(Harbourer of the Deer)

Appendix II: The King's Household at Urbino

Bedchamber

Duke of Mar (arrived in November 1717; away March to May 1718)	(Gentleman)
Lord Edward Drummond (away November 1717 to March 1718; left in April 1718)	(Gentleman)
Lord Clermont (left in April or May 1718)	(Gentleman)
Charles Booth (away August to November 1717; left in May 1718)	(Groom)
Roger Strickland (left in October 1717)	(Groom)
Alan Cameron	(Groom)
John Hay (appointed in August 1717)	(Groom)
James Rodez (temporarily dismissed in July 1717)	(Yeoman of the Robes)
Catherine Macane	(Washerwoman)
Gerald Fitzgerald	(*Valet de Chambre* and Barber)
Thomas Saint-Paul	(*Valet de Chambre* and Barber)
Felix Bonbled	(*Valet de Chambre*)
Michele Vezzosi (appointed by October 1718)	(*Valet de Chambre*)
Jean Legrand	(Servant to the Pages)

Chamber

Duke of Perth (appointed in March 1718)	(Lord Chamberlain/*Maestro di Camera*)
Dominic Sheldon (left in March 1718)	(Vice-Chamberlain)
Father John Brown	(Confessor)

Rev George Barclay (arrived in November (Anglican Chaplain)
  or December 1717)
Rev Patrick Cowper (arrived in October (Anglican Chaplain)
  or November 1717)
Dr Lawrence Wood (left in October 1717) (Physician)
Dr John Blair (left in February 1718)   (Physician)
Dr Charles Maghie (arrived in February (Physician)
  1718)

Secretariat
Duke of Mar (arrived in November 1717; (Secretary of State)
  away March to May 1718)
Robert Creagh (arrived in December   (Under-Secretary)
  1717)
John Paterson   (Under-Secretary)
James Murray (arrived in July 1718)

David Nairne   (Secretary of the Closet)

Household Below Stairs, the Table and the
  Stables
Charles Booth (March to July 1717)   (*Maggiordomo*)
Lord Clermont (July 1717 to April or   (*Maggiordomo*)
  May 1718)
John Hay (April or May 1718 onwards)   (*Maggiordomo*)

Household Below Stairs
Sir William Ellis   (Controller, and Treasurer)
Joseph Martinash   (Assistant)

Charles Macarty   (Yeoman of the Wine Cellar)
Magdalen Rebout   (Scourer)
Francesco Girelli   (2nd assistant in the Wine
                                          Cellar)

Jeremiah Broomer   (Clerk of the Kitchen/*Maestro
                                          di Casa*)

Charles Russel   (his servant)

Richard Bains   (Cooks)
Matthew Creagh
Théophile Lesserteur
James Miner

Pierre Pecquet   (Yeoman Confectioner)
Antonio Seiro   (his servant)
Henry Read   (Confectioner)

Jean Bouzier	(Baker)
Richard Conway	(Kitchen Boys)
Marco Cartolari	
Ignace Faure	

The Stables

James Delattre	(Equerry)
John Hay (until July 1717)	(Equerry)
John Sheridan	(Riding Purveyor)
Lorenzo Montalto	(his servant)
Edmund Butler	(Coachman)
Henry Kerby	(Chairman)
Antoine Brun	(Chairman)
Andrew Simms	(Footmen)
John Morice	
Nicolas Prévot	
Jacques Catillon	
James Kerby	
Francesco Mesi	
Patrick Maguirk (died in September or October 1718)	(Grooms)
Nicholas Clark	
Frank Ridge	
Mark Manning	
Roger Ryan	
John Coghlan	(Helpers)
Lawrence Doyle	
Peter Jolly de Falvie	(Harbourer of the Deer)

Servants of the Duke of Mar

John Barclay	(*Valet de Chambre*)
Laurence Bernardi (left in August 1718)	(*Valet de Chambre*)

Concierge of the Palazzo Ducale/ Guardarobba

Don Francesco Soanti

Appendix III: Salaries and *Pensions* at Urbino

Secretary of State (Duke of Mar)	471. 09. 06
Lord Chamberlain (Duke of Perth)	471. 09. 06
Gentleman of the Bedchamber (Lord Edward Drummond; Lord Clermont)	353. 11. 02
Vice-Chamberlain (Dominic Sheldon)	314. 02. 03
Secretary of the Closet (David Nairne)	205. 03. 02
Groom of the Bedchamber (Charles Booth, Roger Strickland, Alan Cameron, John Hay; with an extra 100. 00. 00 as *Maggiordomo*: Booth, Hay)	204. 02. 03
Peer (Earl of Linlithgow, Earl of Nithsdale, Earl of Panmure, Earl of Southesk, Earl of Winton, Viscount Kilsyth, Viscount Kingston); James Murray	200. 00. 00
Treasurer (Sir William Ellis)	159. 14. 06
Equerry (James Delattre)	117. 12. 10
Physician (Lawrence Wood)	110. 00. 00
Physician (Charles Maghie); *Gentleman (Charles Fleming, Thomas Forster)*	100. 00. 00
Clerk of the Kitchen (Jeremiah Broomer)	98. 10. 07
Riding Purveyor (John Sheridan)	95. 16. 08
Yeoman of the Wine Cellar (Charles Macarty)	79. 07. 01
Yeoman of the Robes (James Rodez); Valet (Gerald Fitzgerald, Thomas Saint-Paul, Felix Bonbled, Michele Vezzosi)	78. 10. 07
Captain Collier	72. 00. 00
Colonel (William Clephane; Donald MacMahon, Sir John O'Brien, John Stewart of Invernity), Gentleman (Alexander Maitland, Sir John Preston)	60. 00. 00
Coachman (Edmund Butler); First Chairman (Henry Kerby)	52. 05. 00
Under-Secretary (Robert Creagh; John Paterson)	50. 00. 00

Washerwoman (Catherine Macane); *Major John Cockburne, Robert Freebairne; George Mackenzie, Major John O'Brien*	45. 00. 00
Yeoman Confectioner (Pierre Pecquet)	44. 13. 09
Baker (Jean Bouzier)	40. 00. 00
Footman (Andrew Simms, John Morice, Nicolas Prévot, Jacques Catillon, James Kerby, Francesco Mesi)	36. 08. 00
Protestant Chaplain (George Barclay, Patrick Cowper); Chairman (Antoine Brun); *William Drummond, James Hay, George Menzies, Captain Charles Wogan (later increased to 60. 00. 00 in 1718)*	35. 00. 00
Groom (Patrick Maguirk, Nicolas Clark, Frank Ridge, Mark Manning, Roger Ryan)	31. 17. 00
Confectioner (Henry Read); Kitchen Boy (Richard Conway, Marco Cartolari, Ignace Faure); *James Edgar*	30. 00. 00
Harbourer of the Deer (Peter Jolly de Falvie)	27. 13. 07
Cook (Matthew Creagh)	27. 06. 00
Assistant to the Treasurer (Joseph Martinash); Cook (Richard Bains)	25. 00. 00
Assistant in the Wine Cellar (Francesco Girelli)	20. 00. 00
Assistant Cook (James Miner); *Robert Watson*	15. 00. 00

Unknown: Confessor (Father John Brown)
                Servant to the Pages (Jean Legrand)
                Scourer (Magdalen Rebout)
                Servant to the Clerk of the Kitchen (Charles Russel)
                Servant to the Yeoman Confectioner (Antonio Seiro)
                Helpers in the Stables (John Coghlan, Lawrence Doyle)
                William Erskine
                John Fotheringham of Powrie
                John Graeme

Appendix IV: The Pensioners and Other People at Urbino

Scottish

Throughout the period July 1717 to October 1718

    Colonel William Clephane

    Major John Cockburne (on a mission to Bologna, August to December 1717)

    Captain Collier

    James Edgar

    Charles Fleming

    Viscount Kilsyth

    Viscount Kingston

    Earl of Linlithgow

    George Menzies

    Earl of Nithsdale

    Sir John Preston

    Robert Watson

    Earl of Winton

Left, but returned

    Earl of Southesk (November 1717; returned October 1718)

    Colonel John Stewart of Invernity (November?? 1717; returned July 1718)

    Duke of Perth (January 1718; returned March 1718, and joined the Household)

Left early and did not return

    William Drummond (October 1717)

    John Fotheringham of Powrie (in 1717)

    James Hay (early? 1718)

    Alexander Maitland (died in September 1717)

    Earl of Panmure (February 1718)

Arrived late
  William Erskine (November 1717)
  John Graeme (November 1717)
  John Carnegy of Boysick (by 1718)
  Mrs Hay = Countess of Inverness (July 1718)
  George Mackenzie (October 1718)
Arrived late and left early
  Robert Freebairne (late 1717 to March 1718)

English
Throughout the period July 1717 to October 1718
  Thomas Forster
Arrived late
  Countess of Nithsdale (October 1718)
Arrived late and left early??
  Charles Radcliffe (or the 4th Earl of Derwentwater)

Irish
Throughout the period July 1717 to October 1718
  Captain (then Major) John O'Brien
  Major (then Colonel) Donald MacMahon
  Captain Charles Wogan (on a mission, August 1717 to April 1718)
Left early
  Captain (then Colonel) Sir John O'Brien (October 1717)

Italian
Throughout the period July 1717 to October 1718
  Michele Vezzosi (appointed *Valet de Chambre* to the King by October
    1718)
Recruited as servants
  Francesco Bartolemeo (Cook to Lord Nithsdale)
  Paolo Antonio de Rossi (Cook to Lord Kilsyth)

A Note on Sources

Many British, Italian and French sources have been used in the preparation of this study of the Stuart court in the Papal States from 1717 to 1719, but the most important are the papers of James III (known as the Stuart Papers); the personal and official papers of Pope Clement XI; and the papers of Filippo Gualterio, Cardinal Protector of England.

The Stuart Papers for the years up to the end of 1718 were published between 1902 and 1923 by the Historical Manuscripts Commission in seven volumes. Volumes IV–VII include most (though not quite all) of the documents from the years 1717 and 1718. With very few exceptions, the Stuart Papers for 1719 onwards remain unpublished and are preserved among the Royal Archives at Windsor Castle (volumes 41–45).

The personal papers of Pope Clement XI, catalogued as the *Fondo Albani* (volumes 165–68), are in the Archivio Segreto Vaticano. The official archives of his papacy are now divided between the Archivio di Stato di Roma and the Archivio Segreto Vaticano. They include the register of presents which he gave, known as the *Registro de' Mandati Camerale* (b.1064–66) now in the Archivio di Stato di Roma, and the archives of the finance departments of the papal court: the supervising *Tesoriere Generale* and, subordinate to that, the *Computisteria Generale* and the *Depositeria Generale*. There was considerable overlap in record-keeping between these departments, so that the same information can sometimes be found in more than one source. The *Giustificazione di Tesoriere* (b.422–23, 427–28, 430, 438, 444) and the *Conti della Depositeria Generale* (b.2017*bis*) are both now in the Archivio di Stato di Roma; the papers of the *Computisteria Generale*, catalogued as *Palazzo Apostolico Computisteria* (volumes 161, 976, 982, 5044), are in the Archivio Segreto Vaticano. The archives of the papal *Segretario di Stato* (*Inghilterra* volume 21) are also in the Archivio Segreto Vaticano.

The papers of Cardinal Gualterio are all in the British Library. They contain his correspondence with James III and Clement XI, and with several Jacobites, but by far the most useful are the regular letters, both official and secret, which he received from David Nairne, the Secretary of the Closet at the Stuart court (Add. MSS 20298, 31259–61). Gualterio did not keep a copy of the letters he sent to Nairne, but the originals have survived among the latter's papers in the Bodleian Library (Carte MSS 257–58).

It should be added that Nairne conducted a very large correspondence, and that some of his letters to other people have also survived. The ones he sent to Thomas Innes at the Collège des Ecossais in Paris, now among the Scottish Catholic Archives in Edinburgh (BL 2/210, 217, 222), provide a valuable supplement to the ones written to Cardinal Gualterio.

In addition to these papers, three diaries have been particularly useful. Dr John Blair wrote detailed descriptions of his journeys with Lord Panmure to Pesaro, to Rome, to Urbino, and finally to Venice in 1717 and 1718. They are now in the Scottish National Archives (GD. 45/26/74). David Nairne wrote a description of James III's first visit to Rome in 1717, which is now in the Bodleian Library

(Carte MSS 208). And Giovanni Gueroli Pucci recorded the details of James III's arrival at Urbino in 1717, and of the entertainments which were provided for him and his courtiers while they were there. The original narrative and three copies are all now in the Biblioteca Universitaria d'Urbino (Fondo del Comune, Rep III and b.167).

One other contemporary source should be mentioned here. In 1724 the philosopher and astronomer Francesco Bianchini arranged the publication in Rome of a new edition of a work which had originally been published in 1587: Bernardino Baldi, *Memorie concernenti La Città di Urbino dedicate alla Sacra Real Maestà di Giacomo III, rè della Gran Brettagna etc.* This book, dedicated to James III by Cardinal Annibale Albani, contains as a frontispiece the engraved portait of James III in his Garter robes by Horthemels, after the original painting by Belle (1714), and includes several engravings which show the Palazzo Ducale as it was when the Stuart court was there. The most important is a ground plan of the first floor where the king's apartment was situated.

Notes

Introduction

1. The legitimate son of James II is referred to here as James III, and not as the Pretender. This is now normal practice in studies of Jacobitism, and the reason for it has already been explained elsewhere (Edward Corp, *A Court in Exile: The Stuarts in France, 1689–1718* (Cambridge University Press, 2004), pp. 9–10). But although James III was the exiled King of Great Britain (*Magnae Britanniae Rex*), he was nearly always referred to in Italy (and in the Italian archives) as *Giacomo III, re d'Inghilterra*. Even the Scots and the Irish at the exiled court normally referred to him as the King of England. Using the name James III in this study of the Jacobites at Urbino is therefore consistent with contemporary practice, but it should not be regarded as implying an exclusive reference to his English or Irish titles. The name James III, as used here, is referring to the third person of that name who was *re della Gran Bretagna*.

1   From Avignon to Pesaro

1. *English Historical Documents vol. VII, 1714–83*, ed. D.B. Horn and Mary Ransome (London, 1957), pp. 913–16. The Article of the treaty which concerned James III is on p. 914.
2. *The Letters of Madame: The Correspondence of Elisabeth-Charlotte of Bavaria, Princesse Palatine, Duchess of Orleans, called "Madame" at the Court of Louis XIV*, trans. and ed. Gertrude S. Stevenson, 2 vols (London, 1924), vol. 2, p. 235, to the Raugravine Louisa, 17 December 1719.
3. The duc de Saint-Simon attended the meeting which discussed the fate of James III, the Dukes of Ormonde and Mar,

> and of all those declared Jacobites who were residing in France or wished to pass through. The Regent committed himself to expelling the former from French territories, and denying entry to the latter.... I argued against the inhumanity of such treatment.... regrettably [James III] left... Avignon and withdrew into Italy [et de tous ceux qui, étant Jacobites déclarés, se tenoient en France ou y voudroient passer. Le Régent s'engageoit à faire sortir les premiers de toutes les terres de la domination de France, et de n'y en souffrir des seconds.... J'y résistai à l'inhumanité de cette proscription.... [Jacques III] partit... d'Avignon, fort à regret, pour se retirer en Italie].
>
> (Louis de Rouvroy, duc de Saint-Simon, *Mémoires*, ed. A. de Boislisle, 41 vols (Paris, 1879–1930), vol. 31, pp. 43–45. See also vol. 30, pp. 5, 144)

4. ASV. Fondo Albani 165, James III to Clement XI, 22 June 1716: "coup fatal un voïage en Italie porteroit à mes interêts".
5. The Regent informed Mary of Modena of his decision to expel her son in October (HMC *Stuart* III, p. 77, Mary of Modena to Mar, 14 October 1716), but his departure had to be delayed until James had recovered from being "cut for a fistula, caused by a long continuance of the piles" (WDA. Epist. Var. 6/29, Ingleton to Mayes, 23 October 1716).
6. "Pesaro is a town in the Dutchy of Urbin subject to the Pope.... In the mercat place... you have a large palais where formerly lodged the Dukes of Urbin now the Cardinal Legat governour of the Dutchy under the Pope" (SNA. GD. 45/26/74, "Journall by Doctor John Blair from Pesaro to Rome, June 1717"). Cardinal Davia was the brother-in-law of Lady Almond, who had been a friend and Lady of the Bedchamber to Mary of Modena. Pope Clement XI's aunt Donna Giulia Albani, who was married to Giovanni Andrea Olivieri, lived in Pesaro in the Palazzo Almerici (which now houses the Biblioteca Oliveriana). It contains a plaque recording the visit that she received from James III. She died in March 1718 (HMC *Stuart* VI, p. 236, Hay to Mar, 31 March 1718).
7. Corp, *A Court in Exile*, pp. 302–05.
8. It is difficult to be sure about all the servants, particularly the footmen and grooms in the Stables, because there is not enough documentary evidence. The people who did not go to Italy were the Earl of Newcastle (Gentleman of the Bedchamber), Richard Trevanion (Groom of the Bedchamber) and John Martinash (Cook). Mr Styles (Page of the Bedchamber: christian name unknown) is never mentioned again, and possibly died at Avignon. Barnaby Hute, the Assistant in the Wine Cellar, seems to have returned to Paris, where he opened a *cabaret* and later provided the premises for the meetings of the Jacobite Masonic Lodge of St Thomas (Corp, *A Court in Exile*, p. 340). It seems that some additional footmen had been sent down from Saint-Germain and that they also went to Italy.
9. BL. Add. MSS 20311, f. 369, anon. (at Lyons) to Gualterio, 16 June 1716; RA. SP 40/149, 281/163, Box 3/83, and 40/150, lists of the people receiving pensions at Avignon, 1716–17.
10. RA. SP 17/55. The list includes the four newly arrived exiles who had been given posts (the Duke of Mar, the Earl Marischal, John Paterson and Dr John Blair) and the two Anglican Chaplains (Charles Leslie and Ezekiel Hamilton).
11. RA. SP 17/55. This list includes John Hay, who had been appointed to be one of the king's Equerries.
12. HMC *Stuart* III, p. 490, Mar to Seaforth, 30 January 1717. For the Highlanders at Toulouse, see Edward Corp, "The Jacobite Presence in Toulouse during the Eighteenth Century", *Diasporas: Histoire et Sociétés* no. 5 (Toulouse, 2004), pp. 124–25.
13. The marquis de Dangeau wrote that "he is sorely missed in Avignon, where his exquisite manners and obliging nature made him very much loved" ["on le regrette fort à Avignon, où il s'étoit fait fort aimer par ses manières polies et obligeantes"] (Philippe de Courcillon, marquis de Dangeau, *Journal*, ed. E. Soulié and L. Dussieux, 19 vols (Paris, 1854–60), vol. 17, p. 21, 10 February 1717).
14. WDA. Epist. Var. 6/39, Ingleton to Mayes, 7 February 1717; HMC *Stuart* IV, p. 90, Mar to Kinnaird, 1 March 1717.

15. Corp, *A Court in Exile*, p. 309.
16. M. Haile, *Mary of Modena* (London, 1907), p. 495, James III to Mary of Modena, 14 March 1717.
17. Edward Corp, *The King over the Water: Portraits of the Stuarts in Exile after 1689* (National Galleries of Scotland, 2001), pp. 57, 107, 111. The painting was commissioned by the Pope:

> When James III, King of Great Britain, came to Italy, crossing the River Panaro and entering the Papal States, he was presented with a letter from the Pope by Don Carlo Albani. This great occasion was celebrated in the presence of the king's court, the Papal ambassador and many other people; and because the Pope had ordered them to produce a painting of it, and had specified that he wanted this done by the Spaniard [Crespi] who was present for the occasion, this man painted them, and he portrayed the king and the important nobles so well that there was none that did not delight in it. [Quando venne in Italia Giacomo terzo, Re della gran Bretagna, nel passar ch'ei fece il Panaro, entrando nel confine dello stato di Santa Chiesa, gli fu presentato da Don Carlo Albani un breve del Papa. Questa solennità so fece all presenza della corte del Re, e di quella dell' ambasciador pontificio, e d'infinte altre persone; e perché il Papa aveva ordinato, che di ciò si facesse una pittura, e avea precisamente ordinato, che la volea dello mano dello Spagnuolo alla solennità condutto, e quindi il tutto ritrasse, e cosi bene ritrasse le principali persone di quella solennità, che non so trovò chi non le ravvisasse].
>
> (G.P. Cavazzoni Zanotti, *Storia dell'Accademia Clementina* (Bologna, 1739), vol. 2, p. 60)

18. The letter specifying the accommodation which James III required for himself and his court has already been summarised in detail in Corp, *A Court in Exile*, pp. 308–09. It is wrongly filed in Archivio di Stato di Bologna (ASB). Assunteria di Magistrati, Affari Diversi 118/19/631, with papers dating from 1726. The details of James's visit to Bologna are given in Affari Diversi 118/18, and ASB. Senato Diari vol. 12 (1714–41), pp. 17–19.
19. Martin Haile, *Queen Mary of Modena* (London, 1905) p. 495, James III to Mary of Modena, 14 March 1717. The old acquaintances from Saint-Germain were a brother of Francesco Riva (Master of the Queen's Robes) and "Miss Ronchi that was", sister of Giuseppe, Giacomo and Peregrino Ronchi (all three in the service of the Queen).
20. Corp, *King over the Water*, pp. 57, 107, 110.
21. BL. Add. MSS 31260, f. 33, Nairne to Gualterio, 22 March 1717: "un voyage ennuÿant de six semaines."
22. For example, the Earl of Panmure travelled separately with Dr John Blair. The latter's diary is in SNA. GD 45/26/74, "Journal by Doctor Blair from Avignon to Pesaro . . . with the Earle of Panmure etc begun ye 8 Feb.ry 1717".
23. SNA. GD 45/26/74, "Journall by Doctor John Blair from Pesaro to Rome, June 1717".
24. Corp, *A Court in Exile*, p. 306. See HMC *Stuart* IV, p. 252, James III to Mar, 19 May 1717: "His Master [Philip V] has consented he should accept what I have given him, provided it be kept private." But see also BL. Add. MSS 20312, f. 16, Alberoni to Nairne, 3 August 1717, expressing the dissatisfaction of Philip V at the favour shown by James III to the Count of Castelblanco.

25. Corp, *A Court in Exile*, p. 309.
26. Ibid., pp. 309–10.
27. Ibid., p. 310. ASV. PAC 976, no. 170/68, a receipt by Booth, 15 June 1717. The title was later changed to *Maggiordomo e Spedizionere* (see Chapter 4). For the list of the king's household at Pesaro, see Appendix I.
28. Edward Corp, "Music at the Stuart Court at Urbino, 1717–18", *Music and Letters* 81, no. 3 (August 2000), p. 354. The operas were *Vespasiano* (Carlo Pallavicino), *Il podestà di Colognole* (pasticcio) and *La fede ne' tradimenti* (pasticcio).
29. HMC *Stuart* IV, p. 285, Paterson to Mar, 29 May 1717. In the middle of May, James referred to "this nasty climate" and commented that "I am just going to call for a fire" (Ibid., p. 252, James III to Mar, 19 May 1717).
30. He took with him Dudley Bagnall (one of the Grooms of the Bedchamber), Colonel Richard Butler (brother of the Earl of Newcastle), the Rev. Ezekiel Hamilton, and David Kennedy. Peter the Great had in fact embarked on his tour of Western Europe. On 11 June 1717, he visited the Château de Saint-Germain, and on the following day spoke with Mary of Modena at Chaillot (John Motley, *The History of the Life of Peter I, Emperor of Russia*, 3 vols (London, 1740), vol. 2, pp. 240–41).
31. Corp, "The Jacobite Presence in Toulouse", p. 128.
32. HMC *Stuart* IV, p. 222, Paterson to Mar, 1 May 1717.
33. Ibid., p. 223, Hay to Mar, 1 May 1717.
34. Ibid., p. 230, Paterson to Mar, 8 May 1717.
35. Ibid., p. 252, James III to Mar, 19 May 1717.
36. Ibid., p. 140, James III to Mar, 27 March 1717.
37. Catherine Macane is shown in the "Liste des Anglois de la Suite de Jacques III Roy d'Angleterre, arrivés a Avignon en 1716" (Bibliothèque Municipale d'Avignon MS. 2827, p. 611). Magdalen Rebout was described in 1720 as being from Avignon and the widow of Stefano Muti, also from Avignon (Archivio Storico Vicariato di Roma: Santi Dodici Apostoli vol. 57, p. 37, Stati d'Anime, 1720). They are the only women included in RA. SP Box 3/90, "A List of the Kings Servants who have been lodged, or have had lodging monie, since His Ma.tie parted from St Germans", undated but probably January 1719.
38. The only Protestants in the Household were Sir William Ellis (Controller, and Treasurer), Charles Leslie, Ezekiel Hamilton and Dr John Blair. The few Catholics among the other courtiers included the Duke of Perth, the Earls of Nithsdale and Winton and Charles Fleming.
39. RA. SP 17/55.
40. ASV. Fondo Albani 168/136, Salviati to Paulucci, 10 June 1716, in which he formally recommended allowing religious toleration for Protestants at Avignon, so as not to hinder a restoration. Also Corp, *A Court in Exile*, p. 305.
41. Dangeau, *Journal*, vol. 17, p. 60, 7 April 1717; C.E. Lart, *The Parochial Registers of Saint-Germain-en-Laye: Jacobite Extracts*, 2 vols (London, 1910, 1912), vol. 2, p. 148, Nairne to Gontieri, 1 April 1717.
42. Biblioteca Universitario d'Urbino, Fondo del Comune, Rep III, 101, p. 400, "Catalogo degli Eminentissimi Legati, e Presidenti della Legazione di Urbino". Only a cardinal could be a Legate, so Salviati had the lesser title of *Presidente*.

43. WDA. Epist. Var. 6/13, Ingleton to Mayes, 3 May 1716. See also Ibid., 6/18, Ingleton to Mayes, 6 July 1716.
44. ASV. Fondo Albani 165, pp. 126, 128, Paulucci to Gontieri, 15 April and 2 May 1716. The specific instructions sent to Father Viganego are at p. 133, and dated 16 May 1716.
45. Haile, *Mary of Modena*, p. 223. See Lart, *Jacobite Extracts*, vol. 2, p. 148, Nairne to Gontieri, 1 April 1717, announcing that Mary of Modena was sending each man a silver watch to thank him for his services.
46. RA. SP 111/80, James III to Ellis, 16 October 1727.
47. Corp, *A Court in Exile*, pp. 324–25; ASV. Fondo Albani 165, Mary of Modena to Cornelio Bentivoglio (Papal Nuncio in France), 5 April 1716, asking him to urge the Pope to give money to James III:

> The pension we receive from the French Court for our living expenses is paid so irregularly that we are at present 8 months in arrears, that is 400,000 francs, with the result that if the butcher and baker did not give me credit, I would be short of even basic necessities [La pension que nous recevons de la Cour de France pour notre subsistance est si mal payée que l'on nous doit actuellement 8 mois d'arrerages, c'est à dire 400,000 francs, si bien que si le boulanger et le boucher ne me donnoit à credit, je manquerois du necessaire].

It should, however, be added that James III received an additional 80,000 *livres* from the Regent while he was at Avignon (HMC *Stuart* V, p. 427, accounts of Dicconson, 31 January 1718), and then a separate secret pension of 300,000 *livres per annum* when he went to Italy (HMC *Stuart* VI, p. 488, James III to the Regent, 28 May 1718; HMC *Stuart* VII, p. 560, James III to Acquaviva, 23 November 1718).

48. The Pope gave James III, 745 Spanish *doble*, the equivalent of 2500 *scudi*, in June 1716 when he had been at Avignon for three months. (ASV. Fondo Albani 165, p. 160; ASR. Cam I: RMC 1064, f. 115, f. 182, f. 263; ASR. Cam I: GT 430, f. 16, no. 3; HMC *Stuart* V, p. 542, Ellis to James III, 27 April 1717). Three months later, at the end of September 1716, he gave him 8873 *livres*, which was intended to be the equivalent of 2500 *scudi*, but which actually realised only 2318 *scudi*. (ASR. Cam I: RMC 1064, f. 182, f. 263; ASR. Cam I: GT 430, f. 16, no. 2). In November 1716, he instructed the *Camera Apostolica* to establish a regular pension for James of 2500 *scudi*, to be paid at the end of each quarter, starting with a payment in January 1717 to cover October, November and December 1716. (ASV. SS: Ingh 21, pp. 240–43 contains the "copie degl'Ordine, e sue Giustificazione, colle quali siè pagato all Mta. del Rè Giacomo d'Inghilterra a l'anno assegnam.to di scudi 10,000". The detailed payments until the summer of 1717 are in ASR. Cam I: RMC 1064, f. 250, f. 257, f. 263, f. 335, f. 373; and ASR. Cam I: GT 430, f. 16, no. 1 (missing), nos. 4, 5).
49. ASR. Cam I: GT 422, f. 17, "la spese fatte in occasione dell'arrivo a Pesaro di Giacomo III d'Inghilterra...dal 27 marzo all 13 maggio 1717"; ASR. Cam I: GT 427, f. 11, "la spese sostenute per mobili...per Giacomo III d'Inghilterra...le riparazioni nell'appartamento a lui destinato, e spese di

lavanderia e di acquisto di stoffe", April to June 1717; ASR. Cam I: RMC 1065, f. 209, "spese di Regalo, mobili provisti, accomodamento di Palazzo, e altre spese recorse in occasione della venuta di Giacomo III", paid on 2 July 1717; Ibid., f. 251, "diverse spese ... mobili provisti per servo il detto Palazzo", paid on 3 August 1717.

50. ASV. Fondo Salviati 36, Nairne to Salviati, 31 August 1716.
51. ASR. Cam I: GT 422, f. 17, "spese per li letti de soldati mandati da Roma e alloggi de medem", March to May 1717; ASR. Cam I: 427, f. 11, "mandati e conti relativi a restauro delle quattro porte di Pesaro e all'alloggiamento dei soldati spediti da Roma in occasione della permanenza del re", April to June 1717; ASR. Cam I: RMC 1065, f. 251, "tanti pagati in Pesaro ... per risercimenti fatti alle Porte della Citta, spese li lettzi e altro per li soldati mandati da Roma per guardia alle d.e Porte", paid on 3 August 1717.
52. For the original portrait, see Corp, *King over the Water*, pp. 46–47, 107, 110; and Corp, *A Court in Exile*, p. 192.
53. Bod. Lib. Rawlinson MSS D.1185, pp. 2194–95, Rawlinson's diary, 27 June 1725.
54. It now belongs to the Museo Civico, and is on loan to the *Prefettura* in the Palazzo Ducale.

2   The King's first visit to Rome

1. WDA. Epist. Var. 6/43, Ingleton to Mayes, 27 March 1717; Dangeau, *Journal*, vol. 17, p. 103, 9 April 1717: "King James is awaited in Rome; throughout the Papal States and in Pesaro, from where he is coming, he has been granted all the honours due to a King; in Rome he will stay at the house of Cardinal Gualterio...; he should be in Rome by now" ["On attend le roi Jacques à Rome; on lui a rendu dans toutes les terres du pape et à Pezaro, d'où il vient, tous les honneurs dus aux grands rois; il logera à Rome chez le Cardinal Gualterio...; il doit être arrivé a Rome présentement"].
2. BL. Add. MSS 31260, f. 67 and f. 75, Nairne to Gualterio, 9 and 14 May 1717.
3. There had been no Cardinal Protector of England since the death of Cardinal Caprara in 1711, although Gualterio had been acting as James III's ambassador at Rome since 1713 (Corp, *A Court in Exile*, p. 67).
4. James also asked Don Carlo Albani to inform the pope of his arrival and to support his requests. See BL. Add. MSS 20312, f. 10, "Mémoire des commissions dont [Jacques III] a chargé Son Excellence Don Carlo Albani, avant son départ pour Rome", Pesaro, 9 May 1717.
5. HMC *Stuart* IV, p. 252, James III to Mar, 19 May 1717.
6. Ibid., p. 267, Paterson to Mar, 22 May 1717.
7. ASV. Fondo Albani 166, p. 25, James III to Gualterio, from Terni, "ce lundi [24 May] à 11 heures du soir", 1717; Ibid., p. 27, Gualterio to Clement XI, 26 May 1717.
8. HMC *Stuart* IV, p. 289, Hay to Mar, 30 May 1717.
9. Ibid., p. 285, Nairne to Paterson, 29 May 1717.
10. ASV. Fondo Albani 166, p. 25, James III to Gualterio, 24 May 1717: "I am bringing only Mr Hay and Porth [*sic*] with me and Nairn [*sic*] will follow, – so if you can find three rooms for them in your Palace that is all that is

necessary" ["Je ne mene avec moi que Mr Hay et Porth [*sic*] et Nairn [*sic*] suivra, – ainsi si vous pourrez trouver trois chambres pour eux dans votre Palais c'est tout ce qu'il faut"].

11. The entrance to the Palazzo Gualterio was in the north wing, immediately opposite the entrance to the Palazzo Ruspoli, across the small Piazza di San Lorenzo in Lucina; or, as Nairne put it, "…Princess Ruspoli whose Palace is right opposite Cardinal Gualterio's" ["…la Princess Ruspoli don't le Palais est tout vis a vis celuy du Cardinal Gualterio"]. The main façade, described by Nairne as "fort longue", was in the east wing, overlooking the Corso (Bod. Lib. Carte MSS 208, f. 352 and f. 354).

12. Bod. Lib. Carte MSS 208, ff. 338–56.

13. ASV. Fondo Albani 166, pp. 25–34.

14. ASV. PAC 161 and 976; ASR. Cam I: RMC 1065; ASV. Fondo Albani 166, pp. 42, 44, two lists of the food and drink sent to the Palazzo Gualterio by the Pope for James III.

15. Bod. Lib. Carte MSS 208, f. 344: "une des plus belles choses de Rome, et qui peut se comparer avec la Galerie de Versailles".

16. ASV. Fondo Salviati 38, f. 2, no. 75.

17. She was born Ippolita Ludovisi in 1663, and had married Gregorio Boncampagni in 1681. She died in 1733.

18. *I David: due pittori tra Sei a Settecento*, ed. Andrea Spiriti and Simona Capelli, exhibition catalogue (Rancate, Pinacoteca Cantonale Giovanni Züst, 2004).

19. BL. Add. MSS 20306, f. 445, Gualterio to Dempster, late February or early March 1718.

20. Bod. Lib. Carte MSS 208, f. 355: "estimé le meilleur peintre de Rome pour les portraits et pour bien attraper la ressemblance."

21. The marquis de Dangeau recorded on two occasions in his diary that the Knights of the Thistle "wore a blue sash like the Knights of the Garter" ["portoient le ruban bleu comme les chevaliers de la Jarretière"] (*Journal*, vol. 15, p. 153, 26 May 1714; and vol. 4, p. 50, 20 March 1692). But no one who had both honours (like the 1st Dukes of Melfort and Perth) could wear them at the same time. It was also necessary to distinguish between them. The duc de Saint-Simon explained: "This Scottish blue sash was at that time of the same colour as that of the Saint-Esprit and like it was worn from right to left; but it was only ever worn underneath the coat, whereas the Garter sash was only ever worn on top" ["Ce cordon bleu d'Ecosse étoit alors de la même couleur et passé de droite à gauche comme celui du Saint-Esprit; mais il ne se portoit jamais que par-dessous, au lieu que celui de la Jarretière ne se porte jamais que par-dessus"] (*Mémoires*, vol. 26, p. 402). The only known portraits which show Jacobite Thistle Knights between 1689 and 1716 are the ones of the 1st Marquis of Seaforth and of his son the 2nd Marquis, now in Fortrose Town Hall (Ross and Cromarty). I am grateful to Andrew McKenzie for giving me photographs). Whereas the one of the 1st Marquis shows him with his *cordon bleu* below his coat, that of the 2nd Marquis (by Sir John de Medina) has the *cordon bleu* prominently displayed on the outside. After 1716 the Thistle was to be suspended from a ribbon, which was now green, worn on the outside around the neck.

22. Corp, *King over the Water*, pp. 57–58.

23. BL. Add. MSS 31260, f. 79, Nairne to Gualterio, 9 July 1717.
24. Corp, *A Court in Exile*, Chapter 8.
25. ASV. Fondo Salviati 38, f. 2, no. 62, "Memoria di Pranzo dato al Re d'Inghilterra", 24 May 1716.
26. ASV. Fondo Salviati 38, f. 3, no. 51, undated: "pour douze violons, qu'ils ont joué [*sic*] à quatre bals que Mgr le Vice Legat a donné au Palais au Roy d'Angleterre dans le carneval".
27. Corp, "Music at the Stuart Court at Urbino", p. 354. See also Chapter 1, note 28.
28. Bod. Lib. Carte MSS. 208, f. 340, f. 344, f. 345, f. 352, f. 354: "on donna des rafraichissements et Mr Scarlatti le jeune [Domenico Scarlatti] grand musicien joua du clavessin et chanta"; "il y avoit deux des meilleurs voix de Rome, et une simphonie admirable"; "la musique de la grande messe"; "une tres belle musique, la meilleure et le plus au goût de S.M. qu'Elle eut encore entendue"; "une Cantata faite exprès pour S.M."; "une musique preparée ou deux filles chanterent 2 ou 3 cantates, une des deux est la meilleure voix de fille qui soit à Rome." The singer on 30 June was described as "a young singer paid by Princess Ruspoli who every Sunday evening has conversation and music in her Palace" ["une cantarina aux gages du Princesse Ruspoli qui a tous les Dimanches au soir conversation et musique dans son Palais"]. The music itself is described as consisting of "sinfonie, concerti" and a cantata by Gasparini entitled "Su la fiorita sponda" in Franco Piperno, "'Su le sponde del Tebro': eventi, mecenati e istituzioni musicali a Roma negli anni di Locatelli. Saggio di cronologia", pp. 793–877 (in vol. 2 of *Intorno a Locatelli: Studi in occasione del tricentenario della nascita di Pietro Antonio Locatelli (1695–1764)*, a cura di Albert Dunning, 2 vols (Lucca, Libreria Musicale Italiana, 1995), at p. 845). According to the same source (p. 846), there was on the same day a "sinfonia e balli, per l'Accademia di lettere ed armi in onore di Giacomo III", at the Collegio Clementino.
29. It cost 4996 *scudi* (ASR. Cam I: RMC 1065, f. 233 and f. 318). The bills were paid on 28 July and 6 October 1717.
30. Bod. Lib. Carte MSS 208, f. 346:

> Aussitôt qu'Elle fut arrivée, on alluma tout au tour du Lac de Castell [*sic*] des feux de distances en distances, et entre autres deux fort belles illuminations, on tira aussi quantité de coups de petits canons et de boêtes qui étoient rangés tout au tour du lac qui a 6 miles de tour, et dont les coteaux au tour font une espece d'amphitheatre, du milieu du lac on tira une Girandola qui fit un tres bel effect des fenêtres du Palais, après quoi le Roy se mit à table.

31. ASV. PAC 976, no. 170/15, "Conto de lavori di Pittura et indoratura fati... per servitio... in occasione della festa fata in Castel Gandolfo per la venuta della Real Maestà d'Inghilterra", 20 June 1717: "Sua Maestà che sbarcha di un vasiello con molte giente e molto poppolo alla sponda del mare che lo ricevani."
32. Bod. Lib. Carte MSS 208, f. 347: "dans l'appartement où S.M. entra... placé sous un Dais."

33. Ibid., f. 346: "toutes les viandes étoient accommodées à la françoise, et il y avoit de très bon vin de champagne"; "dura environ 3 quarts d'heure, et reussit parfaitement bien".

34. ASV. PAC 976, "Ristretti di Pagamenti fatti…in occasione dell'Alloggio fatto nel Palazzo Pontificio di Castel Gandolfo alla Maestà di Giacomo 3ᵉ Re d'Inghilterra nel mese di Giugno 1717". The payments to Domenico Scarlatti for the composition of the cantata, and to his musicians for performing it, with his signed receipts, are no. 170/8 and 52.

35. Reinhard Strohm, *Dramma per musica: Italian Opera Seria of the Eighteenth Century* (New Haven and London, 1997), p. 51.

36. HMC *Stuart* IV, p. 317, James III to Mar, 5 June 1717.

37. Ibid., p. 337, Nairne to Paterson, 11 June 1717. See also HMC *Stuart* VI, p. 291, Nairne to Mar, 10 April 1718: "I am glad you are pleased with Rome, which is more than Mr Booth will allow anything in it deserves, barring St Peter's."

38. The audiences were on Friday 28 May, Saturday 5 June, Sunday 13 June, Monday 21 June, and Saturday 5 July.

39. HMC *Stuart* IV, p. 319, Nairne to Paterson, 5 June 1717.

40. ASV. Fondo Albani 166, f. 70, Gualterio to Clement XI, 7 July 1717.

41. WDA. Epist. Var. 6/54, Nairne to Mayes, 29 July 1717.

42. ASR. Cam I: RMC 1065, f. 173: "cristallo di Montegrandi, e guarnite d'oro." Four days later, on 18 June, James was given "a very lifelike portrait of the Pope in fine tapestry" ["un portrait du Pape, fait du petit point fort beau et fort ressemblant"] (Bod. Lib. Carte MSS 208, f. 348).

43. HMC *Stuart* IV, p. 289, Hay to Mar, 30 May 1717.

44. Ibid., p. 337, Nairne to Paterson, 11 June 1717.

45. Ibid., p. 252, James III to Mar, 19 May 1717.

46. Bod. Lib., Carte MSS 208, f. 344.

47. "Alcune ragioni, per le quali li MyLords Earles della Gran Brittagna pretendono d'essere ommessi al bagio de piede di N.S. con la spada, e cappello". The document has been wrongly filed with the "Leslie Papers, 1643–1711", which form volume 3 of the archives of the Scots College, Rome.

48. "la lingua Italiana non ha una parola propria per esprimere il loro vero grado di nobilità."

49. Bod. Lib. Carte MSS 208, ff. 355–56:

> la visite dura deux heures. Comme S. M. étoit prête à partir, Elle fit entrer les Milords et quelques autres gentilshommes de sa suite qu'Elle presenta à S.S. et ils lui baiserent le pied. Les Milords en consideration de S.M. eurent permission d'entrer avec l'epée et le chapeau. Ils étoient 5 Milords Southesk, Nithesdale, Panmure, Kilseith et Kingston.

50. Ibid., f. 356: "une cassette ou il y avoit un corps saint d'un martir, une autre remplie d'Agnus Dei, un morceau de la vraye croix enchassé dans du cristal et enfermé dans un reliquaire, et un chapelet de lapis lazaris, avec des Indulgences, et les attestations authentiques de tout". The more detailed description of the presents in ASV. Fondo Albani 166, p. 34, specifies that the holy relics given to James III were in fact those of the martyr St. Novico

["di S. Novico martire"], whom I have not been able to identify. James sent "the two boxes containing holy relics and the Agnus Dei medallions" ["les deux boites du corps saint et des Agnus Dei"] to Mary of Modena at Saint-Germain (BL. Add. MSS 31260, f. 79, Nairne to Gualterio, 9 July 1717). The book of attestations was included in the *Royal House of Stuart* Exhibition at the New Gallery, London, in 1889. The catalogue entry for exhibit 518 is "Book in embroidered velvet cover describing relics of Saints [*sic*] given to Prince James in 1717".

51. ASV. PAC 161, no. 157, "Conto de Libri, e stampe fatti sigare...per donare alla Maestà del Rè d'Inghilterra". The books described the architecture, statues, vases, fountains, columns, churches, altars and chapels, palazzi, gardens, galleries, paintings, arches, monuments, ruins and sepulchres of Rome, and cost 278 *scudi*.

52. Bod. Lib. Carte MSS 208, f. 359: "accompagné de Mr Hay dans sa chaise, et de Mr Booth dans une autre, avec 3 ou 4 valets de chambre et autres domestiques."

53. Ibid., f. 359; HMC *Stuart* IV, p. 434, Hay to Mar, 6 July 1717; BL. Add. MSS 31260, f. 79, Nairne to Gualterio, 9 July 1717.

3 The Palazzo ducale

1. SNA. GD 45/26/74, "Journall by Doctor John Blair from Pesaro to Rome, June 1717". When David Nairne arrived at Urbino in July 1717 he took this route and had a very bad fall: "my coach overturned during the last stage through the mountains, and I can still feel the bruise on my head" ["ma chaise ayant versée dans ces montagnes de la derniere poste, je me sens encore de la contusion que j'ay eu a la teste"] (BL. Add. MSS 20298, f. 6, Nairne to Gualterio, 15 July 1717). When he left Urbino for the last time he deliberately went the other way: "The post horses are come...from Fossombrone, which way I am advised to take, the other, straight to Acqualagna, being too dangerous with a French chair. I remember what happened to me coming that way and 'burnt bairns fire dread' " (HMC *Stuart* VII, p. 428, Nairne to Mar, 23 October 1718).

2. Ibid., "Journal from Urbino to Venice by Fossombrone, Ravenna etc, begun the 12th February by Doctor Blair in Company with the Earle of Panmure".

3. Ibid., "Journall by Doctor John Blair from Pesaro to Rome, June 1717".

4. HMC *Stuart* IV, p. 464, Hay to Mar, 23 July 1717. Dr Blair noted that "you easily see by the situation that one cannot easily walk the streets" (see notes 1 and 3).

5. HMC *Stuart* V, p. 368, Mar to Erskine, 4 January 1718. Dr Blair made a similar point in his diary (see notes 1 and 3):

> On the top of one of the hills is the palais.... On top of ye other hill is a convent of Carmes with a small garden whence you have a full view of the country about, none of the most agreeable for excepting one small visto you have of the Adriatique towards Catholica all the rest for twentie miles at least round is nothing but a heap of hills confusedly cast

together without any vale intervening. The most of these are bare and uglie the rest here and there covered with spots of corn, barren planting, and some vines. From this garden you also see towards the west two forts nigh the one to the other built by the late Dukes of Urbin and Toscany to distinguish their Marches and prevent incroachments. Towards the north you see a sharp poynted hill, round which lyes the town and territories of the famous republick of St Marino.

6. HMC *Stuart*, p. 239, Mar to Dillon, 26 November 1717.
7. Ibid., p. 313, Mar to Innes, 24 December 1717.
8. HMC *Stuart* VII, p. 35, Mar to Marischal, 14 July 1718. Dr Blair had a different opinion (see notes 1 and 3): "This place is off all roads and only fitt to stay in during the hott season and then I must say it is very agreeable for all the day you have cool brises and the nights are often tymes prettie sharp even in the midst of summer."
9. HMC *Stuart* VII, p. 99, Mar to Clermont, 29 July 1718.
10. HMC *Stuart* V, p. 463, Mar to Dillon, 12 February 1718.
11. HMC *Stuart* VII, p. 123, James III to Cardinal Albani, 8 August 1718.
12. HMC *Stuart* VI, p. 149, James III to the Duke of Lorraine, 15 March 1718: "nous avons un printemps charmant, qui a succedé aux neiges."
13. Ibid., p. 243, James III to Marischal, 1 April 1718.
14. Ibid., p. 265, James III to Mar, 7 April 1718.
15. Ibid., p. 301, James III to Mar, 12 April 1718.
16. Ibid., p. 306, Mar to James III, 13 April 1718.
17. HMC *Stuart* VII, p. 316, Mar to T.Oglethorpe, 22 September 1718.
18. See note 4.
19. See note 6.
20. See note 5.
21. Unless otherwise shown, all the information about the building is taken from *Il Palazzo di Federico da Montefeltro: restauri e ricerche*, a cura di Maria Luisa Polichetti (Urbino, QuattroVenti, 1985).
22. Biblioteca Universitario d'Urbino, Fondo del Comune Rep III/101/p. 397, "La venuta in Urbino di Giacomo III Stuardi Re della Gran Brettagna, sua permanenza, e partenza.... Malamente il tutto descritto da me Gio. Fortuniano Gueroli Pucci, bèn si la pura verità narrata, e senza alcuna alterazione descritta", 11 July 1717 [hereafter Pucci: I have also consulted three slightly different copies of this narrative, all of them in the Biblioteca Universitario d'Urbino, Fondo del Comune. The references are b.167, f. XI, p. 270 (a copy made in the 1760s), p. 285 (a copy made in 1764), and Rep III/86/no. 5 (a copy made in the nineteenth century)]; ASR. Cam I: RMC 1065, f. 623; ASR. Cam I: GT 428, f. 13, particularly "nota de lavori fatti di Pitura sul Palazzo App.lo per ordine dell.Ill.mo Sig. Marchese Bufalini", 6 June 1717; ASV. Albani 166, p. 66, "Inventario de Parati venuti dà Roma posti nel Palazzo Ap.lico d'Urbino, e che rimangono alla custodia del S.r Fran.co Soanti Guardarobba", undated.
23. HMC *Stuart* IV, p. 437, Salviati to Ellis, 8 July 1717; Pucci, 11 July 1717; ASR. Cam I: RMC 1065, f. 604 and f. 384, payments for the Corsican guards from Pesaro, 9 July 1717 and 11 December 1717; ASR. Cam I: GT 428, f. 13, "Volume formato da documentazione diversa . . . relativa all spese sostenute . . . per

l'arriva e permanenza di Giacomo III d'Inghilterra in Urbino", including "spese per la guardia svizzera". The Corsican guards were commanded by Magior Giacomo Francesco Garrone (ASR. Cam I: RMC 1065, f. 679).

24. Biblioteca Universitario d'Urbino, Fondo del Comune, Rep III/101/p. 402, "Catalogo de' Monsig.ri Governatori, e Vice Legati dello Stato d'Urbino". Anguissola was Vice-Legate from 1713 to 1731.
25. The rooms on the ground floor are all listed and discussed in *Palazzo di Federico da Montefeltro*, pp. 240–45.
26. ASV. Albani 166, p. 66 lists the items sent to Urbino for James III, and shows how they would have been distributed in the various rooms of the *appartamento nobile* if he had lodged there as expected.
27. Biblioteca Universitario d'Urbino, Fondo del Comune, Rep III/101, p. 400, "Catalogo degli Eminent.sme Legati, e Presidenti della Legazione di Urbino". Only a Cardinal could be a Legate, so Salviati was given the lesser title of *Presidente*. Cardinal Davia remained the Legate for the rest of the Romagna.
28. HMC *Stuart* VI, p. 358, James III to Mar, 24 April 1718: "I am drove out of my little room now with the sun."
29. *Urbino: Artistic Guide*, ed. Gabriele Cavalera e Giuseppe Cucco (Urbino, Edizioni d'Alfiere, 2001), p. 43: "This small room takes its name from the fact that James III Stuart once resided in this room as a guest of Clement XI."
30. The apartment of the King can be deduced from various references scattered through the Stuart Papers and the papal archives, particularly ASV. Albani 166, p. 66 and ASR. Cam I: GT 428, f. 13. No awareness at all is shown in *Palazzo di Federico da Montefeltro* that James III used these rooms as his apartment. It merely states that "according to tradition King James III of England was lodged in the small room, known as the golden chamber, for several years from 1717, when he was exiled and took refuge in Italy" ["la tradizione ricorda che nella stanza...nominata 'camerino indorato'...fu alloggiato il Re Giacomo III Stuart dal 1717 per alcuni anni [*sic*], quando si refugiò in Italia perché esiliato"] (p. 245).
31. HMC *Stuart* IV, p. 504, Hay to Mar, 8 August 1717.
32. BL. Add. MSS 31261, f. 80, Nairne to Gualterio, 27 April 1718.
33. HMC *Stuart* V, p. 239, Mar to Dillon, 26 November 1717: "the King goes a promenading for about half a mile or so, but it is on the tops or ridges of hills from one to another, in which I see very little pleasure, and that walking about the large rooms and galleries of the house to me is a much more agreeable exercise".
34. *Palazzo di Federico da Montefeltro*, pp. 246–47: "Accademia degli Assorditi, un'istituzione...che si riuniva per leggere componimenti poetici scritti dai medesimi accademici".
35. BL. Add. MSS 31261, f. 101, Nairne to Gualterio, 27 April 1718.
36. *Palazzo di Federico da Montefeltro*, pp. 247–48.
37. This was Robert Freebairne, who arrived at the end of 1717. When he went to France in March 1718 he left all his belongings with his landlord, and he had to ask for them to be collected and sent on to Rome at the end of the year (HMC *Stuart* VII, p. 534, Freebairne to J. Barclay, 12 November 1718; Ibid., p. 697, Freebairne to Signor Claudio, [12] November 1718).
38. *Palazzo di Federico da Montefeltro*, pp. 237–40.

39. SNA. GD 45/26/74, "Journall by Doctor John Blair from Pesaro to Rome, June 1717".
40. ASR. Cam I: GT 428, f. 13, "Volume formato da documentazione diversa... relativa all spese sostenute... per l'arriva e permanenza di Giacomo III d'Inghilterra in Urbino",
41. ASV. Albani 166, p. 66, "Inventario de Parati venuti dà Roma posti nel Palazzo Ap.lico d'Urbino, e che rimangono alla custodia del S.r Fran.co Soanti Guardarobba", undated. On the second floor, the apartment above that of S. Domenico was given Borghese tapestries, while the one above Salviati's had Barberini and Pamphili tapestries.

4   The Jacobite courtiers

1. See Appendix II for a list of the king's household at Urbino. The list is compiled from many sources, notably RA. SP Box 3/1/90, "A List of the Kings Servants who have been lodged, or have had lodging monie, since His Ma.tie parted from St Germans", undated but probably January 1719.
2. The detailed payments until the end of 1718 are in ASR. Cam I: RMC 1064, f. 428, and RMC 1066, f. 7, f. 54, f. 93, f. 133, f. 166; and ASR. Cam I: GT 430, f. 16, no. 6; and GT 438, f. 6, no. 1–5. At the end of 1717 the Pope placed the Stuart pension on a guaranteed footing by arranging for it to be paid out of the income from the papal institution for lending money to the poor ["li frutti de Luoghi di Monti Camerale"], rather than as a series of one-off payments (ASV. SS: Ingh 21, p. 245, *chirografo* of Clement XI, 30 October 1717; ASR. Cam I: RMC 1064, f. 469; RMC 1066, f. 46).
3. Corp, *A Court in Exile*, p. 306; RA. SP Box 3/1/89, a list of salaries and pensions, July 1717; RA. SP Misc 34, "Salaries of such of His Ma.ties servants as are paid by Establishm.t", November 1722.
4. As against this it should be pointed out that the servants were now paid in Bologna *livres*, not French *livres*. In 1718, 624 Bologna *livres* were worth 520 French *livres* (HMC *Stuart* V, p. 616, Ellis to James III, 26 January 1718).
5. The lists of pensions (in chronological order) are in RA. SP 40/149 (1717), Box 3/1/83 (1718), 281/165 (1718), and 40/150 (1718). See Appendix III for a comparison between the salaries and pensions paid at Urbino.
6. Respectively James Rodez, Thomas Saint-Paul, Gerald Fitzgerald, Felix Bonbled, Jean Legrand and Catherine Macane.
7. Dr Wood left in October and died at Joinville in November or early December 1717. Dr Maghie arrived in February 1718.
8. Perth is described in the papal archives as *Maestro di Camera* (ASV. Albani 168, p. 134, "Corte Nobile di Sua Maestà Britannica in Urbino", 1718). Pucci described him as *Maggiordomo Maggiore* (Biblioteca Universitario d'Urbino, Fondo del Comune, Rep III/86, no. 5, "Nota de Cavalieri Inglesi che furono col Rè della Gran Bretagna Giacomo III in Urbino nell'Anno 1718"). It should be added that, after the the departure of the king, Perth's father (the 1st Duke) had been Lord Chamberlain to Queen Mary at Saint-Germain from 1714 until his death in 1716, when Perth himself had been appointed the queen's Master of the Horse (Corp, *A Court in Exile*, pp. 364–65). It is therefore

possible that Perth was not appointed Lord Chamberlain at Urbino until after news arrived that the queen had died at Saint-Germain in May 1718.

9. At Saint-Germain there had been nine sub-departments: the Kitchen and Pastry, the Confectionary, the Bakehouse, the Cellars, the Chaundry and Buttery, the Ewry and Pantry, the Woodyard, the Larder, and the Silver Scullery.

10. Archivio Storico Vicariato di Roma: Santi Dodici Apostoli, vol. 57, p. 36, Stati d'Anime, 1720.

11. Respectively Richard Bains, Matthew Creagh, Théophile Lesserteur, James Miner, Richard Conway, Marco Cartolari, Ignace Faure and Charles Russel.

12. Respectively Pierre Pecquer, Antonio Seiro and Jean Bouzier.

13. Respectively Francesco Girelli and Magdalen Rebout.

14. The coachman was Edmund Butler, the chairmen were Henry Kerby and Antoine Brun, the Riding Purveyor was John Sheridan, and the Harbourer of the Deer was Peter Jolly de Falvie. For the names of the footmen, grooms and helpers, see Appendix II.

15. His wife Elizabeth, born in 1691, was the daughter of Matthew and Frances Smith, whose son John had been born at the same time as James III in 1688.

16. This needs to be qualified. Nairne informed Gualterio in August 1718 that he used the abbé Buglioni (who was Salviati's secretary) to copy his unimportant letters, but assured him that he wrote and copied all secret correspondence himself (BL. Add. MSS 20298, f. 52, Nairne to Gualterio, 11 August 1718).

17. HMC *Stuart* IV, p. 519, Dillon to Mar, 14 August 1717.

18. See the list in Appendix IV.

19. HMC *Stuart* VII, p. 231, Mar to Gordon, 1 September 1718; Ibid., p. 499, Dicconson to Gordon, October 1718; Ibid., p. 629, Mar to Gordon, 13 December 1718.

20. Colonel William Clephane, Major John Cockburne, Captain Collier, James Edgar, Charles Fleming, Viscount Kilsyth, Viscount Kingston, the Earl of Linlithgow, George Menzies, the Earl of Nithsdale, Sir John Preston, Robert Watson and the Earl of Winton. Further information about these and the other Scottish Jacobites at Urbino can be found in D. Szechi, *1715: The Great Jacobite Rebellion* (Yale University Press, 2006).

21. William Erskine, John Graeme, John Carnegy of Boysick, Marjory Hay and George Mackenzie.

22. William Drummond, John Fotheringham of Powrie, Robert Freebairne, James Hay and the Earl of Panmure.

23. H.C. Stewart, "The Exiled Stewarts [*sic*] in Italy, 1717–1807", *The Scottish Historical Society Miscellany VII*, Third Series, vol. 35 (Edinburgh, 1941), p. 87.

24. Biblioteca Universitario d'Urbino, Fondo del Comune, Rep III/86, no. 5, "Nota de Cavalieri Inglesi che furono col Rè della Gran Bretagna Giacomo III in Urbino nell'Anno 1718".

25. The names in this document are all incorrectly spelt. For example, Panmure appears as "Delmur", Nithsdale as "Nisdel", Winton as "Witton", Southesk as "Sothesch" and Nairne as "Nerni". Derwentwater appears as "Dewentuer".

26. Ibid., HMC *Stuart* V, p. 287, commission dated 16 December 1717.

27. HMC *Stuart* IV, p. 504, Hay to Mar, 8 August 1717; HMC *Stuart* VI, p. 242, Forster to Mar, 1 April 1718.

28. HMC *Stuart* V, p. 140, commission dated 13 October 1717; Ibid., p. 598, Nairne to O'Brien, 19 October 1717.
29. HMC *Stuart* VI, p. 129, Mar to Dillon, 10 March 1718; Ibid., p. 360, Dillon to Mar, 24 April 1718.
30. See, for example, BL. Add. MSS 20298, f. 162, Nairne to Gualterio, undated: "Captain [*sic*] Macmahon, an Irish gentleman who is one of my friends here" ["un gentilhomme Irlandois de mes amis ici le Cap.ne [*sic*] Macmahon"].
31. Ingamells, *Dictionary*, p. 626.
32. See, for example, the lists for 1729 in RA. SP Box 3/78 and RA. SP 136/53.

5   Life at the court

1. Corp, *Court in Exile*, p. 305.
2. BL. Add. MSS 20298, f. 67, Nairne to Gualterio, August 1718: "excepté dans quelques voyages en France, et lorsque le Roy etoit a Rome, je n'ay jamais eu l'honneur d'etre du nombre de ceux qu'il fait prier quelquesfois de manger a sa table pendant qu'il y fait prier tous les jours de petits off[icie]rs et gentilhommes de sa suitte." In another letter, Nairne complained that he and Sir William Ellis both had to eat at the second of the two tables, whereas he had been invited to eat with the king "more than 30 times" ["plus de 30 fois"] in France, presumably at Avignon (BL. Add. MSS 20298, f. 35, Nairne to Gualterio, 7 July 1718).
3. Some of the more senior household servants and pensioners employed their own servants. Some of the latter *were* given board wages. Those for Mar's servants are shown in HMC *Stuart* VI, p. 179, Bernardi to Paterson, 22 March 1718; and HMC *Stuart* VII, p. 246, a bill dated 5 September 1718 for "various small payments for the Duke of Mar from 4 July, and for board wages". Those for Lord Southesk's cook are shown in HMC *Stuart* VI, p. 179, a receipt for board wages from 22 November 1717 to 22 March 1718.
4. Brotherton Library, University of Leeds, MS. Dep 1984/2/5, the inventory after death of the possessions of James II, 22 July 1703. The plate was valued at 2203 *livres*.
5. RA. SP 36/141, "a particular of what is in the five Caisses sent from St. Germains the 26th of Sep.r 1718"; HMC *Stuart* VII, p. 243, Dicconson to James III, 5 September 1718; Ibid., p. 419, Mar to Dicconson, 21 October 1718; Ibid., p. 553, Dicconson to James III, 21 November 1718. See also RA. SP 98/84, "An accompt of what was in the five cases sent from Paris on 26 September 1718 as by an Inventory sent by Mr Diconson", November 1726.
6. HMC *Stuart* V, p. 427, Dicconson's accounts, 30 December 1717. The Pantry plate was valued at 5735 *livres*, and the Scullery plate at 1485 *livres* (see note 4).
7. HMC *Stuart* IV, p. 504, Hay to Mar, 8 August 1717: "we have the finest kind of hare hunting here in the world."
8. HMC *Stuart* V, p. 425, Dicconson's accounts, 12 July 1717; HMC *Stuart* VI, p. 205, Dillon to Mar, 27 March 1718; HMC *Stuart* VII, p. 335, Murray to Hay, 29 September 1718; Ibid., p. 401, James III to Nairne, 18 October 1718.
9. HMC *Stuart* VI, p. 379, James III to Mar, 28 April 1718.
10. HMC *Stuart* V, p. 267, Mar to Marischal, 9 December 1717.

11. HMC *Stuart* VII, p. 671, Cagnoni to Mar, 26 December 1718.
12. Ibid., p. 631, R.Gordon to Mar, 13 December 1718.
13. Pucci, b.167, f. XI, p. 286^r.
14. The route is described on p. 246, and shown in diagram on p. 615, of *Palazzo di Federico da Montefeltro*. The painting by Barocci is reproduced on p. 86 of the *Urbino: Artistic Guide*.
15. HMC *Stuart* IV, p. 230, Paterson to Mar, 8 May 1717; Ibid., p. 245, Paterson to Mar, 15 May 1717.
16. Ibid., p. 392, Mar to Leslie, June 1717.
17. Ibid., p. 445, James III to Mar, 13 July 1717; Ibid., p. 463, Paterson to Barclay, 22 July 1717.
18. Ibid., p. 392, Mar to Leslie, June 1717.
19. Ibid., p. 522, Mar to James III, 15 August 1717; Ibid., p. 528, Cowper to Paterson, 23 August 1717.
20. HMC *Stuart* VII, p. 533, Barclay to Mar, 12 November 1718.
21. HMC *Stuart* V, p. 513, James III to Gaillard, 28 February 1718. There was a Quaker at Urbino, just as there had been at Saint-Germain (Corp, *Court in Exile*, pp. 154–57). This was Robert Watson, who had kept a public house on the estates of Lord Marischal, and been arrested for taking part in the Jacobite rising. Having escaped from prison at Rochester, he had crossed over to France and walked all the way to join the king at Avignon (HMC *Stuart* IV, p. 562, Watson to James III, undated but 1716). He had then walked from Avignon to Rome, and asked the Pope to give him a pass to join the court at Pesaro (Ibid., p. 567, Watson to Clement XI, April 1717). There is a letter from Watson to James III, written at Urbino on 27 July 1718, asking the king to take care of him, because Providence had ordered that his lot was to remain in a foreign country (HMC *Stuart* VII, p. 82). The king gave him a small pension, and even allowed him to remain at the court when it moved to Rome (RA. SP Misc 34, SP Box 3/81, and SP 123/21, pensions paid in Rome in 1722, 1726 and 1729).
22. HMC *Stuart* V, p. 509, Mar to Leslie, 24 February 1718.
23. BL. Add. MSS 31261, f. 8, Nairne to Gualterio, 7 January 1718.
24. BL. Add. MSS 31261, f. 25, Nairne to Gualterio, 27 January 1718. See HMC *Stuart* VI, p. 215, in which Lord Gerard was given a licence by Dr Maghie on 23 March 1718 to eat meat during Lent because of his indisposition.
25. Barclay informed Mar on 1 December 1718 that his "only way of living at Urbino was engaging in a menage with persons who had greater funds than he had" (HMC *Stuart* VII, p. 591).
26. HMC *Stuart* VII, p. 413, Edgar to Paterson, 20 October 1718. For another example, see RA. SP 27/8, Erskine to Paterson, 4 February 1718: "I need say nothing to you of our journey to Fano ... nor how well we lived ...., all our meat right roasted in the juice, and most excellent beef stakes ... – how different from my Lord Panmure's club where everything's roasted to rags." This, however, should be compared with Dr Blair's comment in Chapter 1, p. 6.
27. HMC *Stuart* VII, p. 515, Edgar to Paterson, 9 November 1718. Lord Nithsdale's and Lord Kilsyth's cooks, both from Urbino, were, respectively, Francesco Bartolomeo and Paolo Antonio de Rossi.
28. Ibid., p. 42, Mar to Ormonde, 15 July 1718.

29. HMC *Stuart* VI, p. 242, Forster to Mar, 1 April 1718, refers to coming downstairs from Booth's apartment to "the billiard room".
30. Ibid., p. 265, James III to Mar, 7 April 1718.
31. HMC *Stuart* V, p. 382, Mar to Stewart of Invernity, 11 January 1718. It was not only sports equipment that could not be obtained at Urbino. See HMC *Stuart* VI, p. 383, Paterson to Mar, 28 April 1718: "I wish you would order some of your servants to buy some paper, both for letters and warrants, a hundred or two of good quills, some good ink and two or three pounds of fine wax [in Rome]. This place affords nothing good of any kind."
32. HMC *Stuart* V, p. 413, Stewart of Invernity to Mar, 29 January 1718.
33. Lord Clermont and Lord Edward Drummond each assembled an important library at Saint-Germain. See Edward Corp, "Jacobite Books at Toulouse", *The Journal of the Edinburgh Bibliographical Society*, no. 1 (Edinburgh, 2006), pp. 71–85.
34. HMC *Stuart* V, p. 459, Stewart of Invernity to Mar, 12 February 1718; HMC *Stuart* VI, p. 162, Mar to Stewart of Invernity, 17 March 1718. See also T. Friedman, "A 'Palace Worthy of the Grandeur of the King': Lord Mar's designs for the Old Pretender, 1718–30", *Architectural History*, 29 (1986), pp. 102–33.
35. HMC *Stuart* V, p. 382, Mar to Stewart of Invernity, 11 January 1718.
36. Ibid., p. 487, Mar to Panmure, 17 February 1718.
37. Ingamells, *Dictionary*, p. 63.
38. BL. Add. MSS 31260, f. 159, Nairne to Gualterio, 20 September 1717.
39. Ingamells, *Dictionary*, pp. 761–62.
40. HMC *Stuart* IV, p. 528, Innes to Mar, 22 August 1717.
41. Ibid., p. 542, Sheldon to O'Brien, 29 August 1717; Ibid., p. 547, James III to Origo, 29 August 1717; HMC *Stuart* V, p. 573, "Remarks" by O'Brien, 4 September 1717.
42. M. Ascari, "James III in Bologna: An Illustrated Story", *Royal Stuart Papers* LIX (London, 2001), p. 4.
43. HMC *Stuart* V, p. 577, Peterborough to Sheldon, 11 September 1717.
44. Ibid., p. 584, Sheldon to O'Brien, 27 September 1717; Ibid., p. 93, James III to Origo, 1 October 1717.
45. Ibid., p. 586, account by Sheldon, 5 October 1717; Ibid., p. 136, James III to Origo, 12 October 1717; Ibid., p. 146, Sheldon to O'Brien, 19 October 1717; Ibid., p. 147, James III to Origo, 19 October 1717; Ibid., p. 168, James III to Origo, 28 October 1717.
46. Ascari, "James III in Bologna", p. 6.
47. HMC *Stuart* V, p. 206, Sheldon to Peterborough, 14 November 1717; Ibid., p. 212, Mar to James III, 17 November 1717.
48. For the papal archives concerning this incident, see ASV. Albani 166, ff. 79–127.
49. HMC *Stuart* V, p. 235, Mar to Cockburne, 25 November 1717.
50. Ibid., p. 253, Cockburne to Mar, 4 December 1717. He left Venice for Paris on 1 January (Ibid., p. 353, O'Brien to Paterson, 2 January 1718).
51. Ibid., p. 598, Nairne to O'Brien, 19 October 1717.
52. Francis Strickland had already left Urbino to return to Saint-Germain (Ibid., p. 94, Dillon to James III, 2 October 1717; Ibid., p. 598, Nairne to O'Brien, 19 October 1717).

53. HMC *Stuart* VI, p. 221, James III to Gualterio, 29 March 1718.
54. Copies of the spy's letters to Baylis and to Craggs, undated but December 1718, are among the Stuart Papers, and reproduced in HMC *Stuart* VII, pp. 697–98 (where they are dated November 1718).
55. HMC *Stuart* V, p. 271, Mar to Dillon, 11 December 1717; HMC *Stuart* VI, p. 162, Mar to Stewart of Invernity, 17 March 1718.
56. He was at Urbino in February (John Ingamells, *A Dictionary of British and Irish Travellers in Italy, 1701–1800* (Yale University Press, 1997), p. 721).
57. He came to Urbino with Francis Panton in March (BL. Add. MSS 31261, f. 76, Nairne to Gualterio, 20 March 1718), and again in October 1718 (HMC *Stuart* VII, p. 384, Nairne to Mar, 13 October 1718; Ibid., p. 385, Edgar to Paterson, 14 October 1718). Lord Gerard was at Urbino in March (see note 24).
58. HMC *Stuart* VI, p. 363, James III to Gozzadini, 24 April 1718.
59. Dr Blair noted that

> without the town of Urbino on the one side theres a small convent of Capucins with a little handsome garden. In the church belonging to this convent is a good picture of St Francis and his companion much valued done by Baroci [*sic*]. And on the other side a Convent of Recolets calld here Zocolante where theres also a prettie walk. These two and the Carmes are the only walks to be had about this place.
>
> (SNA. GD 45/26/74, "Journall of Doctor John Blair from Pesaro to Rome, June 1717")

60. Corp, *A Court in Exile*, pp. 245–46.
61. *Urbino: Artistic Guide*, p. 112.
62. Pucci, b.167, f. XI, p. 288ʳ.
63. Anna Fucili Bartolucci, "Urbino e gli Albani", pp. 441–48, in *Arte e Cultura nella Provincia di Pesaro e Urbino dalle Origini a Oggi*, a cura di Franco Battistelli (Venice, Marsilio Editori, 1986), p. 446.
64. The image was reproduced by David in *The Baptism of Charles, Prince of Wales, 31 December 1720* (1725), now in the Scottish National Portrait Gallery. The portrait of James III was not copied by David himself. It is actually based on the engraving by Gabriel Mathieu, a reversed image of the portrait by David which shows the Garter sash falling in the wrong direction. The local artist who copied the engraving has changed the Garter sash to show it falling correctly, from the left shoulder to the right hip. For the engraving, see Richard Sharp, *The Engraved Record of the Jacobite Movement* (Aldershot, 1996), p. 100, no. 156. The Pope's two copies of the engraving are in ASV. Albani 166, f. 53 and f. 54.
65. For the origins of Francesco Girelli and his wife (née Franchetti), see Archivio Storico di Roma: Santi Dodici Apostoli, vol. 65, p. 74 and p. 120, Stati d'Anime, 1735 and 1736.
66. All the male servants were bachelors except those mentioned in notes 67 and 68. The lists are based on the parish registers of Saint-Germain-en-Laye (Hôtel de Ville de Saint-Germain-en-Laye) and Santo Dodici Apostoli in Rome (Archivio Storico Vicariato di Roma).
67. The widowers included David Nairne, Jeremiah Broomer, Edmund Butler, Peter Jolly de Falvie and Roger Ryan.

68. The servants who had come to Urbino without their wives included Lord Edward Drummond, Charles Booth, Gerald Firzgerald, Dr Lawrence Wood, Charles Macarty, Richard Baines, Matthew Creagh, Théophile Lesserteur, James Delattre, John Sheridan, Henry Kerby, Antoine Brun, Andrew Simms, Jacques Catillon, Patrick Maguirk, Nicholas Clark, Frank Ridge and Mark Manning.
69. HMC *Stuart* VI, p. 151, James III to Lady Nithsdale, 16 March 1718.
70. BL. Add. MSS 20298, f. 52, Nairne to Gualterio, 11 August 1718: "un malheureux debauché." Mar's valet was an Italian named Lorenzo Bernardi, who had been born at Bologna,

> whence… he went with his parents to Leghorn, when he was very young and thence, being about 12, went with a Scots merchant to Scotland, where he continued several years and turned Protestant. He came back to Italy and was given up by his parents to the Inquisition, from which he got free by not contradicting them, … saying he was still Roman Catholic, but… he took an opportunity of going into Turkey with a merchant, and went thence to Holland and thence came to France with one of the Czar's people and returned with him to Holland, where he was recommended to [Mar] for his speaking English, Italian and French.

In the summer of 1718 the fact that he was "an apostate" was reported to the Archbishop of Urbino, who passed on the information to the Inquisition because "he [Bernardi] was the Pope's subject" (HMC *Stuart* VII, p. 143, Mar to West, 12 August 1718). Mar persuaded the king to send a long letter to Cardinal Gualterio, asking him to defend him (BL. Add. MSS 31255, f. 127, James III to Gualterio, 31 July 1718), which prompted Nairne to comment secretly how much he disapproved of a man who merited so little being so strongly supported: "it is the sort of thing which really pains me" ["ce sont de ces sortes de choses là qui me font une vray douleur"] (BL. Add. MSS 20298, f. 41, Nairne to Gualterio, 4 August 1718). Gualterio replied that under the circumstances it was completely out of the question for him to defend the valet against the Inquisition, and advised the king to dismiss Bernardi and drop the matter (BL. Add. MSS 31261, f. 193, Nairne to Gualterio, 11 August 1718). The king agreed, particularly as Bernardi "seemed no wise inclined to return into the Church" (HMC *Stuart* VII, p. 124, James III to Gualterio, 8 August 1718), and Nairne thanked Gualterio for his reply, commenting that the king should never have become involved in a question of this sort (BL. Add. MSS 20298, f. 52, Nairne to Gualterio, 11 August 1718).

71. BL. Add. MSS 20298, f. 52, Nairne to Gualterio, 11 August 1718: "Il y d'autres gens ici, gentilhommes même de la suitte du Roy, dont la conduitte donne un peu de scandale."
72. BL. Add. MSS 20298, f. 92, Nairne to Gualterio, 9 October 1718: "quelques jeunes gens de notre cour."
73. BL. Add. MSS 31261, f. 249, Nairne to Gualterio, 13 October 1718.
74. HMC *Stuart* VII, p. 73, Mar to Ormonde, 22 July 1718.
75. Ibid., p. 277, W.Drummond to Mar, 14 December 1718.

76. HMC *Stuart* V, p. 488, Mar to Panmure, 17 February 1718: Perth "went to Fano some days ago, gallanting some ladies". The ladies were his own wife, and his cousin the Duchess of St Andrews, who was leaving with her husband for France.

77. HMC *Stuart* VI, p. 235, Hay to Mar, 31 March 1718:

> He [Perth] walked above two hours on the ramparts with my lady, where…there was a great many tears shed on both sides, and…he has both given himself the trouble to take leave in all its forms…. I fancy his good nature may engage him to endeavour to please his companion as well as himself, and you know how difficult it is to satisfy a large voracious stomach.

78. Ibid., p. 399, Gordon to Mar, 3 May 1718; HMC *Stuart* VII, p. 43, Mar to Ormonde, 15 July 1718.

79. BL. Add. MSS 20298, f. 47, Nairne to Gualterio, 7 August 1718.

80. BL. Add. MSS 31261, f. 244, Nairne to Gualterio, 6 October 1718; HMC *Stuart* VII, p. 365, Nairne to Mar, 8 October 1718. The arrival of Lady Nithsdale meant that her husband was obliged to move into a larger apartment in the Palazzo Ducale. See Ibid., p. 414, Edgar to Paterson, 20 October 1718: Lord Southesk "has changed his lodgings to where Lord Nithsdale was."

81. Ibid., p. 320, Duchess of Mar to Mar, 23 September 1718.

82. BL. Add. MSS 31261, f. 281, Nairne to Gualterio, 22 November 1718.

83. BL. Add. MSS 20298, f. 47, Nairne to Gualterio, 7 August 1718.

84. BL. Add. MSS 20298, f. 67, Nairne to Gualterio, August 1718.

85. HMC *Stuart* VII, p. 419, Mar to Dicconson, 21 October 1718. She was looked after when she arrived and was given a permanent post at the court. It was also noted that John Graeme was now at Urbino with his "mistress" (HMC *Stuart*, p. 384, Nairne to Paterson, 13 October 1718).

86. Ibid., p. 484, James III to Dicconson, 2 November 1718.

6 Friction and frustration

1. Biblioteca Universitario d'Urbino, Fondo del Comune, Rep III/86, no. 5, "Nota de Cavalieri Inglesi che furono col Rè della Gran Bretagna Giacomo III in Urbino nell'Anno 1718".

2. Marquis de Ruvigny and Raineval, *The Jacobite Peerage* (Edinburgh, 1904), p. 240; HMC *Stuart* VII, p. 435, Booth to Mar, 24 October 1718.

3. RA. SP Box 3/1/89, a list of salaries and pensions, July 1717.

4. Hay's salary was increased from 117 *livres per annum* to 204 *livres per annum*.

5. HMC *Stuart* IV, p. 445, James III to Mar, 13 July 1717, with postscript of 16 July.

6. Ibid., p. 464, Hay to Mar, 23 July 1717. Hay's warrant to be a groom is actually dated February 1718 (HMC *Stuart* V, p. 526).

7. BL. Add. MSS 38851, f. 109, James III to Dillon, 30 July 1717. Although it seems that Booth would have kept his salary (the salary of an Equerry was only 117 *livres p.a.*, whereas that of a Groom of the Bedchamber was 204 *livres p.a.*), he would have experienced a significant loss of status.

8. Ibid.
9. HMC *Stuart* IV, p. 504, Hay to Mar, 8 August 1717.
10. BL. Add. MSS 38851, f. 109, James III to Dillon, 30 July 1717. This was obviously a reference to Lord Edward Drummond, Dominic Sheldon (Dillon's brother-in-law) and Roger Strickland.
11. BL. Add. MSS 31260, f. 178 and f. 180, Nairne to Gualterio, 7 and 10 October 1717.
12. BL. Add. MSS 31260, f. 222, Nairne to Gualterio, 23 November 1717; BL. Add. MSS 31261, f. 60, Nairne to Gualterio, 10 March 1718.
13. HMC *Stuart* V, p. 360, Mar to Straiton, 3 January 1718.
14. Ibid., p. 373, James III to Dillon, 7 January 1718.
15. Ibid., p. 442, Mar to Ogilvie, 5 February 1718.
16. Ibid., p. 513, James III to Gaillard, 28 February 1718: "j'ay trouvé une probité inconnüe parmi la plupart de nos St. Germanois."
17. HMC *Stuart* VI, p. 102, James III to Ormonde, 7 March 1718.
18. Ibid., p. 175, James III to Sheldon, 20 March 1718.
19. Ibid., p. 242, Forster to Mar, 1 April 1718.
20. Ibid., p. 311, Paterson to Mar, 14 April 1718.
21. Ibid., p. 301, James III to Mar, 12 April 1718.
22. When Middleton heard what had happened he wrote to James III that "if six and thirty years service to three Kings may merit anything, I make it all over to the old woman [Lady Middleton] and her children.... Your Majesty has promised them your favour and protection. I depend on it" (Ibid., p. 463, Middleton to James III, 23 May 1718).
23. Ibid., p. 379, James III to Mar, 28 April 1718. Shortly afterwards the king made the following comment about the open hostility between Hay and Clermont: "John [Hay] ... is in a very good way and walks about ... as narrow as a knife. Clermont is in steel, so you see how the troublesome planets reign here."
24. Ibid., p. 174, James III to Ormonde, 20 March 1718; SCA. BL 2/222/11, Nairne to T.Innes, 5 May 1718. After his return to Saint-Germain, Booth was reported to have stated that "nobody [was] taken notice of with [Mar] except the Scots" (HMC *Stuart* VII, A.Graeme to Mar, 27 August 1718).
25. HMC *Stuart* VII, p. 361, warrant in the handwriting of James III, 5 October 1718.
26. His assistant was Joseph, son of John Martinash.
27. At the end of June 1718, when he had just received his papal pension for April, May and June, the king had 174,570 Bologna *livres*. He spent 18,684 during July, and a further 18,594 during August, so that he had 137,291 Bologna *livres* by the beginning of September. Ellis' accounts at Urbino can be studied in HMC *Stuart* V, pp. 563 (31 July 1717), 570 (11 August 1717), 573 (7 September 1717), 582 (14 September 1717), 584 (27 September 1717), 586 (5 October 1717), 600 (31 October 1717), 602 (5 November 1717), 616 (26 January 1718); and HMC *Stuart* VII, pp. 54 (=RA. SP 33/113, 17 July 1718), 131 (10 August 1718), 268 (10 September 1718), 387 (14 October 1718), 589 (=RA. SP 39/64, November 1718).
28. HMC *Stuart* VII, p. 201, Mar to Dicconson, 25 August 1718.
29. SCA. BL 2/217/2, Nairne to T.Innes, 6 November 1717.

30. HMC *10th Report* (London, 1885), p. 170, Mar to Gordon, undated but 1717 (before November); HMC *Stuart* IV, p. 448, Paterson to Mar, 13 July 1717. When Mar was in Rome he needed Stewart of Invernity and Erskine to interpret for him in French, so that he could conduct the king's business (HMC *Stuart* VI, p. 221 and p. 223, James III to Gualterio and Imperiali, 29 March 1718; Ibid., p. 262, Mar to James III, 6 April 1718).

31. David asked to be given this warrant in February, and Nairne replied that "since His Majesty sees no problem with it, I found he was quite happy to grant him this favour" ["comme S.M. n'y voit point d'inconvenient, je l'ay trouvé assés disposé a luy accorder cette grace"] (BL. Add. MSS 31261, f. 37, Nairne to Gualterio, 13 February 1718. Also BL. Add. MSS 31261, f. 44, Nairne to Gualterio, 20 February 1718).

32. HMC *Stuart* VII, p. 1, Mar to Dillon, 1 July 1718.

33. BL. Add. MSS 31261, f. 64, Nairne to Gualterio, 13 March 1718: "qu'il peut conter sur la patente puisque S.M. l'a promis."

34. BL. Add. MSS. 31261, f. 78, Nairne to Gualterio, 24 March 1718: "Milord Duc de Mar a été si occupé d'autres affaires plus importantes depuis quelques tems qu'il n'a pû y songer plutôt."

35. BL. Add. MSS 31261, f. 80, Nairne to Gualterio, 27 March 1718: "sans me mesler d'en fournir un modele dans un bureau de Secretaire d'Etat protestant, ou je n'ay ni n'aurai s'il plait a Dieu jamais aucune inspection (mais ceci est dit seulement en confiance a V[otre] E[xcellence]". When he received his warrant, David wrote to Nairne (whom he addressed as "Vossignoria Illustrissima"), and said that he hoped he might one day use his pencil to depict the king no longer away from his palace, but in London itself, having triumphed over his enemies (RA. SP 29/130, David to Nairne, 9 April 1718).

36. SCA. BL 2/222/12, Nairne to T.Innes, 11 May 1718, with postscript of 12 May.

37. Corp, *A Court in Exile*, p. 326.

38. SCA. BL 2/222/11, Nairne to T.Innes, 5 May 1718.

39. BL. Add. MSS 20298, f. 33, Nairne to Gualterio, 1 July 1718. After this date Nairne's secret letters are in BL. Add. MSS 20298, his official letters in BL. Add. MSS 31261.

40. BL. Add. MSS 20298, f. 35, Nairne to Gualterio, 7 July 1718:

> A l'egard de Milord Mar nous vivons a cette heure assés bien ensemble, il a vû que le Roy m'a fait l'honneur de me venir voir plusieurs fois pendant mon indisposition, il y est venu aussi et s'etant apperçu aussi bien que le Roy que je ne pretendois point recevoir des ordres de luy, quand nous traittons d'affaire ensemble il agit a cette heure avec moy avec plus de civilité, ainsi j'ay conservé mon independence, et je ne crois a l'heure qu'il est que ni luy ni le Roy me meprise au point de me mettre sur le pied de commis.

41. Biblioteca Universitario d'Urbino, Fondo del Comune, Rep III/86, no. 5, "Nota de Cavalieri Inglesi che furono col Rè della Gran Bretagna Giacomo III in Urbino nell'Anno 1718."

42. HMC *Stuart* VI, p. 268, Oxford to Mar, 27 March 1718; Ibid., p. 345, J.Menzies to Mar, 10 April 1718.

43. BL. Add. MSS 20298, f. 41, Nairne to Gualterio, 30 July or 4 August 1718:

> Le Roy continue toujours d'agir avec moy avec...confiance de bonté et d'egards..., mais il a encore une confiance plus intime de coeur et d'inclination et d'un autre coté qui absorbe tout. Monsr. Mâtre [i.e. Mar] est l'oracle et Mr Hays [*sic*] qui est un jeune homme d'un merite et d'une capacité assés mediocre a tout pouvoir dans sa maison, et il n'a rien de caché pour luy. Milord Clermont et le pauvre Mr Booth ont été ecarté pour faire place a luy qui certainement n'a ni l'experience ni l'esprit solide de l'un ni l'autre, mais ce n'est pas toujours le vray merite qui est le regle des inclinations.... Mr Murray qui a veritablement de la capacité et du genie pour les affaires mais qui est encore jeune, et qui se croit beaucoup plus capable qu'il n'est et se donne de grandes airs de Ministre, a aussi toute la confiance tout comme beau frere de Mons.r Hays, que comme un homme entierement devoué a Milord Mar. Voila ce que je vois;" "je me tiens retiré et ne vais chez le Roy que quand il m'appelle, et ne me merle que de ce qui regarde mon employ.... Il est vray que dans des affaires importantes il ne paroit pas avoir du secret pour moy, et qu'il a la bonté de demander souvent mon sentiment, et quand Mil.d Mar...s'ouvre avec moy, nous nous entretenons ensemble avec toute sorte d'aisance mais j'evite de paroitre curieux de son confiance.... sa propre inclination...n'est pas certainem.t du coté ni des catholiques ni des vieux domestiques don't il a une bonne partie ecartée, et je ne scais pas comment je n'ay pas deja eu le sort des autres. Mais je conte que mon tour viendra.... beaucoup de choses...me font de la peine non par rapport a moy mais par rapport au bien du service.... Je ne m'ouvre qu'a V[otre] E[xcellence].... J'espere qu'Elle aura la bonté de bruler cette lettre.

44. BL. Add. MSS 20298, f. 47, Nairne to Gualterio, 7 August 1718:

> il me croit asses philosophe pour etre insensible a tout ce qui me regarde.... Il distribue tous les jours quelques faveurs a d'autres et il me les confie, mais c'est toute la part qu'il m'y donne, et je ne dis rien, mais je n'en pense pas moins. Au reste je verrai recompenser tout le monde et passer devant moy tous les plus nouveaux venus.

45. BL. Add. MSS 20298, f. 78, Nairne to Gualterio, September 1718: "le favori", "sa femme", "le beau frere".

46. BL. Add. MSS 31261, f. 258, Nairne to Gualterio, 20 October 1718: "je prens le part du *silence respectueux.*"

47. BL. Add. MSS 31255, f. 169, James III to Gualterio, 4 October 1718: "un vieux et fidele domestique"; "un peu ombrageux."

48. BL. Add. MSS 20298, f. 88, Nairne to Gualterio, 2 October 1718: "tous les honneurs imaginables."

49. HMC *Stuart* VII, p. 389, Mar to H.Paterson, 15 October 1718.

50. Ingamells, *Dictionary*, p. 879.

51. HMC *Stuart* V, p. 453, Southesk to Paterson, 10 February 1718.

52. HMC *Stuart* V, p. 204, Southesk to Paterson, 13 November 1717. Nairne described himself as a "little man". See BL. Add. MSS 31259, f. 124, Nairne to Gualterio, 26 August 1717: "The Earl of Douglas is a little man of about my height" ["Le Comte de Douglas est un petit homme un peu de ma hauteur"]. Despite this hostility, Southesk was willing to "club" with Lord Edward Drummond when he visited Rome a few months later (HMC *Stuart* V, p. 436, Redmond to Paterson, 5 February 1718).
53. Ibid., p. 453, Southesk to Paterson, 10 February 1718.
54. HMC *Stuart* VI, p. 162, Mar to Stewart of Invernity, 17 March 1718.
55. HMC *Stuart* VII, p. 385, Edgar to Paterson, 14 October 1718; Ibid., p. 400, James III to Nairne, 18 October 1718; Ibid., p. 414, Edgar to Paterson, 20 October 1718.
56. HMC *Stuart* VI, p. 151, James III to Lady Nithsdale, 16 March 1718.
57. Ibid., p. 521, Panmure to James III, 13 June 1718.
58. HMC *Stuart* V, p. 464, Mar to Dillon, 12 February 1718:

    Lord Panmure left us to-day for Venice, whence he goes to Paris.... I cannot say he is in a very good humour, being desirous to be informed of everything.... He fancies there are secrets where there are none, and that he is not let into them, which made him very peevish.

    HMC *Stuart* VI, p. 90, Mar to H.Paterson, 5 March 1718. See BL. Add. MSS 31260, f. 164, Nairne to Gualterio, 25 September 1717: Panmure "has not the qualities to be as circumspect as he should be" ["n'a pas les qualités requises pour agir avec toute la circumspection qu'il faut avoir"].
59. HMC *Stuart* VI, p. 415, Panmure to Mar, 9 May 1718.
60. HMC *Stuart* VII, p. 7, Panmure to Mar, 4 July 1718; Ibid., p. 21, Mar to Panmure, 8 July 1718.
61. HMC *Stuart* VI, p. 250, Panmure to Mar, 4 April 1718.
62. Ibid., p. 546, Panmure to Mar, 18 June 1718.
63. Ibid., p. 333, Mar to James III, 20 April 1718.
64. HMC *Stuart* V, p. 267, Mar to Marischal, 9 December 1717.
65. HMC *Stuart* VII, p. 424, A.Graeme to Mar, 22 October 1718.
66. Mar had ignored Seaforth's letters, and then pretended that he had never received them: HMC *Stuart* VII, p. 288, Seaforth to Mar, 16 September 1718; Ibid., p. 387, Mar to Seaforth, 14 October 1718.
67. HMC *Stuart* VII, p. 600, Campbell of Glendarule to Mar, 4 December 1718.
68. Ibid., p. 366, Seaforth to James III, 8 October 1718.
69. Ibid., p. 672, Mar to Seaforth, 27 December 1718.
70. Ibid., p. 673, Mar to Campbell of Glendarule, 27 December 1718. By this time Marischal had joined the Duke of Ormonde in Spain and was preparing to command the military expedition to Scotland.
71. Corp, *A Court in Exile*, p. 365.
72. Hay referred to Perth somewhat disrespectfully as "the *Cordon Verte*": HMC *Stuart* VI, p. 235, Hay to Mar, 31 March 1718. See also Ibid., p. 243, Forster to Mar, 1 April 1718. Nairne complained that Perth was badly treated by the new favourites: BL. Add. MSS 20298, f. 88, Nairne to Gualterio, 2 October 1718.
73. HMC *Stuart* V, p. 487, Mar to Panmure, 17 February 1718.

7 The music of the court

1. Pucci, b.167, f. XI, p. 286^v.
2. She had died in 1709 after giving birth to a son, Giacomo. Gualterio gave Nairne an introduction to Camillo Staccoli, and described the family as "one of the most distinguished in Urbino" ["une des meilleurs maisons d'Urbino"] (Bod. Lib. Carte MSS 257, f. 229, Gualterio to Nairne, 28 September 1717).
3. Lucrezia Staccoli's niece, Lucrezia Antaldi (born c.1691), married Marchese Filippo Legnani of Bologna and became one of the Ladies of the Bedchamber to Queen Maria Clementina.
4. Pucci, b.167, f. XI, p. 287^r:

> Precedeva in primo luogo il canto di molti musici, e virtuose forastiere, e d.o divertimento durava a piacere di S.M., di poi palzava da sedere, e con somma gentilezza sinchinava a tutte le Dame, come il simile faceva nella sua venuta, non volendo che gli cavalieri d'Urbino so movessero, ma che restassaro a servire le Dame. Fornavono poi Milordi, e Cavalieri dopo l'accompagnamento alla Conversazione, quale eradi doppio divertimento di giuoco, e di ballo con l'intervento di tutte le Dame, e Cavalieri della città con rinfreschi dupplicati sinella permanenza del Rè, come dopo, che il deseriverto si farebbe un sommo torto alla somma generosità di d.o Cavaliere Sig.r Castellano Guido Bonaventura.

5. HMC *Stuart* IV, p. 504, Hay to Mar, 8 August 1717.
6. *Palazzo di Federico da Montefeltro*, p. 226.
7. BL. Add. MSS 31260, f. 191, Nairne to Gualterio, 17 October 1717: "quelques belles voix de femme."
8. BL. Add. MSS 31261, f. 40, Nairne to Gualterio, 17 February 1718.
9. Edward Corp, "Music at the Stuart Court at Urbino, 1717–18", pp. 351–63, *Music and Letters* 81/3 (Oxford, August 2000), at pp. 356–57; Edward Corp, "A Possible Origin for the Berkeley Castle Manuscript of Italian Arias and Cantatas: The Stuart Court at Urbino", pp. 13–21, *Studi Vivaldiani* 5 (Venice, 2005), at pp. 15–17.
10. NLS. MS. 9474 (from *La Merope*) and 9475 (unidentified).
11. They are described in Faun Tanenbaum Tiedge and Michael Talbot, "The Berkeley Castle Manuscript: Arias and Cantatas by Vivaldi and his Italian Contemporaries", *Studi Vivaldiani* 3 (Venice, 2003), pp. 33–87.
12. Corp, *A Court in Exile*, Chapter 8.
13. HMC *Stuart* V, p. 267, Mar to Nicolini, 9 December 1717.
14. Ibid., p. 368, Mar to J.Erskine, 4 January 1718. For the identities of "Painter" and "Mitchell's Jack", see HMC *Stuart* VII, p. 639, Mar to Maule, 16 December 1718.
15. HMC *Stuart* V, p. 340, Mar to Ormonde, 28 December 1717.
16. Ibid., p. 454, James III to Prince de Vaudémont, 10 February 1718: "nous n'avons ici presqu'aucune companie ou amusement, si ce n'est quelque petite musique Italienne, que je commence a gouter beaucoup."
17. Ibid., p. 382, Mar to Stewart of Invernity, 11 January 1718.
18. Corp, "Music at the Stuart Court at Urbino", p. 356.
19. HMC *Stuart* V, p. 384, Redmond to Paterson, 14 January 1718.

20. Ibid., p. 429, Forster to Mar, 1 February 1718. Dr Blair recorded that "the theatre is very large; the decorations were handsome and the musick excellent. They had several choice voices which sung charmingly, ten trible viols, 3 basses and one hautbois. My Lord Panmure said he had never heard any play better on the hautbois and was charmed with one solo he plaid on that instrument. We pay'd 3 paolis each for the Opera [libretto] and a paolis for a seat in the parterre for the boxes were all filled before we came" (SNA. GD 45/26/74, "Journal from Urbino to Venice by Fossombrone, Ravenna etc, begun the 12th Febry by Doctor Blair in Company with the Earle of Panmure").
21. HMC *Stuart* VI, p. 93, St. Andrews to Nairne, 6 March 1718.
22. HMC Stuart V, p. 487, St. Andrews to Mar, 17 February 1718.
23. Pucci, b.167, f. XI, p. 287^v: "Per commodo di S.M., come per li suoi cavalieri fa fatto un casino grande a piedi della platea del teatro a spese della Reverenda Camera."
24. Corp, "Music at the Stuart Court at Urbino", pp. 356–57.
25. HMC *Stuart* VI, p. 101, Mar to Tullibardine, 6 March 1718. It might be coincidence, but this visit to Fano took place at the same time as the king began to show his dissatisfaction with the people and things he had liked at Saint-Germain. See Ibid., p. 107, James III to Oxford, 8 March 1718: "the persons I have lived almost all my life with, of whom I own I am surfeited".
26. BL. Add. MSS 31261, f. 50, Nairne to Gualterio, 24 February 1718.
27. RA. SP Misc 32, account book, 22 February 1718.
28. Ibid., p. 130, Mar to Panmure, 10 March 1718; Ibid., p. 136, Mar to Ormonde, 11 March 1718.
29. Ibid., p. 149, James III to Duke of Lorraine, 15 March 1718: "We have had more comedies here, and what are called *gioci di forze*, which are as surprising as they are odd" ["Nous avons eu encore des comedies ici, et ce qu'on appelle ici gioci di forze, qui sont aussi surprenans que singuliers"].
30. Claudio Sartori, *I libretti italiani a stampa dalle origini al 1800*, 6 vols (Cuneo, Bertola & Locatelli, 1990–1992), with two additional volumes of indexes (ibid., 1993–1994), vol. 5, p. 104 and p. 188.
31. HMC *Stuart* VI, p. 162, Mar to Stewart of Invernity, 17 March 1718.
32. RA. SP Misc 20, p. 77, Book of Entries and Warrants, 21 February 1718.
33. BL. Add. MSS 31261, f. 70, Nairne to Gualterio, 20 March 1718: "il a été l'autre soir une petite conversation chez Madame [Lucrezia] Staccoli ou cette Dame a chanté elle meme fort bien, et S.M. y a entendu pour la premiere fois un fameux musicien nommé Tempeste que M. le President a fait venir ici expres et qui y restera quelque tems pour faire plaisir a S.M. qui commence a beaucoup gouter la musique Italienne." See also BL. Add. MSS 20298, f. 22, Nairne to Gualterio, 24 March 1718.
34. HMC *Stuart* VI, p. 204, Mar to Dillon, 26 March 1718.
35. Clari's setting of the libretti was performed at Florence in 1709 and at Lucca in 1720. Lotti's setting was performed in Rome in 1703 (see note 30).
36. Pucci, b.167, f. XI, p. 288^r: "Sbaraglia e Tempesta [*sic*] i quali soprendentemente cantarano, essendovi intervenuta la Maesta Sua, a di cui onore era

frato fatto, nel solito Palchettone, siccome pure tutte le Dame e Cavaglieri di della Città che forastieri."

37. HMC *Stuart* VI, p. 235, Hay to Mar, 31 March 1718; Ibid., p. 237, Paterson to Mar, 31 March 1718; Ibid., p. 242, Forster to Mar, 1 April 1718; Ibid., p. 262, Mar to James III, 6 April 1718.

38. Ibid., p. 265, James III to Mar, 7 April 1718.

39. Ibid., p. 266, Paterson to Mar, 7 April 1718.

40. Pucci, b.167, f. XI, p. 288^r: "m[edesim]o Monarca stredo al luogo polito del Teatro con Mons. Pres[ident]e e suoi Cavalieri, le Dame, e cavalieri d'Urbino stavano nella platea con il solito bell'ordine distributi."

41. RA. SP Misc 32, account book, 5 April 1718.

42. HMC *Stuart* VI, p. 265, James III to Mar, 7 April 1718.

43. Pucci, b.167, f. XI, pp. 288^v–289^r: "le lamentazioni in canto fermo con cembalo, ed altri instrumenti composte du nuova musica del Sig.r D. Gabrielle Balami".

44. HMC *Stuart* VI, p. 311, Hay to Mar, 14 April 1718.

45. Ibid., p. 319, James III to Mar, 17 April 1718.

46. Pucci, b.167, f. XI, p. 288^r: "con una musica assai sontuosa per esservi ancera in citta li Musici di grido fatto venire dal Sig.re Alam[ann]o Salviati."

47. HMC *Stuart* VI, p. 352, Nairne to Mar, 23 April 1718; Ibid., p. 359, Paterson to Mar, 24 April 1718.

48. Ibid., p. 381, Hay to Mar, 28 April 1718.

49. Pucci, b.167, f. XI, p. 289^r: "con l'eccellente suo canto, e con la sua maestria nel suonare il Liuto diede il più bel risalto e contento a tanto nobile adunanza, ed a Sua Maestà Britannica che ripatutamente gli fece plauso."

50. HMC *Stuart* VI, p. 379, James III to Mar, 28 April 1718.

51. Ibid., p. 381, Hay to Mar, 28 April 1718.

52. Ibid., p. 389, Paterson to Mar, 28 April 1718.

53. HMC *Stuart* VII, p. 384, Nairne to Paterson, 13 October 1718.

54. Ibid., p. 367, Nairne to Paterson, 9 October 1718.

55. Pucci, b.167, f. XI, p. 289^v.

56. RA. SP 31/85, "Note of monie to be given to different people upon account of their mourning", 23 May 1718.

57. He was given 167 *livres* (RA. SP Misc 32, account book, 22 May 1718).

58. Pucci, b.167, f. XI, p. 289^v: "con suntuoza musica".

59. Ibid.: "con la Messa Cantata, ed un generale officio di Messe basse, col dire, che così era il costume alla Francese."

60. Ibid., p. 290^v.

61. HMC *Stuart* VII, p. 43, Mar to Ormonde, 15 July 1718. Albani was still at Urbino in October, with his wife Teresa, his mother-in-law (Contessa Borromeo), and his sister-in-law and her husband (Marchesa and Marchese Bentivoglio) (BL. Add. MSS 31261, f. 258, Nairne to Gualterio, 16 October 1718; HMC *Stuart* VII, p. 422, C.Albani to James III, 22 October 1718).

62. HMC *Stuart* VII, p. 90, Erskine to Paterson, 27 July 1718.

63. Ibid., p. 365 Nairne to Paterson, 8 October 1718, with postscript of 9 October.

64. Ibid., p. 367, Nairne to Paterson, 9 October 1718.

65. Ibid., p. 384, Nairne to Paterson, 13 October 1718.
66. Ibid., p. 402, Mar to Nairne, 18 October 1718.

8 James III and the Papacy

1. For the entertainment provided for James III by the Ruspolis in June 1717, see p. 25.
2. James III and the Colonna family were both descended from the two sisters of Cardinal Mazarin.
3. BL. Add. MSS 20298, f. 6, Nairne to Gualterio, 15 July 1717; BL. Add. MSS 20312, f. 96, Marchesa di Cavailla to Nairne, 30 October 1717; BL. Add. MSS 31260, f. 79, f. 156, f. 174 and f. 260, Nairne to Gualterio, 9 July, 20 September, 3 October and 26 December 1717; BL. Add. MSS 31261, f. 27 and f. 64, Nairne to Gualterio, 30 January and 13 March 1718. The lists of people who were to receive copies, which were enclosed with the last two letters, have been wrongly filed at, respectively, BL. Add. MSS 30260, f. 163 and Add. MSS 20313, f. 269.
4. BL. Add. MSS 31260, f. 180, Nairne to Gualterio, 10 October 1717.
5. RA. SP 24/107, David to Nairne, 1 December 1717; BL. Add. MSS 31260, f. 240, 5 December 1717.
6. BL. Add. MSS 31261, f. 27, f. 46 and f. 40 [sic], Nairne to Gualterio, 30 January, 10 February and 17 February 1718.
7. HMC *Stuart* V, p. 497, James III to Principessa di Piombino, 21 February 1718; Ibid., p. 122, James III to Sacripanti, 10 March 1718; Ibid., p. 151, James III to Principessa Colonna, 15 March 1718; BL. Add. MSS 21312, C.Albani to Nairne, 23 March 1718; HMC *Stuart* VI, p. 223, James III to Imperiali, 29 March 1718.
8. BL. Add. MSS 31260, f. 248, Nairne to Gualterio, 16 December 1717.
9. BL. Add. MSS 31261, f. 27 and f. 54, Nairne to Gualterio, 30 January and 3 March 1718; BL. Add. MSS 20306, f. 445, Gualterio to Dempster, late February or early March 1718.
10. BL. Add. MSS 31261, f. 64, Nairne to Gualterio, 13 March 1718.
11. For example, the copy which was in the Threipland collection, sold by Christie's in 1993 as part of the Fingask Castle sale (lot 246).
12. HMC *Stuart* VI, p. 584, Redmond to Mar, 27 June 1718.
13. RA. SP 27/26, David to Nairne, 9 February 1718.
14. BL. Add. MSS 31261, f. 103, Nairne to Gualterio, 21 April 1718:

> V[otre] E[xcellence] verra par la lettre cy jointe de M. de Cavailla que le portrait du Roy qu'elle luy a envoyé pour Mad. son epouse est arrivé a bon port et a été reçu avec beaucoup de plaisir, et que la peinture a fait honneur a Mr David a la cour de Turin, ou la Reine Elle meme l'a vû avec plaisir et l'a loué.

See also C.E. Lart, *The Parochial Registers of Saint-Germain-en-Laye: Jacobite Extracts*, 2 vols (London, 1910, 1912), vol. 2, p. 149, Nairne to Gontieri, 16 June 1718.
15. HMC *Stuart* VII, p. 55, James III to F.Colonna, 17 July 1718.

16. Late in April 1718, Salviati's two nephews, the sons of his brother the Duke of Salviati, arrived from Florence and spent several days in Urbino on their way to Rome (HMC *Stuart* VI, p. 359, Paterson to Mar, 24 April 1718; Ibid., p. 381, Hay to Mar, 28 April 1718).
17. Ibid., p. 436, James III to Sacripanti, 15 May 1718.
18. ASV. Albani 166, p. 149, James III to Clement XI, 1 June 1718. This request was not granted until the following year (RA. SP 43/22 and 65, Nairne to James III, 1 and 22 April 1719).
19. In fact Salviati became such an enthusiastic supporter of the Jacobite cause that he had to be dissuaded from asking the Pope for the rank of Papal Nuncio to the court of James III, which would have risked offending Gualterio (BL. Add. MSS 20298, f. 67, Nairne to Gualterio, August 1718).
20. BL. Add. MSS 20313, f. 99, Gualterio to Nairne, 21 June 1718.
21. BL. Add. MSS 20312, f. 241, Nairne to Gazola, 12 June 1718:

> par rapport au ceremonial don't Elle n'est pas assés instruite pour pouvoir se regler presentement surtout quand il s'agit de changer un stile dont ses predecesseurs se sont toujours servis jusqu'au present tant envers Mg. le Duc de Modene son oncle qu'envers S.A.S..

22. BL. Add. MSS. 31261, f. 133, Nairne to Gualterio, 30 June 1718:

> Dans l'ignorance où on a esté a St. Germain du veritable ceremonial d'Angleterre, on a cru que le plus seur estoit de se regler sur celuy de France, et effectivement je n'ay jamais vû depuis trente ans de Protocole dans le Secretairerie du Roy que celuy qu'on eut de Mons.r de Torcy.

23. HMC *Stuart* VI, p. 564, James III to Ormonde, 23 June 1718.
24. HMC *Stuart* VII, p. 77, Marriage Contract, 22 July 1718.
25. HMC *Stuart* V, p. 443, James III to Imperiali, 6 February 1718.
26. Ibid., p. 496, James III to Gualterio, 21 February 1718.
27. HMC *Stuart* VI, p. 220, James III to Gualterio, 29 March 1718; Ibid., p. 223, James III to Imperiali, 29 March 1718.
28. Ibid., p. 246, James III to Mar, 3 April 1718; Ibid., p. 290, James III to Mar, 10 April 1718; Ibid., p. 310, James III to Ormonde, 14 April 1718.
29. ASV. Albani 166, p. 147, James III to A.Albani, 24 April 1718.
30. HMC *Stuart* VI, p. 373, James III to Dillon, 27 April 1718.
31. Ibid., p. 373, James III to Mar, 28 April 1718.
32. HMC *Stuart* VII, p. 35, Mar to Marischal, 14 July 1718.
33. BL. Add. MSS 31255, f. 119, James III to Gualterio, 14 July 1718.
34. HMC *Stuart* VII, p. 74, Mar to Dillon, 22 July 1718; BL. Add. MSS 31255, f. 124, James III to Gualterio, 24 July 1718; HMC *Stuart* VII, p. 91, James III to Dicconson, 28 July 1718; Ibid., p. 99, Mar to Clermont, 29 July 1718; Ibid., p. 136, Mar to Jermingham, 11 August 1718; Ibid., p. 340, Mar to Marischal, 30 September 1718.
35. Ibid., p. 122, James III to A.Albani, 8 August 1718.
36. Ibid., p. 124, James III to Gualterio, 8 August 1718.
37. ASV. Albani 166, p. 152, James III to Clement XI, 7 August 1718.
38. ASV. Albani 166, pp. 166–176.

39. HMC *Stuart* VII, p. 283, James III to A.Albani, 15 September 1718.
40. Ibid., p. 352, James III to Gualterio, 3 October 1718.

9   The planned move to Castel Gandolfo

1. HMC *Stuart* VII, p. 245, Mar to O'Reilly, 5 September 1718.
2. Ibid., p. 248, James III to Murray, 5 September 1718. The king emphasised that he was very much opposed to the idea of being married by proxy, and that he would do everything he could to avoid it. His original intention was to send Mar to greet the Princess and her mother at Trento (BL. Add. MSS 31255, f. 157, James III to Gualterio, 4 September 1718).
3. Ibid., p. 264, Hay to James III, 9 September 1718; Ibid., p. 293, Elizabeth Sobieska to James III, 18 September 1718; Ibid., p. 297, Hay to James III, 19 September 1718.
4. Ibid., p. 334, James III to Hay, 29 September 1718.
5. Ibid., p. 336, Hay to James III, 29 September 1718.
6. HMC *Stuart* V, p. 397, Lady Nithsdale to James III, 19 January 1718.
7. HMC *Stuart* VI, p. 151, James III to Lady Nithsdale, 16 March 1718; Ibid., p. 367, Mary of Modena to Lady Nithsdale, 26 April 1718.
8. HMC *Stuart* VII, p. 292, Mar to Lady Murray, 17 September 1718. See also ibid., p. 353, Mar to Drummond, 3 October 1718.
9. Ibid., p. 379, Trant to James III, 12 October 1718.
10. Ibid., p. 396, Mar to Lady Carrington, 17 October 1718; Ibid., p. 635, James III to Mlle de Chausseraye, 15 December 1718.
11. Ibid., p. 604, Mar to R.Strickland, 5 December 1718.
12. Ibid., p. 66, Colgrave to James III, 20 July 1718.
13. RA. SP Box 3/1/88, James III to Dicconson, undated (August 1718).
14. HMC *Stuart* VII, p. 331, Caryll to Mar, 27 September 1718.
15. Ibid., p. 396, Mrs Nugent to James III, 16 October 1718.
16. Ibid., p. 612, Contessa Molza to James III, 6 December 1718.
17. Ibid., p. 543, James III to Dillon, 15 November 1718.
18. Ibid., p. 369, Lady Murray to Mar, 9 October 1718.
19. BL. Add. MSS 20298, f. 33, Nairne to Gualterio, 1 July 1718:

> J'avoue en confiance a V.E. a qui je ne peux rien cacher, que je ne peux pas fermer les yeux a tout ce que je vois faire tous les jours de plaisirs effectifs et non de simples paroles a d'autres favoris nouveaux.... Et V.E. verra que leurs femmes leurs parens leurs amis seront preferés a tous quand nous aurons le bonheur d'avoir une Reine, et qu'on ne pensera seulem.t pas a donner la moindre place a ma fille ainée quoique filliolle du Roy et D[emoise]lle asses bien elevée pour etre capable de remplir une poste telle qu'avoit M.e Molza ou d'etre fille d'honneur, si on ne met dans l'autre poste que des femmes mariées.

20. BL. Add. MSS 20298, f. 41, Nairne to Gualterio, 4 August 1718: "La femme de Mr Hays [sic] est deja asseurée d'etre auprès de la Reine quand nous en aurons une, et la D[uche]sse de Mar d'etre dame d'honneur quand elle voudra venir."

21. HMC *Stuart* VI, p. 484, James III to Middleton, Sheldon, Dillon and Dicconson, 27 May 1718; HMC *Stuart* VII, p. 91, James III to Dicconson, 28 July 1718; Ibid., p. 192, Dicconson to James III, 22 August 1718.
22. Ibid., p. 1, Mar to Dillon, 1 July 1718.
23. Ibid., p. 243, Dicconson to James III, 5 September 1718.
24. Ibid., p. 242, Clermont to Hay, 4 September 1718; Ibid., p. 254, James III to Dicconson, 7 September 1718; Ibid., p. 358, Dicconson to James III, 3 October 1718.
25. RA. SP 36/141, "a particular of what is in the five Caisses sent from St Germans the 26th of Sept.r 1718". The other items included

> a little strong box in which is an ivory box representing the passion, an embroiderd tabby box in which is a Silver Chappel, two aprons and a Silver Key said to be good for women with child. A little black Japan-celler, a holy-water pott garnish'd with precious stones, an embroidered box with a St. Suares . . . , and a pair of Snaffers, two Etuis for Neck-laces, a little Clock garnish'd with philigrin work, . . . , a Christal pyramede in a case, [and] a pair of shoes for the King.

26. RA. SP Box 4/2/1, "An Inventory of w. was in y. strong box sent to Rome", annotated by Ellis to show those things which were "with ye Queen". One item which was not given to the queen is described as "la tête du feu roi de France [Louis XIV] en forme de médaillon". This medallion showing the head of Louis XIV measures 12 centimetres in height, and is now in a private collection in Paris. On the back is written (in capital letters): "Re Giacom d'Inghiltera" [sic].
27. RA. SP Box 4/2/2–5.
28. HMC *Stuart* VII, p. 264, A.Albani to James III, 10 September 1718.
29. RA. SP 36/7, "Distribution of the appartments at Castle Gandolfo for the King and his familie", 5 September 1718; RA. SP 38/51, Bonbled's "letter from Rome with an accompt of the furniture demanded for Castello, recd Novem 1st, 1718".
30. ASV. Albani 166, p. 202, "Descrizzione fatta con il Ministro della Maestà del Rè d'Inghilterra delle cose da farsi nel Palazzo Pontificio di Castel Gandolfo", 14 September 1718. Bonbled had already submitted his report to the king and Mar at Urbino, and Mar had substantially increased the number of chimneys needed (RA. SP 36/7 and 8). Mar had also recommended that one of the lavatories should be moved: "There is a house of office behind the great round stairs as I remember the plan, w.ch I am perswaded will stinck the whole house near it, so I wish you could find another place for that convenience to shut up the other" (RA. SP 36/45, Mar to Bonbled, 11 September 1718).
31. HMC *Stuart* VII, p. 283, James III to A.Albani, 15 September 1718.
32. Ibid., p. 285, Mar to Panmure, 15 September 1718.
33. Ibid., p. 316, Mar to T.Oglethorpe, 22 September 1718.
34. Ibid., p. 322, "Heads to be spoke of by the King to Don Carlo [Albani]", 25 September 1718.
35. RA. SP 36/151, Mar to Bonbled, 28 September 1718.
36. HMC *Stuart* VII, p. 352, James III to Gualterio, 3 October 1718.
37. Ibid., p. 384, Nairne to Mar, 13 October 1718; RA. SP 37/143, Bonbled to Nairne, 22 October 1718; RA. SP 38/51, received 1 November 1718; HMC

Stuart VII, p. 504, Nairne to James III, 8 November 1718. The pope said that "Bonbled had asked dividing galleries and making rooms of them and making so many alterations of stairs and chimneys and other things, that were not practicable" (Ibid., p. 461, Nairne to James III, 19 October 1718). See also p. 488.
38. Ibid., p. 514, Bonbled to Nairne, 9 November 1718.
39. Ibid., p. 384, Nairne to Mar, 13 October 1718; Ibid., p. 420, 21 October 1718.
40. Ibid., p. 492, James III to Nairne, 3 November 1718; Ibid., p. 509, Murray to Ormonde, 9 November 1718:

> after he [the Pope] promised the King the use of the house, people were employed to persuade him not to go there, alleging the air was bad in the winter and fifty other things equally frivolous. When it was found he was not to be diverted in this manner from going, they thought to have stopped his journey by refusing to make chimneys and other preparations which were absolutely necessary to make the house habitable during the winter, but ... they found too that this little art was without effect, for he acquainted the Pope it was his positive resolution to pass the winter in or about Rome.

10 The King's second visit to Rome

1. HMC *Stuart* VII, p. 348, James III to Origo, 2 October 1718.
2. Ibid., p. 348, James III to Patrizi, 2 October 1718.
3. BL. Add. MSS 20298, f. 88, Nairne to Gualterio, 2 October 1718. Apart from Sir William Ellis and James Delattre, Nairne was the only senior member of the court who was not invited.
4. HMC *Stuart* VII, p. 299, Hay to James III, 19 September 1718.
5. BL. Add. MSS 31261, f. 244, Nairne to Gualterio, 6 October 1718: "Madame Nidsdale [*sic*] qui est arrivée ces jours cy et qui est ... Cath[olique] estant fille du feu Duc de Powis, a pressé fortement d'avoir l'honneur d'etre du voyage, mais le Roy ne luy a pas voulu permettre, ainsi il n'y a que Madame Hay qui a cette avantage."
6. HMC *Stuart* VII, p. 334, Murray to Hay, 29 September 1718.
7. For the detailed account of Perth's meeting with Cardinal Origo, see Ascari, "James III in Bologna", pp. 6–7.
8. BL. Add. MSS 31261, f. 244, Nairne to Gualterio, 6 October 1718; Pucci, b.167, f. XI, p. 291^r, 6 October 1718.
9. HMC *Stuart* VII, p. 384, Nairne to Mar, 13 October 1718.
10. Ascari, "James III in Bologna", p. 7. For the king's meeting with Cardinal Origo and Cardinal Boncampagni on 9 and 10 October, see Ascari, pp. 7–8.
11. HMC *Stuart* VII, p. 377, Murray to Mar, 12 October 1718. See ASV. Albani 168, p. 137, "Spese fatte per il preparam.to dell'Alloggia di S.M. del Rè d'Inghilterra ... nel Palazzo del Sig.re Marchese Onofrio Benilacqua", 2–20 October 1718.
12. HMC *Stuart* VII, p. 390, Mar to H.Paterson, 15 October 1718, with a postscript of 18 October.
13. Ibid., p. 402, Mar to Dillon, 18 October 1718, with a postscript of 19 October.

14. Matthew Creagh, the cook, was left behind in Ferrara with the footman (Ibid., p. 423, M.Creagh to Mrs Creagh, 10 November 1718).
15. BL. Add. MSS 31261, f. 258, Nairne to Gualterio, 20 October 1718:

> Je n'ay pas la vanite de me croire absolument necessaire auprés du Roi, le jeune ami de Mar [i.e. Murray] est plus que capable de remplir mon poste et on luy en fera jouir tous les honneurs les plus etendus avec plaisir, les quels on n'a jamais accordés a moy qu'a demi.

16. HMC *Stuart* VII, p. 413, Edgar to Paterson, 20 October 1718.
17. Pucci, b.167, f. XI, p. 291^r, 22 October 1718.
18. HMC *Stuart* VII, p. 399, James III to Nairne, 18 October 1718.
19. Ibid., p. 401, James III to C.Albani, 18 October 1718: "16 jours depuis l'arrest sans que j'apprenne la moindre nouvelle que par le public et sans avoir receu des lettres ni de Mr Hay ni des Princesses ni d'aucun de leur suite".
20. Ibid., p. 408, James III to Clement XI, 19 October 1718.
21. Ibid., pp. 457, 484, 502, 513, Nairne to James III, 29 October, 2, 4 (missing), 8, 9 November 1718; Ibid., pp. 428, 463, 490, 490, 495, Nairne to Mar, 23, 29 October 1718, 2, 2, 5 November 1718. Nairne also wrote four letters to Gualterio during the same period: BL. Add. MSS 31261, ff. 262, 264, 266, 270, 29 October, 1, 4, 9 November 1718.
22. HMC *Stuart* VII, p. 495, Clement XI to James III, 5 November 1718.
23. Ibid., pp. 417, 421, 491, 492, James III to Nairne, 21, 22, 25 (missing) October, 2 (missing), 3, 4 November 1718.
24. Ibid., p. 492, James III to Nairne, 4 November 1718.
25. Ibid., p. 503, Nairne to James III, 8 November 1718. See also BL. Add. MSS 31261, f. 270, Nairne to Gualterio, 9 November 1718:

> He tells me to continue making as much fuss as possible about this, which is embarrassing since it is not really in my nature to make trouble, and I am not really convinced that it is in the King's interest or appropriate for me to be complaining about the Emperor [Il me dit de continuer de faire tout le bruit que je pourrai sur cette affaire, cela m'embarasse car le bruit n'est pas mon caractere, et je ne suis pas persuadé que ce soit ni du service du Roy ni convenable a moy de criailler contre l'Empereur].

26. HMC *Stuart* VII, p. 400.
27. Ibid., p. 402, Mar to Nairne, 18 October 1718.
28. The Corsican guards, however, were not withdrawn until 22 May 1719 (Pucci, b.167, f. XI, p. 291^r).
29. HMC *Stuart* VII, p. 429, Nithsdale to Mar, 23 October 1718; Ibid., p. 432, Clephane to Mar, 24 October 1718; Ibid., p. 446, Clephane to Mar, 27 October 1718; Ibid., p. 522, Nithsdale to Mar, 10 November 1718; Ibid., p. 572, Ellis to Mar, 25 November 1718. Linlithgow, Cockburn, Cameron, Graham and Preston left on Monday, 24 November. Collier, Menzies and James Hay travelled together, as did Kingston and Fleming. The Nithsdales travelled with Kilsyth and Anthoine Brun, the king's chairman. Clephane, Stewart of Inverinity and Mackenzie formed another group.

30. Ibid., p. 448, Ellis to Mar, 28 October 1718; Ibid., p. 489, Nairne to James III, 2 November 1718.
31. Ibid., p. 463, Nairne to Mar, 29 October 1718; Ibid., p. 497, Nairne to Mar, 5 November 1718.
32. Ibid., p. 504, Nairne to James III, 8 November 1718. See also ibid., p. 516, Ellis to Paterson, 9 November 1718. RA. SP 40/129 contains "a list of ye goods yt came from Urbino". There was a series of numbered boxes belonging to the following named people:

> Lord Mareschal [who had left the court in May 1717], Lord Winton, [Richard] Baines [cook], Matthew Creagh [cook], [Jeremiah] Broomer [Clerk of the Kitchen], [James] Miner [cook], [Théophile] Leserteur [cook], F[ather] Brown, Nairne, Murray, [Michele] Vezzosi [*valet de chambre*], Perth, Madalena [Rebout, scourer], [Edmund] Butler [coachman], Paterson, [Anthoine] Le Brun [chairman], Hay, [Andrew] Symes [footman], Gen. Foster, [James] Delattre [Equerry], Rob. Creagh, [Charles] Macarty [Yeoman of the Wine Cellar], [Jacques] Catillon [footman], Duke of Ormond [who had left the court in April 1717], Dr. Barclay [Anglican Chaplain], Mr. [Gerard] Fitzgerald [*valet de chambre* and barber], [Henry] Kerby ye Father [chairman], Ellis, [Joseph] Martinash [assistant to Ellis], [John] Sheridan [Riding Purveyor].

This list, which takes no account of rank or status, shows how the household servants were regarded as being members of a single "family". The pensioners were responsible for transporting their own possessions.
33. HMC *Stuart* VII, p. 515, Edgar to Paterson, 9 November 1718.
34. Ibid., p. 489, Nairne to James III, 2 November 1718.
35. Ibid., p. 463, Nairne to James III, 29 October 1718.
36. Ibid., p. 504, Nairne to James III, 8 November 1718.
37. Ibid., p. 489, Nairne to James III, 2 November 1718; Ibid., p. 490, Nairne to Mar, 2 November 1718; Ibid., p. 496, Nairne to Mar, 5 November 1718; Ibid., p. 504, Nairne to James III, 8 November 1718.
38. Ibid., p. 427, James III to Inverness, 23 October 1718.
39. Ibid., p. 483, James III to Ormonde, 2 November 1718.
40. Ibid., p. 482, Duchess of Mar to Mar, 1 November 1718.
41. Ibid., p. 483, James III to Ormonde, 2 November 1718.
42. Ibid., p. 502, James III to Mar, 8 November 1718.
43. Ibid., p. 508, Murray to Mar, 9 November 1718. Also ibid., p. 502, James III to Mar, 8 November 1718.
44. Ibid., p. 543, James III to Dillon, 15 November 1718.
45. Ibid., postscript.
46. BL. Add. MSS 31261, f. 275, Nairne to Gualterio, 16 November 1718.
47. HMC *Stuart* VII, p. 536, Mar to Ormonde, 14 November 1718.
48. Ibid., p. 391, Mar to H.Paterson, 15 October 1718, with postscript of 18 October. Mar had returned to Bologna on the 9th, shortly after the departure of the king and Inverness, but before the departure of Murray and Lady Inverness (Ibid., p. 536, Mar to Ormonde, 14 November 1718).
49. Ibid., p. 550, note of the papers and other things packed up by John Paterson at Urbino, 19 November 1718; Ibid., p. 571, Buglioni to Paterson, 25 November 1718; Ibid., p. 636, Buglioni to Paterson, 15 December 1718.

50. BL. Add. MSS 31261, f. 284, Nairne to Gualterio, 26 November 1718; HMC
    Stuart VII, p. 579, Mar to Dillon, 29 November 1718. There is a letter written
    by Matthew Creagh, the cook whom Murray had left behind at Ferrara, to
    his wife Julienne at Saint-Germain, which is rather surprisingly among the
    Stuart Papers. It explains that he had been sent to Ferrara "to make the nec-
    essary preparations for food" and that he had been left stranded there for
    "more than a month without seeing the King" (Ibid., p. 523, M.Creagh to
    Mrs Creagh, 10 November 1718).
51. BL. Add. MSS 31261, f. 275, Nairne to Gualterio, 16 November 1718. Nairne
    had been living in the Palazzo, but had to give up his apartment to the
    Invernesses.
52. HMC *Stuart* VII, p. 698, anon. to Craggs, undated but December
    1718: "Paterson, Mar's under-secretary, who has private lodgings of
    his own".
53. BL. Add. MSS 31261, f. 305, Nairne to Gualterio, 5 January 1719. Another
    reason for the economies was that the Regent had stopped paying the
    secret pension of 300,000 *livres per annum* which had started when the
    king left Avignon (HMC *Stuart* VII, p. 474, Dillon to James III, 1 November
    1718; Ibid., p. 560, James III to Acquaviva, 23 November 1718. See p. 161,
    note 47).
54. BL. Add. MSS 20298, f. 112, Nairne to Gualterio, 7 January 1719.
55. BL. Add. MSS 20298, f. 110, Nairne to Gualterio, 10 January 1719: "depuis
    que je suis a Rome on m'a retranché table bois et chandle avec environ 20
    livres par mois..., et je ne scais si le retranchement se bornera là, mais
    je scais que les nouveaux directeurs favoris de la famille feront ce qu'ils
    voudront."
56. HMC *Stuart* VII, p. 533, Barclay to Mar, 12 November 1718.
57. Ibid., p. 639, Mar to Maule, 16 December 1718.
58. Ibid., p. 516, Edgar to Paterson, 9 November 1718.
59. BL. Add. MSS 31261, f. 300 and f. 303, Nairne to Gualterio, 28 December
    1718 and 4 January 1719.
60. BL. Add. MSS 31261, f. 307, Nairne to Gualterio, 7 January 1719.
61. BL. Add. MSS 31261, f. 311, Nairne to Gualterio, 11 January 1719; BL. Add.
    MSS 20298, f. 116, Nairne to Gualterio, 14 January 1719; Corp, "Music at the
    Stuart Court at Urbino", p. 358.
62. BL. Add. MSS 31261, f. 314, Nairne to Gualterio, 18 January 1719: "prefere
    avec la generalité de Rome celuy de Liberti."
63. The painting is in the collection of the Earl of Mar and Kellie.
64. Corp, *King over the Water*, p. 58, fig. 38. The painting is at Holyroodhouse,
    Edinburgh.

11   The Palazzo Del Re

1. Ibid., p. 521, Mar to James III, 10 November 1718.
2. HMC *Stuart* VII, p. 484, Nairne to James III, 2 November 1718, at pp. 487–89.
   The possibility of acquiring a palazzo for James III was first mentioned by
   Nairne in his discussion with the pope on 31 October. Cardinal Acquaviva

was strongly in favour of the Palazzo Riario, but Nairne and Francesco Bianchini of the *Camera Apostolica* agreed that the Piazza dei SS. Apostoli would be a much more suitable location.

3. Ibid., p. 497, Nairne to Mar, 5 November 1718.
4. BL. Add. MSS 31261, f. 279, Nairne to Gualterio, 19 November 1718.
5. BL. Add. MSS 31261, f. 284, Nairne to Gualterio, 26 November 1718; BL. Add. MSS 31255, f. 175, James III to Gualterio, 30 November 1718.
6. BL. Add. MSS 31261, f. 286, Nairne to Gualterio, 30 November 1718.
7. BL. Add. MSS 31261, f. 290, Nairne to Gualterio, 7 December 1718.
8. HMC *Stuart* VII, p. 624, Mar to Dillon, 13 December 1718. See also BL. Add. MSS 31255, f. 177, James III to Gualterio, 17 December 1718: "I hope to be in my new residence by the middle of next month" ["j'espere etre dans ma nouvelle maison à la moitié du mois prochain]".
9. Ibid., p. 645, Corradini to James III, 18 December 1718.
10. Ibid., p. 662, G.B.Muti to *Camera Apostolica*, 22 December 1718; ASR. Cam I: GT 444, f. 9, "istromento rogito", 22 December 1718.
11. BL. Add. MSS 20298, f. 103, Nairne to Gualterio, 31 December 1718: "on travaille a la nouvelle maison du Roy mais cet ouvrage va a la maniere du pais – *piano.*"
12. BL. Add. MSS 31261, f. 303, Nairne to Gualterio, 4 January 1719.
13. The rent was not actually paid until 24 January (ASR. Cam I: CDG 2017bis/13/8, pp. 1–2).
14. BL. Add. MSS 31261, f. 307, Nairne to Gualterio, 7 January 1719.
15. ASV. PAC 982, "Prima Parte pagamenti fatti...per...il Re d'Inghilterra".
16. HMC *Stuart* VII, p. 624, Mar to Dillon, 13 December 1718.
17. BL. Add. MSS 31261, f. 294, Nairne to Gualterio, 14 December 1718: "quoique de peu d'apparence aura beaucoup de commodité."
18. H. Tayler, *Lady Nithsdale and her Family* (London, 1939), p. 115, Lady Nithsdale to Lady Traquair, 3 January 1719.
19. Alessandro Specchi had previously worked for the Albani family at Urbino (Bartolucci, "Urbino e gli Albani", p. 443).
20. ASR. Cam I: CDG 2017bis/13/7 and 8, "Entrata ed uscita delle spese in conto della Maestà di Giacomo III d'Inghilterra"; ASV. PAC 982, "Prima Parte pagamenti fatti... per...il Re d'Inghilterra". Most of the detailed information has been published in Rossella Pantanella, "Palazzo Muti a piazza SS. Apostoli residenza degli Stuart a Roma", *Storia dell'arte* pp. 307–28, at pp. 316–25. The archives refer specifically to work carried out for "il Sig. Duca de Mare" [Mar], "il Sig.r Secretario di S.Mtà" [Nairne], "il Tesoriere di Sua Maestà" [Ellis] and "Monsù Bomble" [Bonbled].
21. On 9 February there was a delivery of all the plate belonging to Cardinal D'Adda, who had just died and left it to the king in his will (BL. Add. MSS 31261, f. 319 and f. 321, Nairne to Gualterio, 28 January and 1 February 1719; RA. SP Misc 33, p. 145, a list of the plate bequeathed to James III by Cardinal Ferdinando D'Adda, 9 February 1719). Then, on the following day, all the plate from Saint-Germain and Urbino was delivered into the hands of the appropriate servants in the Household Below Stairs: the Scullery plate to Matthew Creagh (cook), the Backstairs plate to Gerald Fitzgerald (*valet de chambre* and barber), the Pantry plate and porcelain to Pierre Pecquet (Yeoman Confectioner), and some more to Charles Macarty (Yeoman of the

Wine Cellar) (RA. SP Misc 33, pp. 143–44, 147, 149, 151, 153, six lists of the plate delivered, 10 February 1719).
22. BL. Add. MSS 31261, f. 324, Nairne to Gualterio, 12 February 1719.
23. HMC *Stuart* VII, p. 662, G.B.Muti to *Camera Apostolica*, 22 December 1718.

12   Changes at the court during the nineteen

1. HMC *Stuart* VII, p. 644, Ormonde to James III, 17 December 1718.
2. Ibid., p. 661, Ormonde to James III, 22 December 1718.
3. Henrietta Tayler, *The Jacobite Court at Rome in 1719* (Edinburgh, 1938), p. 14 and p. 151, Murray to James III, 23 February 1719.
4. M. Haile, *James Francis Edward, The Old Chevalier* (London, 1907), p. 263.
5. According to Lord Pitsligo, the only people with whom Murray was not "at odds" were John Carnegy and Robert Freebairne, and also Thomas Forster who "paid him a considerable deference, being much charmed as was supposed with his sister" (Tayler, *Jacobite Court at Rome*, p. 87). Carnegy and Murray were old friends, and had worked closely together when they were both Members of Parliament at Westminster.
6. HMC *Stuart* VI, p. 268, Oxford to Mar, 27 March 1718 O.S.; Ibid., p. 345, J. Menzies to Mar, 10 April 1718 O.S.; Ibid., p. 416, Panmure to Mar, 9 May 1718; HMC *Stuart* VII, p. 465, Ogilvie to Mar, 29 October 1718.
7. HMC *Stuart* VII, p. 583, Mar to Ogilvie, 29 November 1718.
8. Tayler, *Jacobite Court at Rome*, pp. 143–45, Mar to James III, 4 February 1719.
9. Ibid., pp. 146–47, Mar to Pitsligo, 7 February 1719.
10. Bod. Lib. Carte MSS 208, f. 321, "Power given to Mr Murray when the King parted for Spain to open letters", 2 February 1719.
11. RA. SP 42/18, "Directions for Sir William Ellis", undated. The wives were Mary Fitzgerald (née Gordon, a cousin of David Nairne) and Anna Vezzosi (née Robertson).
12. BL. Add. MSS 31255, f.178, James III to Gualterio, 7 February 1719: "J'ay laissé entre les mains de Nairne une espece de lettre de créance pour luy au Pape . . . . je vous recommande ce vieux et fidele domestique qui vous rendra compte de luy meme."
13. ASV. Albani 167, p. 19, James III to Clement XI, 7 February 1719: "notre Ministre et Protecteur de notre Royaume d'Angleterre"; "notre ainé et fidele sujet le Chevalier David Nairne notre Secretaire du Cabinet, et de notre Conseil Privé"; "Nous la [Votre Sainteté] supplions de le recevoir et de l'ecouter favorablement, et le regarder comme un de nos plus anciens et plus fideles sujets et serviteurs Catholiques en qui V.S. peut avoir une pleine confiance."
14. ASV. Albani 167, p. 20, James III to Clement XI, 7 February 1719: "Je supplie Votre Sainteté de vouloir bien permettre ma famille de demeurer dans la maison quelle a eu la bonté de me donner pour ma demeure dans cette ville, jusque a ce que je sois en estat de leur envoyer mes ordres, et d'informer V.S. de mes demarches ulterieurs."
15. ASV. Albani 167, p. 22, James III to Clement XI, 8 February 1719.
16. ASV. Albani 167, p. 25, Nairne to Clement XI, 8 February 1719 (Gualterio's copy is at BL. Add. MSS 20313, f. 70). The Jacobites included Lord Richard Howard and Lord William Drummond (both priests in Rome), Father John

Ingleton (the king's former preceptor), Father Thaddeus Connel (his former chaplain), Charles Booth (whose sons were being educated at Saint-Omer), the English, Scottish and Irish Colleges in Rome, Father Lawrence Mayes and Father William Stuart (the Agents of the English and Scottish Catholic Clergy in Rome) and the Duke of St. Andrews (called here the Count of Castelblanco). The Italians included Alamanno Salviati and his secretary (Abbate Buglioni), Lodovico Anguissola (the Vice-Legate at Urbino) and the officials of the *Camera Apostolica* with whom Nairne had negotiated when selecting a palazzo for the court, notably Francesco Bianchini (see note 58).

17. His letters describing his journey and plans are in HMC *Stuart* VII, pp. 525, 552, 585, 607, 612, 639, 650 and 688.
18. BL. Add. MSS 31261, f. 315, Nairne to Gualterio, 21 January 1719.
19. Bod. Lib. Carte MSS 258, f. 321, Gualterio to Nairne, 24 January 1719: "lors que les affairs seront entre vous et moy seuls S.M. peut estre tranquille sur le secret."
20. Bod. Lib. Carte MSS 208, f. 321, "Power given to Mr Murray when the King parted for Spain ... to solemnise the King's marriage with the Princess", 2 February 1719.
21. BL. Add. MSS 20298, f. 119, Nairne to Gualterio, 9 February 1719.
22. BL. Add. MSS 31261, f. 328, Nairne to Gualterio, 18 February 1719.
23. RA. SP 42/57, Nairne to James III, 23 February 1719; ASV. Albani 166, p. 128, memorandum by Nairne "on the capture and imprisonment of Princesse Clementine Sobieski, showing why the Pope should intervene", minuted by James III: "Mémoire pour Sa Sainteté sur l'affaire de mon marriage"; RA. SP 42/72, Nairne to James III, 3 March 1719.
24. BL. Add. MSS 20298, f. 121, Nairne to Gualterio, 2 March 1719.
25. BL. Add. MSS 31261, f. 329, Nairne to Gualterio, 22 March 1719.
26. Bod. Lib. Carte MSS 258, f. 326, Gualterio to Nairne, 31 January 1719; Ibid., f. 340, Gualterio to Nairne, 16 March 1719: "my sincere attachment which has never altered" ["mon attachement sincere et qui n'a jamais changé"].
27. Tayler, *Jacobite Court at Rome*, p. 148, Murray to Mar, 11 February 1719.
28. Ibid., p. 149, Edgar to Paterson, 22 February 1719.
29. Ibid., pp. 64–65.
30. Ibid., p. 151, Murray to James III, 23 February 1719.
31. Ibid., p. 152, Murray to James III, 23 February 1719. Inverness' elder brother, the 7th Earl of Kinnoul, was later appointed British ambassador at Constantinople. Murray's elder brother David, the Master of Stormont, visited Rome in the spring of 1719 and succeeded his father as the 6th Viscount Stormont in 1731. David Murray's son, the 7th Viscount, was later appointed British minister at Warsaw and ambassador at both Vienna and Paris (Ibid., pp. 17 and 29, and p. 164, Mar to James III, 23 March 1719).
32. BL. Add. MSS 20298, f. 121, Nairne to Gualterio, 2 March 1719: "intention de me mettre toujours entierrement sous la dependance et la protection de V[otre] E[xcellence]."
33. ASV. Albani 167, p. 23, James III to Clement XI, 17 March 1719.
34. Maria Josefa Carpio, *España y los Ultimos Estuardos* (Madrid, 1952), p. 126.
35. RA. SP 42/106, Mar to Panmure, 21 March 1719.
36. Tayler, *Jacobite Court at Rome*, p. 154, Murray to James III, 17 March 1719.
37. Ibid., p. 156, Mar to James III, 23 March 1719.

38. BL. Add. MSS 20298, f. 124, Nairne to Gualterio, 18 March 1719: "je n'ay vu le Duc de Mar qu'une fois depuis son arrivée et il m'a fait beaucoup d'honnetetê"; "comme un simple particulier et un serviteur congedié ou disgracié."
39. RA. SP 42/97, Nairne to James III, 18 March 1719.
40. RA. SP 43/22, Nairne to James III, 1 April 1719.
41. This time Mar resigned as Secretary of State, and sent the seals to the king in Spain (Tayler, *Jacobite Court at Rome*, pp. 170–72, Mar to James III, 3 July 1719).
42. RA. SP 44/107, Mar to James III, 9 September 1719.
43. RA. SP 43/94, James III to Dicconson, 22 May 1719; RA. SP 44/17, James III to Dicconson, 16 July 1719.
44. The escape is described in Peggy Miller, *A Wife for the Pretender* (London, 1965).
45. ASV. Albani 167, p. 31, Gualterio to Clement XI, 5 May 1719.
46. RA. SP 47/92, James III to Dicconson, 15 June 1720.
47. ASV. Albani 168, p. 143, "Regalo mandato alla Principessa Clementina Sobieski sposa del Rè d'Inghilterra", 16 May 1719.
48. Lord Pitsligo, "A Narrative of the Secret History of the Court in Rome", 16 September 1720, in Tayler, *Jacobite Court at Rome*, pp. 49–107, at p. 54.
49. Ibid., pp. 55–67, Pitsligo to James III, 19 June 1719. In a letter of 5 June, Murray even wrote to the king that the Duchess was "under more than suspicion of never having been and not being of your interest" (Ibid., p. 169).
50. Ibid., p. 67.
51. RA. SP 43/65, Nairne to James III, 22 April 1719.
52. RA. SP 43/71, Nairne to James III, 25 April 1719.
53. See BL. Add. MSS 31255, f. 180, James III to Gualterio, 23 April 1719, in which the king described Murray as "sage et prudent".
54. BL. Add. MSS 20298, f. 127, Nairne to Gualterio, 12 June 1719: "il est vray que je ne suis plus utile au service du Roy"; "tout vieux, inutile, et mauvais courtisan."
55. RA. SP 43/117, Nairne to James III, 17 June 1719.
56. RA. SP 44/6, Nairne to James III, 20 June 1719. The docket is at RA. SP 43/125.
57. ASR. Cam I: CDG 2017bis/13/8, pp. 8–9; ASV. PAC 982, partly printed in Pantanella, "Palazzo Muti a piazza SS. Apostoli", pp. 326–27.
58. *Intorno a Locatelli*, vol. 2, p. 852. The cantata was commissioned by Francesco Bianchini, a *cameriere d'onore* in the *Camera Apostolica*, who had become a particular friend of Sir David Nairne and other Jacobites. It was scored for three voices (*Genio Celeste, Astrea* and *Tevere*) and chorus, and its libretto was dedicated by Bianchini to James III and printed "in Roma per Antonio de Rossi nella Strada del Seminario Romano, vicino alle Rotonde" (information from the notes of the late Jean Lionnet, preserved at the Centre de Musique Baroque de Versailles). Nairne described Bianchini as "truly zealous and a sincere well-wisher of the King's and ready to give himself any trouble to serve him" (HMC *Stuart* VII, p. 491, Nairne to Mar, 2 November 1718). Shortly before the performance of the cantata, Nairne recorded that "as for good Mr Bianch[ini] here he talks of nothing els" than his hopes that the king would be restored: "He is now gone to the Country to render what service he can to Mrs Martel [i.e. the Duchess of Mar] who is gone there for 3 or 4

days with several other Company to see the curiositys" (RA. SP 43/79, Nairne to James III, 29 April 1719).
59. Tayler, *Jacobite Court at Rome*, p. 69.
60. RA. SP 44/38, Nairne to James III, 12 August 1719:

> I must say that the Card.l is extreme civil and obliging, and ready to do me any kindness upon all occasions and assures me his friendship for me is not changd in the least, tho' I cannot without being blind but perceive that his confidence in many things is not the same it was formerly when he saw I had the honour to be intirely trusted by your Ma.ty which he has perhaps some grounds given him to doubt of at present for reasons which I shall not penetrat into.... perhaps I might be of a little more use...than I am, if I were a little more authorised and less dependent, and had not to writhe against all the present appearances which can give little or no notion to this Court [i.e. the Quirinale] of my being thorowly trusted and imployd by Yr Ma.tyt when they see and know very well that I meddle with nothing.

61. Edward Gregg, "The Jacobite Career of John, Earl of Mar", in Eveline Cruickshanks, ed., *Ideology and Conspiracy: Aspects of Jacobitism, 1689–1759*, pp. 179–200, at p. 186.
62. RA. SP 44/38, Nairne to James III, 12 August 1719.
63. Ibid.
64. RA. SP 44/66, Nairne to James III, August 1719 (no date given).
65. RA. SP 44/38, Nairne to James III, 12 August 1719.
66. HMC *Stuart* VII, p. 298, Hay to James III, 19 September 1718.
67. Tayler, *Jacobite Court at Rome*, p. 174, Murray to James III, 26 August 1719.

13   The King's marriage at Montefiascone

1. ASV. Albani 168, p. 145.
2. BL. Add. MSS 31255, f. 191, James III to Gualterio, 2 September 1719. James gave his opinion of Bishop Bonaventura in this letter: "I have found no one in Italy who has shown me such kindness" ["je n'ay point trouvé son pareil en Italie a mon egard"].
3. Reproduced in *Souvenir of the British Section of the International Fine Arts Exhibition* (Rome, 1911), no.18.
4. Corp, *King over the Water*, p. 73, fig.60. The painting is in the Scottish National Portrait Gallery.
5. Corp, "Music at Urbino", p. 362.
6. HMC *Stuart* VII, p. 322, "Heads to be spoke of by the King to Don Carlo [Albani]", 25 September 1718.
7. Tayler, *Jacobite Court at Rome*, p. 175, Murray to James III, 28 August 1719.
8. RA. SP 44/66, Nairne to James III, August 1719 (no date given).
9. BL. Add. MSS 31255, f. 191, James III to Gualterio, 2 September 1719:

> J'ay bien parlé a Murray sur mon retour a Rome et je vous avoue que je trouve mes raisons...pour ce retour plus fortes que toutes celles qui s'y

opposent. Ainsi je vous prie de presser fortement l'ameublement de la maison, et de ne point donner de repos au Pape sur cela. Serait il possible que S.S. ne nous fasse aucun present comme il faut a l'heure qu'il est.

The draft is in RA. SP 44/88.

10. RA. SP 44/103, James III to Gualterio, 8 September 1719: "au bout du compte rien moins qu'une defense positive de S.S. nous empechera de venir a Rome, et je ne puis croire qu'Elle veuille jamais se faire un si grand tort dans le monde que de nous traitter avec tant de dureté."

11. It should be added that the Palazzo del Re had actually been rented for a minimum of three years (HMC *Stuart* VII, p. 662, G.B. Muti to *Camera Apostolica*, 22 December 1718; ASR. Cam I: GT 444, f. 9, "istromento rogito", 22 December 1718), and that the second instalment of rent had been paid in July 1719 (ASR. Cam I: CDG 2017bis/ 13/8, p. 8).

12. ASR. Cam I: CDG 2017bis/13/8, pp. 9–10; ASV. PAC 982, partly printed in Pantanella, "Palazzo Muti a piazza SS. Apostoli", pp. 327–28.

13. Tayler, *Lady Nithsdale*, p. 132, Nithsdale to Lady Traquair, 13 September 1719.

14. Tayler, *Jacobite Court at Rome*, p. 57, Duchess of Mar, 13 September 1719.

15. RA. SP 44/126, Nairne to Clephane, 16 September 1719. The draft is in the handwriting of Murray.

16. RA. SP 44/125, Nairne to Nithsdale, 16 September 1719. See also RA. SP 45/11, Nairne to Howard, 27 September 1719, for a similar letter. These drafts were all written by Murray and sent "by direction".

17. Tayler, *Lady Nithsdale*, p. 133, Lady Nithsdale to Lady Traquair, 10 October 1719.

18. RA. SP 44/127, Nairne to Mackenzie, 16 September 1719.

19. RA. SP 44/139, Nairne to Pitsligo, 23 September 1719.

20. Tayler, *Jacobite Court at Rome*, pp. 71–74.

21. Ibid., pp. 75–77, James III to Pitsligo, 30 September 1719.

22. BL. Add. MSS 31261, f. 354, Nairne to Gualterio, 1 October 1719. He was given the apartment occupied by Murray, who was given a room in the one occupied by Lord and Lady Inverness. The king described the accommodation for Gualterio as "two uncomfortable rooms" ["deux mauvaises chambres"] (BL. Add. MSS 31255, f. 199, James III to Gualterio, 23 September 1719).

23. BL. Add. MSS 31262, f. 9, Murray to Gualterio, 10 October 1719: "J'ay lieu de croire que le Roy a entré dans sa lettre a V.E. dans les details assez particuliers, et ainsi je prens la liberté de supplier tres humblement V.E. de ne pas communiquer le contenu a Mons.r Nairne quoiqu'il en soit le Porteur."

24. BL. Add. MSS 20298, f. 143, Nairne to Gualterio, 11 October 1719: "sur ce qui me regarde personellement je scais passer bien des choses qui ne sont pas trop agréables, pour ne pas troubler la paix de personne, mais je ne les sens pas moins."

25. Tayler, *Jacobite Court at Rome*, p. 177, James III to Mar, 26 September 1719.

26. Ibid., p. 179, James III to Mar, 5 October 1719.

27. Ibid., pp. 182, 185, 186 and 188, Mar to James III, 15 October, 4 and 18 November and 8 December 1719; and p. 190, James III to Mar, 29 December 1719.

28. Ibid., pp. 78–83, Pitsligo to Nairne, 7 October 1719.
29. Ibid., pp. 84–94; Alastair and Henrietta Tayler, *The Stuart Papers at Windsor* (London, 1939), pp. 58–59.
30. Tayler, *Lady Nithsdale*, p. 133, Lady Nithsdale to Lady Traquair, 10 October 1719.
31. BL. Add. MSS 31261, f. 254, Nairne to Gualterio, 18 October 1719:

> Je serai trop heureux et trop content de quitter et la Cour et la Vie quand la providence le voudra...ayant peu de credit que j'en ay, et n'ayant peut etre que trop fait connoitre que j'ai le malheur de ne pouvoir pas approuver tout ce que je vois, et d'etre par consequent un peu suspect.

32. Bod. Lib. Carte MSS 258, f. 394, Gualterio to Nairne, 24 October 1719: "vous avez toute la part aux bonnes graces et a la confiance de S.M.."
33. When the king had left for Spain in February he had increased Nairne's salary from 205 to 240 *livres* each month, but had arranged that this should no longer be paid by Ellis out of the monthly pension from the Pope, but rather by Gualterio out of the *luoghi di monti* in Rome which James had inherited from Mary of Modena (BL. Add. MSS 31255, f. 178, James III to Gualterio, 7 February 1719). In fact the king's *luoghi di monti* did not yield enough money to pay this amount (RA. SP 44/38, Nairne to James III, 12 August 1719), and anyway Gualterio did not have a procuration to allow him to draw any money from them (RA. SP 44/66, Nairne to James III, August 1719). As a result Gualterio had had to pay Nairne out of his own pocket, and by September (when he gave Nairne that month's money in advance) he had given him his salary for eight months (BL. Add. MSS 31261, f. 333, Nairne to Gualterio, 3 September 1719). Gualterio told the king that there was absolutely no need to repay him the money he had given to Nairne (BL. Add. MSS 31261, f. 353, Nairne to Gualterio, 27 September 1719), and when he came to Montefiascone at the beginning of October the king told him that he would now start paying Nairne himself (Bod. Lib. Carte MSS 258, f. 392, Gualterio to Nairne, 17 October 1719). The king then reduced Nairne's salary by a half, from 240 to 120 *livres* each month. As Nairne put it in one of his secret letters, he was now to get "20 écus a month from Sir William Ellis instead of the 40 which I was receiving from Y[our] E[xcellency]" ["20 écus par mois par les mains du Chev.r Ellis au lieu des 40 que je recevois de V.E.]". (BL. Add. MSS 31261, f. 254, Nairne to Gualterio, 18 October 1719.) But by the beginning of November, when he knew he had been demoted, he had still not received even this amount:

> since the payment which Y[our] E[xcellency] so kindly ordered to be given me, I have not had a single shilling from the King and nobody has even mentioned it, although the family here is being paid at the moment. I would be glad to be mistaken and pleasantly surprised if, having waited as long as I have, I am not the only member of the family here to have his salary cut and to be reduced from 40 to 20 ecus a month. [depuis le payment que V.E. eut la bonté de m'ordonner, je n'ay pas touché un sols du Roy et on ne m'en parle seulem.t pas quoique on paye la famille

ici actuellement.... je serai bien trompé et agreablement si après avoir attendu tant que je pourrai je n'ay pas l'honneur d'etre le seul ici de la famille qui serai retranché et reduit de 40 a 20 Ecus par mois.]
(BL. Add. MSS 20298, f. 148, Nairne to Gualterio, 4 November 1719)

34. RA. SP 45/71, James III to Sheldon, 26 October 1719. When Lord Pitsligo arrived in Paris he was surprised to find that both Dillon and Innes had already seen copies of his correspondence. Dillon spoke strongly against Murray and said he had written to the king to say he was too severe with his Scottish subjects. Pitsligo also saw Lord Panmure whom "I found very much discontented with the new set about the King" (Tayler, *Jacobite Court at Rome*, p. 98).

35. BL. Add. MSS 31262, f. 11, Murray to Gualterio, 27 October 1719: "quoique la Reine trouvera a la fin apres tout ce que c'est passe son appartment sans meubles."

36. RA. SP 45/76, receipts by Pierre Pecquet, Henry Read and Sarah Maguirk, 29 October 1719; RA. SP 45/84, 85, two inventories by Ellis of "Pieces of Plate and other things deliverd for ye Queen", 6 November 1719.

37. BL. Add. MSS 31261, f. 359, Nairne to Gualterio, 1 November 1719: "la Reine a trouvé son appartement assés bien meublé, et celuy du Roy est fort bien et on peut dire que L[eurs] M[ajestés] sont logées asses proprement et tres commodement". James III had decided that, if the queen's apartment was not properly furnished, he would have to rent additional items from "les Juifs" in Rome (BL. Add. MSS 31255, f. 195 and f. 203, James III to Gualterio, 16 September and 27 October 1719). It seems that that was not necessary.

38. BL. Add. MSS 31261, f. 357, Nairne to Gualterio, 28 October 1719.

39. "Mr McMahon said...the Q. herself was plagued by him [Murray] and his sister who together with Mr Hay [*sic*] had all the management of the K's family and did several things contrary to her inclination" (Pitsligo's "Narrative", 16 September 1720, in Tayler, *Jacobite Court at Rome*, p. 89).

40.   The substance of what I learnt from Sir Charles Wogan and Sir John Misset was that the Q was very much disgusted with Mr Murray and his sister, and also with Mr Hay [*sic*] though she was acquainted with his management later.... He said the Q was not not only angry with Mr Murray but despised him.

(Ibid., p. 95)

See also the comments by Lord Richard Howard that "the Pope's own relations were angry", that "Cardinal Albani expresst himself very earnestly", that "the Italians said he [the king] was led by two boys", and that "Cardinal Acquaviva took notice of Mr Murray's ill manners" (Ibid., p. 81).

Index